I0825484

FUTURE RELIC

FAILURES, DISASTERS, DETOURS, AND HOW I MADE A CAREER AS AN ARTIST

DANIEL ARSHAM

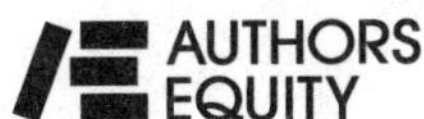

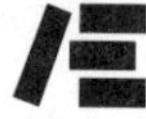

AUTHORS EQUITY
1123 BROADWAY, SUITE 1008
NEW YORK, NEW YORK 10010

COVER AND BOOK DESIGN BY HOUSE INDUSTRIES.

MOST AUTHORS EQUITY BOOKS ARE AVAILABLE AT A DISCOUNT WHEN PURCHASED IN QUANTITY FOR SALES PROMOTIONS OR CORPORATE USE. SPECIAL EDITIONS, WHICH INCLUDE PERSONALIZED COVERS, EXCERPTS, AND CORPORATE IMPRINTS, CAN BE CREATED WHEN PURCHASED IN LARGE QUANTITIES. FOR MORE INFORMATION, PLEASE EMAIL INFO@AUTHORSEQUITY.COM.

LIBRARY OF CONGRESS CONTROL NUMBER: 2025945812

PRINT ISBN 9798893310900
EBOOK ISBN 9798893310979

PRINTED IN THE UNITED STATES OF AMERICA

FIRST PRINTING

WWW.AUTHORSEQUITY.COM

THIS BOOK IS DEDICATED
TO ALL WHO BELIEVED IN ME,
WHOSE FAITH LIT THE PATH
WHEN IT WAS STILL
IN SHADOW.

AND TO YOU, THE READER,
WHO CARRIES THAT LIGHT
FORWARD SIMPLY BY
HOLDING THESE PAGES.

CONTENTS

CHAPTER I

WHY THIS BOOK?

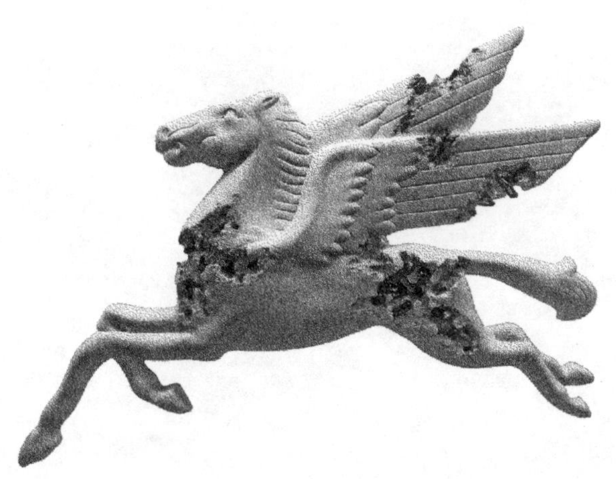

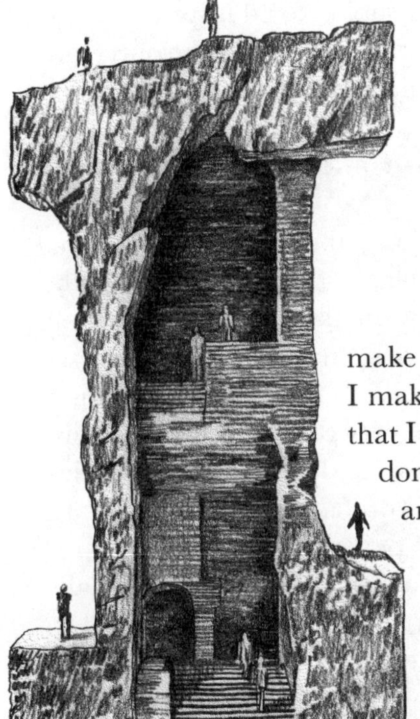

make most of the things I make for the simple reason that I wish they existed. They don't, so I make them exist, and it's the same with this book. As I look back at all of my experiences—the ups and downs of my career, my triumphs and failures, the dreams that have come true and those that haven't (yet), what I've seen and felt and learned, the people I've met and worked with and how they've influenced me—I believe with absolute certainty that this type of resource, this type of book from a working artist, is something I could've used along the way. It would have helped.

If you want to be a working professional artist of any kind—a visual artist or musician or writer or filmmaker or designer—there are many things you're going to have to learn that nobody teaches you. Stuff that's not covered in books or in school. For visual artists it's how to get a gallery, how to start and run a studio, how much a show costs to make and to put up. How an artist gets paid. For all kinds of artists there are all the crucial intangibles: how to deal with rejection, make failure your teacher and your friend, how to surrender to and really live the creative process, how to listen to your mentors, and how to find your people—those who support and inspire you.

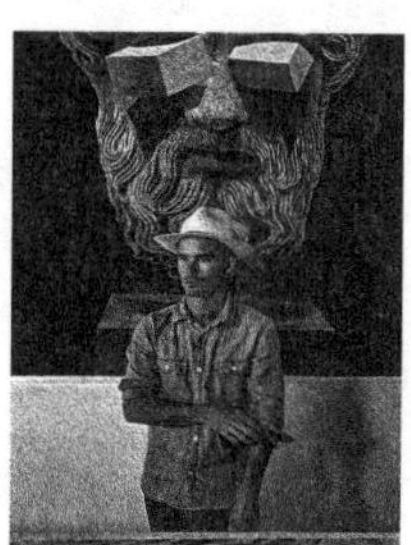

Early on, in the studio.

Hopefully this book will become a resource for others who are taking the creative path. If my story can help one young artist realize their full potential and make their dreams come true, I'll consider it a huge success.

The complicated thing about writing this book is that I haven't had a clear, straight, smooth path. I knew from very early on that I wanted to be a capital-*A* Artist—and, yes, that's really the way I thought about it: an Artist. But wanting something and actually doing it are very different things. There have been failures, disasters, detours, and obstacles the size of mountains. You can't look at my life in detail, either from my perspective or from thirty thousand feet, and see a straight line. I know that's not unique: It's the path of the creative life.

It seems crazy when I reflect back on what I expected coming out of high school and even art school. What I *actually* encountered, what I did, how I did it, and what I had to deal with coming up bear no resemblance to what I thought the steps would be.

As I said, I make things that I wish existed, and I wish a book like this had existed for me. It might not have made the way easier, but it would have helped prepare me for just how uphill it would be.

Over the years, I had a lot of conversations with my mentor. We discussed life, art, business, music—everything. Once or twice a month he would send text messages. Sometimes the messages would be about one of the specific issues that kept creeping up in my life. Other times, the texts would be very open and general. I've kept all of them, and I'll go back to certain ones in moments of doubt or at times when I need inspiration.

My mentor gives it to me straight. Who he is—that's less important than what he shares with me. What matters is that he is one in a long line of important influences and people who've helped me find my path over the years. And what matters is that one of his messages was the true spark for this book, for creating this resource and telling my story: "In the story of your life, if it all came easy and fast it would be very boring. Embrace that difficulty and disappointment. It will make for a great story one day."

That piece of advice was the push I needed. I hope this book can be the push you might need. As I start, I'm nervous. As with any piece I create, I'm putting myself out there, and I want it to connect with as many people as possible. But this book is different from other things I create. It's not an exhibition at a gallery; it's my story. I want to offer advice, but you need to know where that advice comes from. So I'm sharing things I haven't shared before, events from my personal life.

I can tell you what I *don't* want this to be. There's a whole pile of books that claim to describe the typical path—*This is the way it's supposed to be done* and all that shit. But none of those books read or feel like they are written by artists (even though some of them are).

I didn't want to write the kind of cliché that I hate. Instead, what I've tried to offer is just this: the raw practical realities of how I've made my own way,

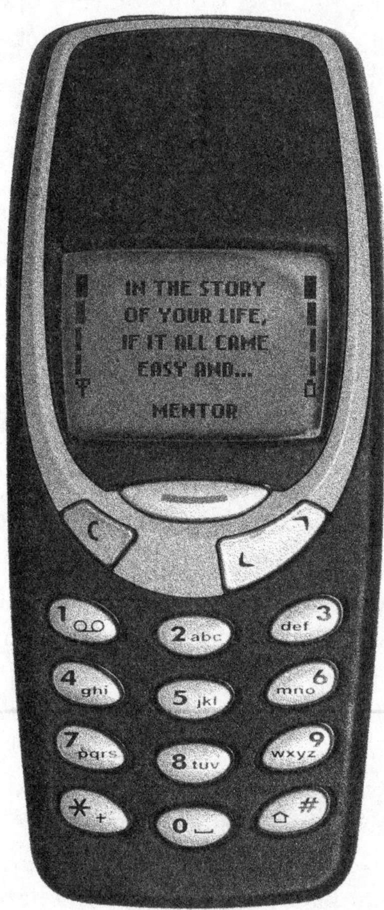

MENTOR NOTE

“IN THE STORY OF YOUR LIFE, IF IT ALL CAME EASY AND FAST IT WOULD BE VERY BORING.

EMBRACE THAT DIFFICULTY AND DISAPPOINTMENT. IT WILL MAKE FOR A GREAT STORY ONE DAY.”

MENTOR NOTE

and the practical and spiritual advice I wish I'd gotten while doing it.

When people look at one of my artworks or come to an exhibition, what they're seeing is only the end of my journey. They're seeing only that final moment, when I've arrived at this place in the here and now. Someone who sees me in the present sees only my success. They don't know the struggles that went into doing what I do. *I've got all this, and I've accomplished all that.* Some, when they see only the final result and not the journey, get pissed off. Jealousy and all of this other baggage come when they see where I've arrived but not how I got here, when they think it was easy for me.

Here's the reality. For every show I have ever done, I worked my ass off. I grinded to get to the end point. And that's what the next generation of artists needs to understand. After I graduated from Cooper Union, I lived in my studio. Not a studio apartment—don't get that wrong. I lived where I worked, in a shitty cinder-block warehouse, on a shitty block in the Greenpoint neighborhood of Brooklyn. The heat barely worked. It would get cold as fuck. It seemed like I'd wear damn near everything I owned in the winter just to stay warm. There was no shower and no kitchen. It was a shithole. I never celebrated my birthday. I never went on a vacation. The idea of a vacation never entered my mind. I had a place where I could get my work done, and that's what mattered.

My entire focus was on my work, and that's the way it needs to be if you're going to make it in the capital-*A* Art World, or really in any creative world. Otherwise, someone else will do the grind and take your spot. Having a nice place to live isn't the most important thing. Having a place to create and to make your work is the most important. Intention was behind everything I did early in my career—I knew where I wanted to go, and I was willing to do the work to try to get there.

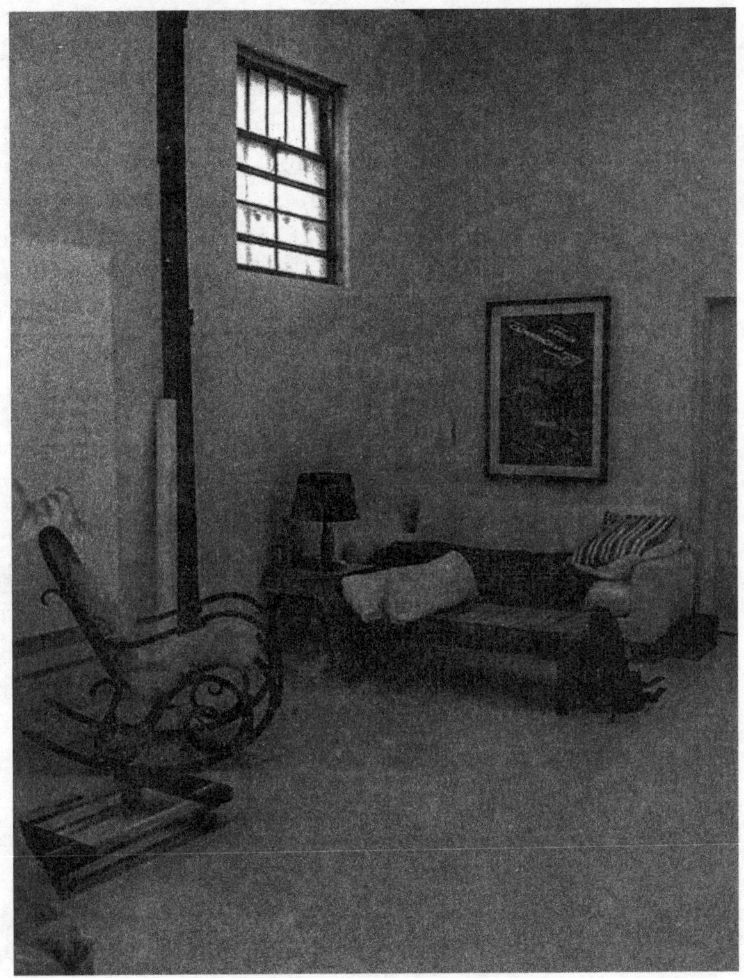

Live-in studio.

There's a creative process I've used thousands of times to make art, and I applied it to making this book. I started by making recordings. Putting down my memories, like I was sketching out a piece or putting down ideas for an installation, talking it out for myself so I could one day talk it out with you. Just like when I'm making a piece of art, I had to adjust along the way. I began on a traditional chronological path, talking about my earliest experiences. High school, photography, art, graffiti, girls. But I knew soon enough that that was all wrong. Nothing wrong with the stories, but telling them in a straight line through time creates the illusion that the actual experience was linear. It wasn't.

I had to take a step back and think about the books that have made the biggest impact on me. There are books about art, of course, but also books about history and business and philosophy. Books that don't just tell you what happened but make you think about why. Many of the books that have hit me right in the chest are about understanding human nature and our essential desire for agency, for power. We often associate power with domination, danger, and evil, but there's more to it. Any scenario in life contains a power dynamic. Either you're exercising power or it's being exercised upon you.

You have to understand this in order to play the game of life or of business or of art. Most people don't want to. They want to avoid it. But avoiding the game of power is death in the Art World or in any creative world. The game is there. Either you play it or it plays you.

When younger artists ask me some version of "How do you get there?" they want a list of steps they can tick off to become successful. It doesn't work that way. It's not just what you do or make, it's about what you're willing to endure. Most people aren't willing to experience failure for ten years, to fail over and over again with no real assurance that they're ever going to make it. But that's what it takes. That's the grind. That's what it is. Sure, there are some one-hit wonders and people who come smoking hot out of school, but that wasn't my experience, and it isn't most artists' journey. You are going to have to work your ass off. You are going to get kicked in the teeth. I have been, many times. I wouldn't want it any other way.

I have a friend who is an amazing artist. He's one of the most talented people I know, and he still lives in a small one-room studio in Brooklyn. For two decades he's poured his soul into his work, and nobody gives a fuck. His is not an uncommon story. Most people who want to be artists will never make it past that life of the grind and barely getting by. Seeing that among my peers solidified in me the conviction that, in addition to working to make the best art I could, I also needed to be very intentional in understanding the business of art. But even if you theoretically do everything right in trying to plan your career, there's no assurance. There's no guarantee it's going to work, or that you will ever be successful.

> "THERE IS NO TALENT WITHOUT DEDICATION TO CRAFT.
>
> THERE IS NO GENIUS WITHOUT PUTTING IN IMMENSE WORK.
>
> THERE IS NO MASTERY WITHOUT SACRIFICE."
>
> MENTOR NOTE

My mentor always said to *be* the thing that you want to be. If you want to be an artist, you have to fully embody being an artist and put everything on the line. *Live that life.* Risk it all. Even though it still might not work out.

I want everyone reading to understand some truths about the Art World and being an

Artist—capital A's all around. There are so many things that you don't learn in art school that you need to know. The practicalities, the small things that make a massive difference.

I was fortunate enough to go to Cooper Union, a great art school that built me up through fundamentals. They taught me how to paint, how to draw a straight line—the technical skills I needed. Even to this day I can draw a fifteen-foot line that's perfectly straight. (Am I going to use that skill on anything upcoming? No, I can't see myself using it anytime soon, but it's there if I need it, and it's pretty fucking cool.)

But I didn't learn everything I needed to know while I was in school. Nobody taught me how to form a business, create an LLC, register my copyrights, negotiate a contract, or find a gallery. Those are only a handful of the steps that I was completely ignorant about coming out of Cooper. The biggest one of all—getting your work into a museum—seemed like a far-off fantasy not at all attached to reality. None of these skills or goals were remotely discussed at Cooper, and I doubt they were at other art schools.

A few years ago, in a full-circle moment, I was invited back to Cooper as a visiting professor. As I instructed those young artists, I became increasingly concerned that there were still no business skills on the curriculum. I talked to the president of Cooper about what I thought they should do, like bringing in a counselor to prepare the students for the real life of an artist. But just talking about it isn't good enough, and that's why I'm here. That's why I'm writing this book. I want this book to pick up the slack.

This is a guide for my teenage self, my twenty-something self, for me at my lowest points and at my highest too. It's for that kid who knew art was where he had to go, what he had to commit to. He had the dream that I've now lived. This is what I wish he'd known.

"BEING AN ARTIST IS LIKE THIS:

IT WILL NOT LOVE YOU BACK.

IT WILL DISAPPOINT YOU IMMENSELY.

YOU'LL NEVER KNOW WHEN IT'S DONE.

IT WILL BE THE MOST FRUSTRATING EXPERIENCE OF YOUR ENTIRE LIFE.

BUT IF YOU STAY WITH IT, IT WILL BECOME PART OF YOU.

YOU WILL LOVE EVERY PART OF IT.

IT WILL BE A MIRROR THAT REFLECTS THE PARTS OF YOURSELF THAT YOU HIDE FROM OTHERS.

IT WILL BE THE MOST MAGICAL CONDUIT FOR YOUR DREAMS."

MENTOR NOTE

CHAPTER II

WHY THE ART WORLD SUCKS AND WHY IT'S NECESSARY

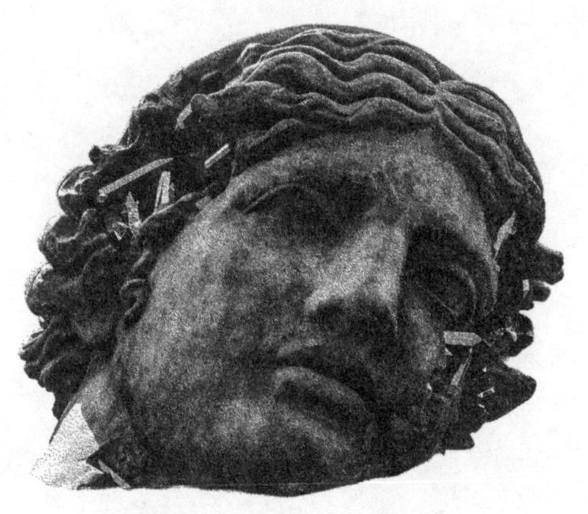

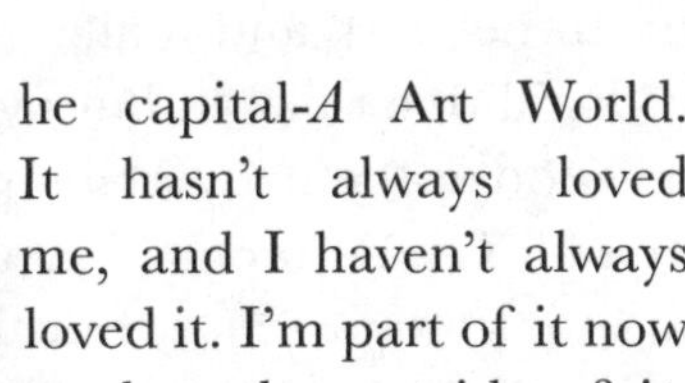

he capital-*A* Art World. It hasn't always loved me, and I haven't always loved it. I'm part of it now but also outside of it. By choice.

When I was in art school at Cooper Union, I would go to galleries in Chelsea, in Manhattan. You'd walk in the door, and there was always a beautiful woman at the desk. The guy in a suit standing outside was clearly the guard. He'd barely open the door for a scruffy-ass-looking art school kid like me. I always thought that was super intimidating. When people talk about the Art World, they might imagine it as one cohesive group of people. An organization that is working together. At least that's how I imagined it: a sort of unified team who all understand what they're going to like, what they'll favor or not favor, who will make it and who won't. Collective groupthink.

When I was young, I thought those people—that *important* group of people who ran the Art World—were the ones I needed to please. They would be the ones to say whether the things I was creating were going to be relevant or not. I felt that I needed that audience. And because that Art World exists in actual physical places, I would go to a gallery and watch the power dynamic on display. I'd literally see Larry Gagosian walking through the space with Damien Hirst or Jeff Koons, and I always thought those were the people who were running shit, that good Art was defined by them.

"WHENEVER YOU THINK OF QUITTING, THINK ABOUT ALL THE PEOPLE WHO WOULD LOVE TO SEE YOU FAIL."

MENTOR NOTE

Early in my career I thought, *I have to do that too. I have to be part of this club.* I was obsessed with the idea that I had to go out and meet all these people and try to network and make them like me. But I hated it. I still don't like it, but over time I learned how to be good at the networking part while still *seeming* like myself. Over time, as I realized what it would take to fit into their space, I decided that I'd rather enter through the back door and create my own space.

Over the years, particularly after meeting and working with Emmanuel Perrotin, the art dealer who would give me my first solo show, I got a whole new perspective on that world. I realized that it is *very* small and *very* insular. This was reinforced when I began working with people who were famous and big in the world outside of the Art World. Pharrell Williams and Virgil Abloh wanted to touch the Art World but came at it from the outside. Virgil could touch fashion, *and* he could touch music. He could touch stage design, *and* he could touch architecture, furniture design, and all these other things. It was inspiring to see someone create in so many different spaces, and it was frustrating for me to be locked into the monotony of producing exhibitions that were going to be seen by only this insulated Art World.

At the first three exhibitions I did—2005 at Emmanuel's gallery in Paris, 2008 in Amsterdam, and Paris again in 2009—I saw all the same people. The same critics talking to each other about the same artists who nobody in the outside world has ever heard of (or would care if they had). I realized then that the people who were cocooned in this world had no influence at all on the greater culture. Capital-*A* Art World people don't have any relevance for normal people who are not interested, for whatever reason, in being part of the insular community.

At some point I realized I didn't care about that insular community either. It boiled down to the fact that they're not the kind of people I would like to hang out with and be around. There's a ton of ego and bluster and money and networking and favors and all kinds of bullshit that happens behind the scenes, and I just couldn't stay interested. I realized that I had to make a choice: Either I had to find a way to play that game or I had to break its rules and play a different game.

This realization happened around the same time Instagram was starting to take off, and I began to see this as the opening I wanted to explore, a way to expand the pool of people who could see my work. For me, and for artists all over the world, this was a game changer. It was an invitation to break the rules.

If you trace art and artists all the way back to the Renaissance, which is when artists first started to become *famous*, all of the famous artists of the time had the blessing of gatekeepers—royal families, wealthy families, or the Church. Those gatekeepers picked the artists that the public was going to follow. If you go through the seventeenth and eighteenth centuries, it was still the same system, the same types of gatekeepers. In the nineteenth century, salons and galleries became another type of gatekeeper system, arbiters of taste who decided who would be successful. Even when the gatekeepers changed, the essential elitism and insularity remained: an echo chamber of the same people talking to one another about the same artists.

The Art World is counterintuitive. In some ways, you think of it as a huge behemoth. This Godzilla of culture. There are art museums in almost every major city in the world. Artists like Leonardo da Vinci, Van Gogh, Picasso, Pollock, and Warhol are household names. Art seems omnipresent and *big*. But at the same time, the group of people deciding who becomes iconic is very, very small.

Richard Prince is one of the most famous, most revered, and most expensive artists in the world today. He is also one of my favorites. For years he's talked about making art for a specific, intimate audience: "There's about 250 people out there. You spend so much time alone, you do art in private for the private."[1] Thinking that way has obviously worked for him. His entire approach revolves around appropriation and bringing low culture into high-culture art. He takes low-American imagery, like photos of biker chicks, images of naughty nurses from fifties pulp book covers, actual Dodge Challengers, and he turns them into art. At the macro level, it's a very interesting perspective and not dissimilar from some of what I do. But where we differ is in how we engage with the audience. For him it's the 250 people, the Art World. For me, I want to reach as many people as possible.

Instagram made it possible. When I post a work of my art on Instagram, more people see it in an hour than would see it in a year in a museum. Hundreds of thousands more see it than if it were in any gallery in the world. People get to see it and judge it for themselves, without the approval of critics or other Art

1 *Marvin Heiferman, interview with Richard Prince,* Bomb, *July 1, 1988, https://bombmagazine.org/articles/1988/07/01/richard-prince.*

World gatekeepers. The critics are a prime example of how irrelevant and insulated the art community has become in the larger world. Though the job is to be a critic, to *critique*, their main objective seems to be to grow their own followers, maybe because some of them are angry artists who never made it out of the studio. They win attention by being controversial and loud, by always having the hottest take. The critiques themselves tend to be less about art and more about the artists and their lives, including takedowns of anyone who uses social media or venues outside of the Art World, or any artist who is able to support themselves financially. If you criticize my art, I won't argue with you. But criticizing artists, including me, for engaging directly with people in the real world? Most critics have lost the plot.

"PEOPLE SAY NOT TO WASTE TIME ON THE CRITICS. I SUGGEST YOU DO THE OPPOSITE. WHATEVER IT IS THEY ARE HATING ON IS WORKING. DO MORE OF THAT."

MENTOR NOTE

If the Art World considers those critics part of the 250 to impress, then it's not for me, and I know I'm not for them. I've had enough interactions with real people outside of that world to believe I'm on the right path. When I walk down the street, people who have nothing to do with the Art World will stop me to talk. They know my work and have been impacted by it. They've understood it. It's changed their perspective on how they interpret culture, what they think is interesting. In some cases, it's brought them to a gallery for the first and maybe the only time in their lives. The possibility that maybe I've had an impact on their lives? That's the real thrill for me. Those are the people I care about and who I create for, not the 250.

History is not determined by critics, and it's not determined by what's in vogue at a particular moment. It's determined by how many people you have a lasting impact on. In my opinion, Manet was the most important painter of the nineteenth century, not just because his art is great, and not just because of his technical innovation and the new ground he broke, but also because he was the most viewed painter of his time. He was prolific. When he rejected the idea of the traditional salon and opened his own space, twenty thousand people came, while only four thousand went to the official salon. They went to Manet's salon because, despite being rejected by the Art World at the time, his work touched people's souls in a way the officially "accepted" art did not.

If there's a choice between creating work that achieves high success in a small world or becoming a significant cultural figure in the rest of the world, which would you pick? My choice is to try to reach everyone else, and if that means I'm also going to piss people off, including a good portion of the Art World with a capital *A*, I'm okay with it.

I set myself a target of engaging in the commercial world outside of fine art, and I succeeded. But even though I was really excited about making sneakers with Adidas and jewelry with Tiffany, cars with Porsche and clothes with Kith, everyone I knew in the Art World, including Emmanuel, was really critical. They all asked why I wanted to be so commercial. Why I wanted my name in ads on billboards. Why I was willing to diminish the value of my work. My response was always the same: audience. Those collaborations grow my audience. And they speak to normal people. That's who I want to reach.

"YOU MIGHT NEED TO TRY 100 TIMES AND FAIL 99 OF THEM.

THE REASON THEY SAY MOST ARTISTS NEVER ACHIEVE SUCCESS IS THAT THEY QUIT ON THE 98TH ATTEMPT OR WELL BEFORE.

PERSISTENCE IS KEY."

MENTOR NOTE

Andy Warhol made paintings of Campbell's soup and Coke cans. He appeared in any film or TV show that would have him, including *Tootsie* and *The Love Boat*. If he were alive today, he would be designing Nike sneakers and making streetwear, designing jewelry for rappers and endorsing energy drinks. Warhol realized that art is about life and everything that's in it. If our lives were surrounded by and dominated by consumer culture, then that was a prime vehicle for creating expression and investigating

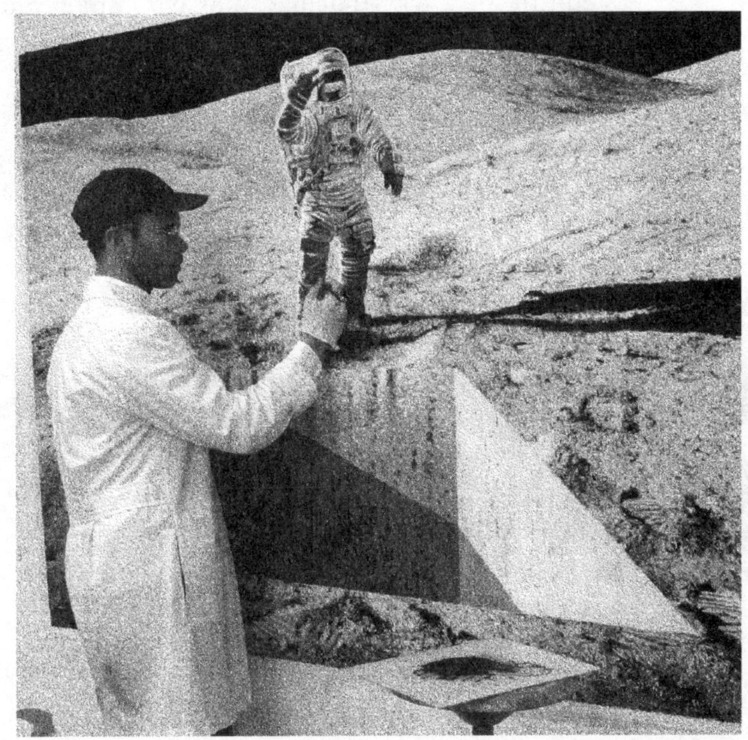

In the studio.

human experience. He also understood business and commerce. Late in his career, he was having a hard time selling his paintings the usual way, so he switched almost his entire artistic practice to making portraits for rich people. Experts basically considered them worthless, but now all those pieces are worth huge sums. Warhol embraced and celebrated commercial culture in a way that had massive impact and also made him massively famous. Imagine if he had listened to all the critics.

Ultimately, and not surprisingly, the Art World's business model is controlled by short-term economics—how much a painting is worth at any given moment, and who is smart enough to buy low and sell high. That's a model that can be dangerous for artists. Because the *buy low, sell high* model rules, the Art World always wants the young, the new, the hot, the soon-to-be very valuable. Young artists can be on top one day and utterly tossed aside the next, and that's almost impossible to come back from. It's precarious. You want a career, and quick money and fame are alluring. Nobody ever thinks they'll be the one to get rejected after all those early accolades.

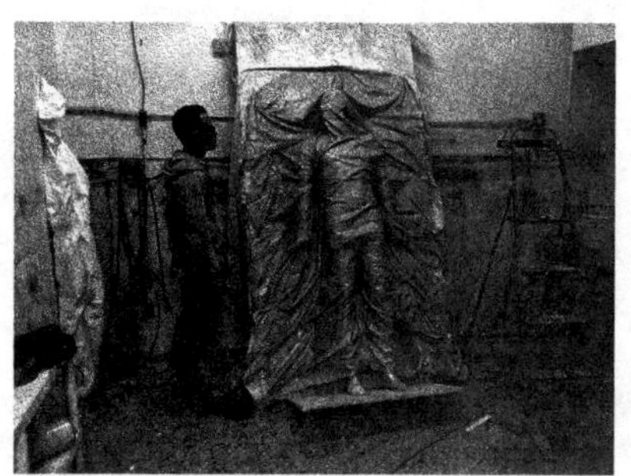

In the studio, 2013.

So yeah, there are a lot of reasons why I think the Art World sucks. But I also know the ways in which it's necessary. When the model provides an artist with more than just short-term money, that's when the Art World is at its best and completely necessary for artists. I was really lucky to have Emmanuel as my dealer from early on. His approach is different: He makes long-term bets. He believes in nurturing an artist over time to bring out the best in them, that the money will follow when the work is great. For me, taking the slower approach was the right one, even though I didn't know it at the time, and even though I wanted everything to go faster. Emmanuel forced me to learn to be a professional artist while I was learning to be an Artist. He taught me to be patient and play the long game, with a large body of work in multiple media, while always making the main focus of my work my paintings and sculpture.

One of the reasons artists go to art school is because they hate the idea of working normal jobs, of engaging in *business*. But once you're successful, that's exactly what you have to do. It can be immensely helpful to be guided in setting up a business for yourself by someone who really knows how to do it.

Working in the Art World also taught me how to be a better artist. While my instincts can be broad, having a dealer with a refined eye and a knowledge of art history and the market has helped me sharpen my ideas and make sure I am following through with the best of them.

While I do want to reach as broad an audience as possible, I know that the reason I can do so with authenticity and authority is partly because of the capital-*A* Art World. The approval and attention I get from inside it opens doors for me in the worlds outside, worlds like design and fashion. And the work I do outside boosts my profile and creates more demand, and that helps strengthen my position inside. Each side feeds the other, which is actually perfect. I get to do what I want to do, and that works to further my greater goals and make more of my dreams come true.

CHAPTER III

ORIGINS

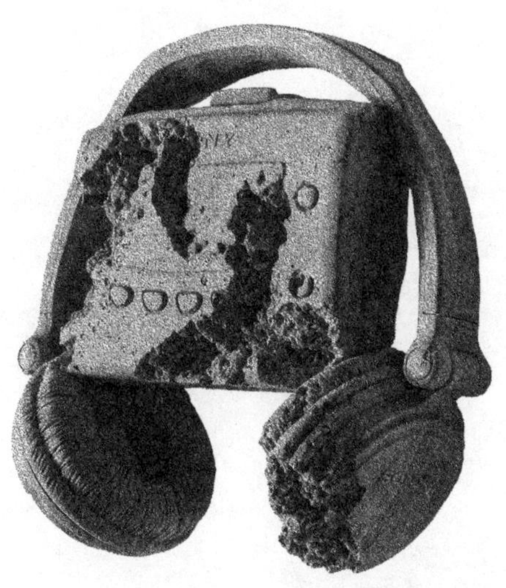

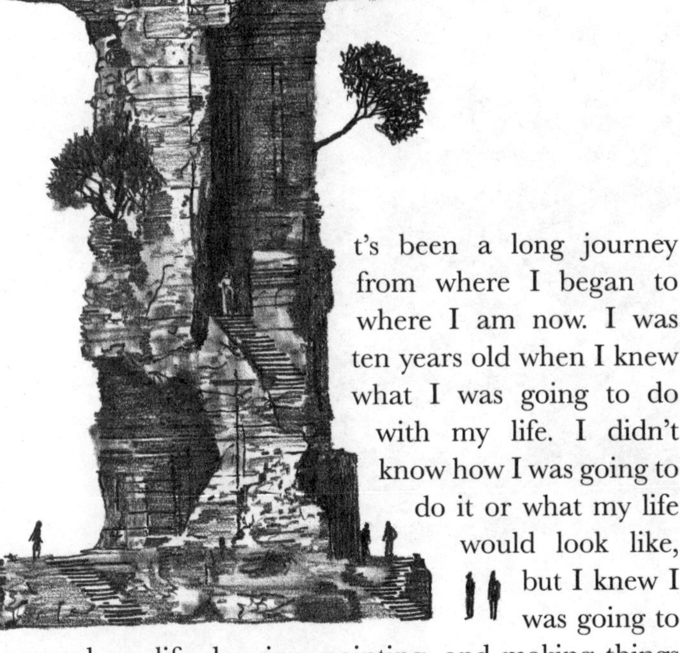

t's been a long journey from where I began to where I am now. I was ten years old when I knew what I was going to do with my life. I didn't know how I was going to do it or what my life would look like, but I knew I was going to spend my life drawing, painting, and making things that brought me joy. I knew I was going to be an artist. My parents also knew. My grandparents. My fourth-grade teacher knew. My family didn't come from an artistic background—there were no artists in our history—so this would be a new path for an Arsham.

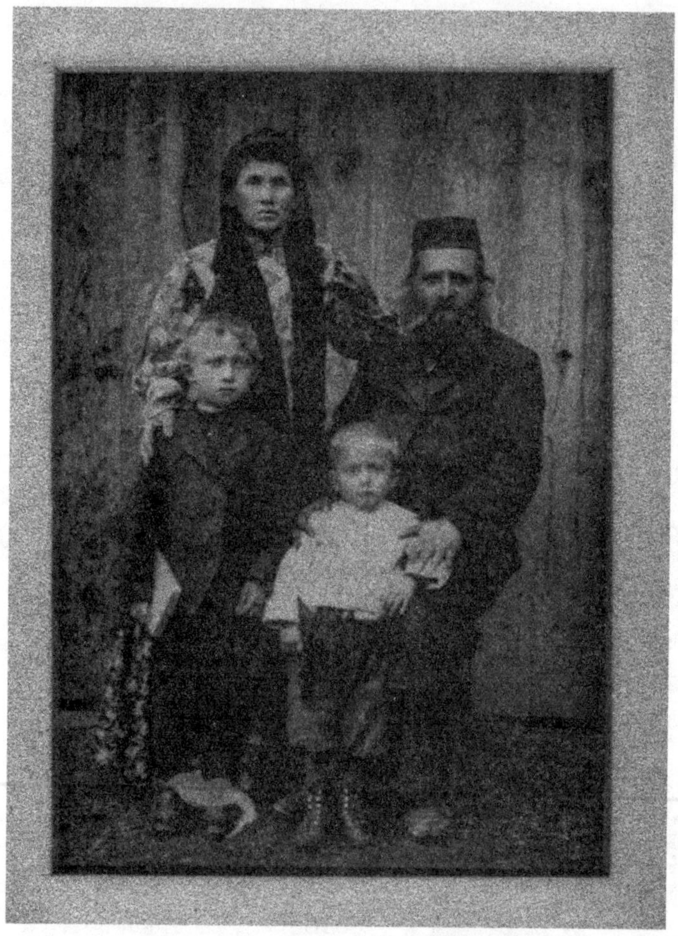

My paternal great-grandparents in Ukraine.

I was born in Cleveland, which I still consider home, even though I moved away at a young age. My great-grandfather and two of his three brothers emigrated from Ukraine in 1909. They chose Cleveland because at the time it was a booming city with plenty of jobs. Their father had been a tailor, and they started a business turning leftover scraps from clothing manufacturing into fabric for car seats for Detroit-based automakers. They called it, logically, Arsham Brothers. Early car seats were usually covered with wool, and they were itchy and felt terrible. The brothers recycled the clothing fabric into softer seat yarn for more expensive models of cars. The business was just enough to support the three families. They tried for years to get their fourth brother to join them, but he didn't want to leave Ukraine. He was later murdered by the Nazis in the Holocaust.

When World War II started, my grandfather Edwin and his brother joined the military. Edwin flew on supply planes for the Navy in China and India. After returning from the war, he gave his shares in the family business to his brothers and started selling life insurance. He was adamant about achieving financial success, however humble it might have been at the time. Meanwhile, car companies were using better materials for their seats, and so the family business grew. They all got married and started having families, becoming part of the growing middle class. The Arsham clan became quite large, and almost all of my relatives still live in Cleveland. If you ever come across an Arsham in Cleveland, tell them I say hello. They are good, decent, hardworking people.

My mother had a very different background. Her father was a diplomat in the State Department, and her family moved all over the world because of his job. She spent a large chunk of her childhood in Germany, with other stops in Sri Lanka, Brazil, and Mexico. She moved to Ohio for college and met my dad when they were in their twenties. They got married and had me. They're a great pair and balance each other out. Both had a huge influence on me. I got my working-class work ethic from my dad and my fascination with art, culture, and travel from my mom.

My dad got transferred to Miami in 1985, when I was five. My mom started working at the University of Miami law school. When we arrived, it was a bit of a shock. Cleveland was a cold Rust Belt city with a traditional urban center. Miami was a warm, bright, sunny urban sprawl. If Cleveland had a color, it would be a cool gray, whereas Miami was blue—even the light felt blue. I still remember the first time we pulled into our new suburban neighborhood. There was a large sign that said THE CROSSING, with a picture of a bird flying over a lake, and the community actually had birds and a lake. For a little kid coming from the Midwest, it was thrilling, as if I had suddenly been sent to a new and different and very exciting world.

I had a pretty standard childhood. I had school and neighborhood friends. I played soccer and basketball, though I was deeply average at both. I played video games, rode BMX bikes, and watched movies on old VHS tapes and on what was the new technology at the time—DVDs. My first memory of art is of making drawings. I was seven or eight. It was a rainy Florida day, and I had just finished watching *Star Wars* for the seventy-fifth time. R2-D2 was my favorite character, so I pressed Pause on the VCR and picked up a pencil and gave it a shot. It wasn't great, but it wasn't terrible, and I enjoyed the process, the focus, trying for the precision that I didn't yet have the skills to do. The most important thing was that I loved it. Drawings started pouring out of me. I drew cars, bikes, sneakers, characters from films, TV shows, and video games—basically all of my favorite things. I drew on the bus to school and on the bus home.

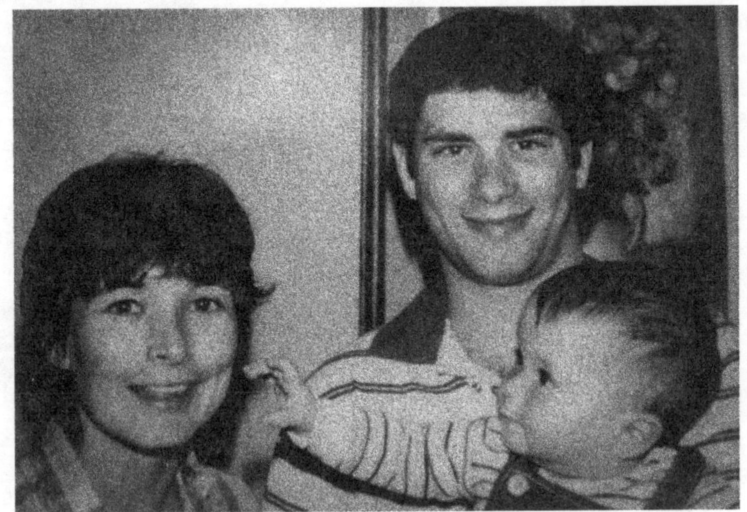

With my parents in 1981.

I drew in class when I was bored, which was most of the time, and many of my memories of that time revolve around making drawings.

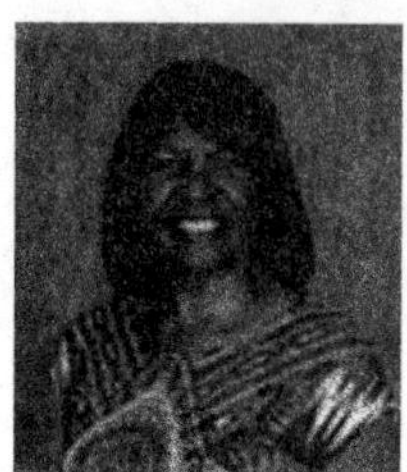
Miss Perry.

In fourth grade, my art teacher, Miss Perry, noticed my drawings, and she was the first person to tell me that I might be pretty good at it. Miss Perry was a Black woman who always dressed in bright colors and wore flowered headscarves. She made cutouts with scissors and paper and cardboard, intricately crafted snowflakes and dolls, animals and birds. I thought of her as an Artist with a capital *A*. When she told me I showed talent for drawing, I thought she was joking. I didn't think my drawings were that interesting or special. I was just screwing around and doodling. She called my parents and shared her thoughts. She told them there was a special art school in Miami I should apply to. My parents, who always seemed interested in my drawings but weren't in a position to judge their quality, followed her recommendation. Much to my surprise, I was accepted. And to this day I owe Miss Perry a debt of gratitude for encouraging me, for talking to my parents, and for recommending me to the new school. That one act of kindness from my fourth-grade art teacher was transformational; it shaped my entire life.

R. R. Moton Elementary School was a magnet school in a rough part of town, one of the poorest neighborhoods in Miami. Most of the kids in the neighborhood were Black or Latino. The white kids, like me, were almost all bused in from the suburbs. Once in school, the groups mixed together—Black, white, Cuban, Dominican, Puerto Rican, Haitian, Jamaican. An average lunchroom table was like a meeting at the U.N., and that was the point, or at least part of it: that magnet schools integrated communities in ways that neighborhood schools, especially in an ethnically divided city like Miami, couldn't. I had my first real experiences with hip-hop and streetwear as fashion, both of which have become part of my work and part of my life. And jewelry—street jewelry and high classic jewelry—was a constant topic of conversation, even though not one kid could have afforded any of it. Given my mother's international background, she was thrilled with my new school. And my father was happy because for the first time in my life, I was excited to go to school every day.

One of the things I loved and still remember was being exposed to different media of art making. I drew, I painted in acrylic, I painted in oil, I drew with crayons, I made pottery and ceramics. And though it was drawing that brought me to R. R. Moton, I spent most of my time there working in photography. Until I started there, I never thought of photography as art. I knew it existed as art and that there were artists who worked in it, but I mostly thought of photography as family portraits, advertisements, posters. It was the medium I had the least experience with but was most excited to learn about and try to work in.

I got my first camera when I was eleven, a birthday gift from my dad's father, my grandfather Edwin. He started shooting pictures during World War II as a hobby to distract himself from what was going on in the world, and he was a really great amateur photographer. To this day, I have all these memories of him with his camera around his neck. Always shooting photos, always working away in his basement darkroom. The camera he gave me was fully manual, a Pentax K1000. It was the perfect student camera. Indestructible and heavy, a beautiful and functional object. I loved that camera, and I still have it. I still use it when I need a certain type of raw analog look. It came with the standard 35-millimeter lens, so I didn't have a huge visual range when I started, but I knew I could earn money to buy different lenses and have the capability to shoot different perspectives. Before I went to shoot with it for the first time,

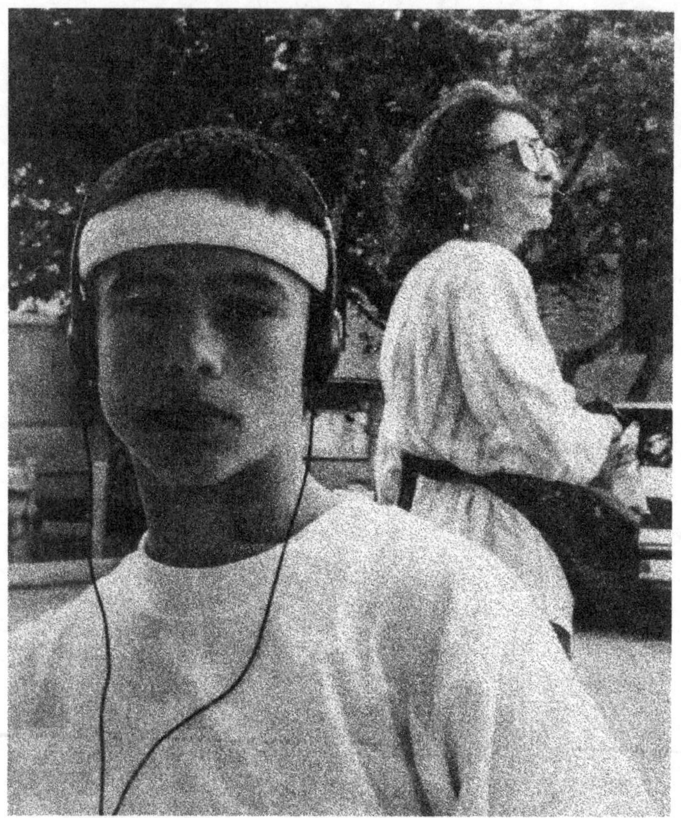

Self-portrait taken with first camera, a Pentax K1000.

my grandfather gave me some advice, which I still believe in and which really applies to any kind of art making: Anyone can take a picture, but not everyone can make a memorable image.

With that in mind, I started thinking about what kind of photos I wanted to take. Because you had to buy film, and developing it was either very time-consuming or very expensive, you had to plan carefully. There were no digital cameras, there were no cell phones, much less smartphones with high-powered cameras. My Pentax went with me everywhere, often hanging around my neck. When I saw an image I liked or thought would make a cool photo, I would look through the viewfinder, adjust the lens and sharpen the focus, and take the picture, even though there was no film in the camera. I was sharpening my eye and practicing image making before it started costing me, or my parents, money.

While I was working on my eye and learning how to really use the camera, I started to learn how to develop film and make prints. At the time, it was by far the most complicated part of making art, or of making anything, that I had ever undertaken. I also started looking at photography books in the school library. I wanted to see what other artists did with their cameras—real artists, artists like Cartier-Bresson and Avedon who were good and important enough to have their work published, and good and important enough to have their books in a middle school library.

My first big series of photos was a series of doors. These were in some ways the first real works of art I ever made—the first things I created with the idea that they would be displayed, and people would see them and judge them. I had learned that many artists, writers, and musicians, people in all creative fields, make art out of what they see around them every day. *Make what you know.* And what I knew best was my neighborhood, the housing development where I lived and spent all of my time outside of school.

All the houses were essentially identical, with each floor plan a mirror of its neighbor. So the doorways all looked the same, but with the entrances positioned differently. And the structure of each door was the same, but they were painted different colors, with different tiles on the entryways. They had different doorbells. The knockers were different, and some had plants right outside. Every few houses, there was some kind of kitschy little suburban lawn sculpture thing, like a gnome or a pink flamingo. I saw the doors every day and was fascinated by these small but awesome nonconformities. I framed the photos all exactly the same, emphasizing the identical aspect. I found a kind of beauty in that quality of sameness and variation. And because I was young, I thought the doors were a great, very deep, and very profound metaphor for humanity—that we are all in some way the same, despite being so different.

I shot two rolls of twenty-four exposures, knowing I wouldn't keep all of them and that not all of them would be very good, or good at all. Then I had to go into the darkroom, which was a delicate, involved, and meticulous process that required controlled lighting, precise timing, and the use of specific types of toxic chemicals. And you had to do it all in a very dark room where you couldn't really see, even after your eyes had adjusted. Once you were in the darkroom, you had to remove the film from the camera without touching the negative or allowing it to touch anything else. There was a whole process to developing the film. When you had the negatives done, you had to load the film negative into an enlarger, a device that projects the image onto photographic paper, and focus the image within the enlarger. From there you chose the negatives you wanted to print, and after you chose them, you had to expose a test strip of photographic paper to light in increments to determine the correct exposure time. Once you'd determined that, you developed the test strip in chemical baths to make sure you were correct. If you were, you placed a full sheet of photographic paper under the enlarger and exposed the paper to light for the amount of time determined for proper exposure. When that step was finished, you immersed the exposed paper in the developer to bring out the image, and once the image appeared, you fixed the image in a fixer solution to develop it and make it permanent. After it developed, you rinsed the print thoroughly in water to remove chemical residues and dried the print using a drying rack or press. It was a ton of complicated work for a kid. And I loved it. I loved the entire process. It took hours, and if you made a single mistake, the image was ruined. The demanding and meticulous nature of the work was great for me to learn; it would serve me well for the rest of my life.

The door photos, a series of twelve prints, are what really started it all for me as an artist. It was the first time I had made Art with a capital *A*. Before that series, I had made all my drawings and paintings because I loved making them, but not with the idea that they would be shown anywhere or be seen by anyone. I drew and painted because those were activities that brought me joy, the same way other kids might find joy playing sports or video games. But with the doors, from the moment I started thinking about them and figuring out how to make and present them and going through the long, incredibly involved, and difficult process, I was making Art. And I loved it even more than doing it for fun or for myself.

I only have one of those pictures left in my possession; it's hanging in my dad's house. I wish I still had the whole series, but I have no idea where they ended up, and I no longer have the negatives.

Even though most of them are gone, the door photos taught me an incredibly important lesson: that I could create Art. And I could create Art from things that were around me every day. And just by paying a little more attention than everyone else, I could make something unique and special.

Aside from teaching me skills and processes that I would carry with me for the rest of my life, going to art school so early changed me in several ways. Before I started at R. R. Moton, I was a shy, awkward, introverted kid without much social success. That part didn't change much—I didn't become more outgoing or more handsome or a better athlete. But I found my people: other kids who were into art or music or dance or film or all of them. Other kids who were shy, awkward, and introverted. Other kids who felt like, for whatever reason, they didn't fit in. When we hung out, we talked about drawing and painting and photography. We went to museums together. And when we got older, we started making art together.

After I finished at R. R. Moton, I went to a middle school called Southwood, which was in southwest Miami, another neighborhood very different from my own. Southwood was a huge school, but it too had a magnet section for visual art, theater, and dance. I had loved the focus at R. R. Moton, but now I had the confidence to want to be in a bigger space and have friends of all kinds. Within my first few days at Southwood, I met Jacob, who went by Jack. He was a Cuban kid in the ninth grade, two years older than me—a large gap when you're that age. Jack saw me sitting alone in the lunchroom and came over to the otherwise empty table and sat with me. It might have been the Nirvana shirt, the JanSport backpack with a Nine Inch Nails patch, the Jordan 3s, or the JNCO jeans I was rocking at the time, but he saw something in me that made him believe we'd get along. And we did, and I'm happy I met him, because Jack introduced me to graffiti and skating.

Jack had been *writing graf* for a couple of years. He wasn't naturally an artist, but he loved art and making art as much as anyone I've ever known. I met other Southwood graffiti kids, and we started a crew. We named it TSC. We hung out after school and on weekends, came up with ideas together, shared drawings, worked on drawings together, and went out and created massive pieces on walls all over Miami. As I learned from Jack, choosing your tag was the most important thing you would ever do in graffiti. It was your public-facing name and the focus of your art—your entire reputation was based on it, and it was a representation of your style and ideas. If you were really good, it was a chance to create your own design language.

Some of the core members of TSC, who are still my friends to this day, went by the tags ATOMIC, QUAKE, RAVI, and DTEK. The tag I chose was WHEN, or sometimes WEN. While some people chose a word they loved or one that was directly representative of some part of their life, my tag was an abstract idea, a conceptual conceit. To me, when I painted WHEN, it meant I was literally capturing a moment, creating a memory. And I imagined it would invoke memories for other people when they saw it. I loved how the letters looked and how they sat together when they were drawn or painted, and I varied how it looked by using different combinations of upper- and lowercase letters. I felt good when I chose my tag, and I felt great when I would draw or paint it somewhere. The conceit worked. I still have the memories. And I hope and believe I always will. *When. WHEN. wen.*

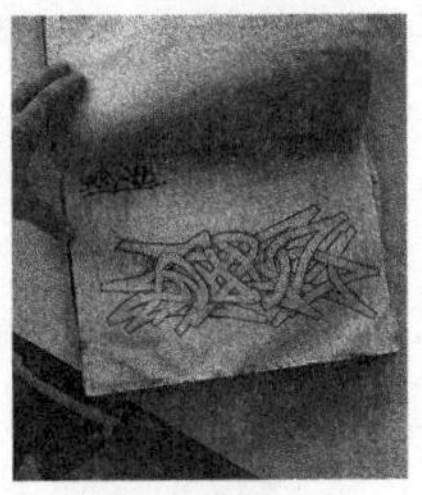

A sketch of one of my early graffiti pieces.

I had always been a good, well-behaved kid. I had never been in trouble, never had any issues at school. So on top of the joy of being in a crew and having a group of new friends and making art with them, there was an added thrill and risk to writing graffiti, given the simple and basic fact that it was illegal. And none of us cared at all, as long as we didn't get caught. In my mind, and in the minds of most graffiti writers, we were simply creating and displaying art. The thought that we were defacing property never even entered our minds. We appreciated and critiqued all the other writers' work. We made work that was for anyone to see. It didn't rely on any gallery or museum to give us space to show. We made our own gallery. It may have been on the side of some train tracks or behind a dumpster at the supermarket, but we were expressing ourselves artistically. We wouldn't go out and just drop a bunch of individual tags or write nonsense on the sides of people's houses. We would go to forgotten or neglected places and create really extravagant, collaborative graffiti pieces. In reality, most of the places were not places we were likely to get caught. The threat seemed minimal.

Part of being in a crew, and part of being in TSC, was proving yourself. To be a full member of the crew, you had to earn a belt buckle with your tag on it. One of the guys in our crew, Adam, had a cousin in New York who would get them made and send them down for each crew member who earned one. Though we claimed they were gold, they were made of shiny brass, with whatever tag in big, bold letters. I had never wanted anything more in my life. But in order to get one, you had to tag something really dangerous and illegal, and you had to do it without getting caught.

To earn my buckle, I was given the task of tagging the back of a highway sign that was suspended in the air over an eight-lane highway. Everyone else in TSC had already done their thing and had their buckles, and I was the last one who needed to complete a mission. I knew that

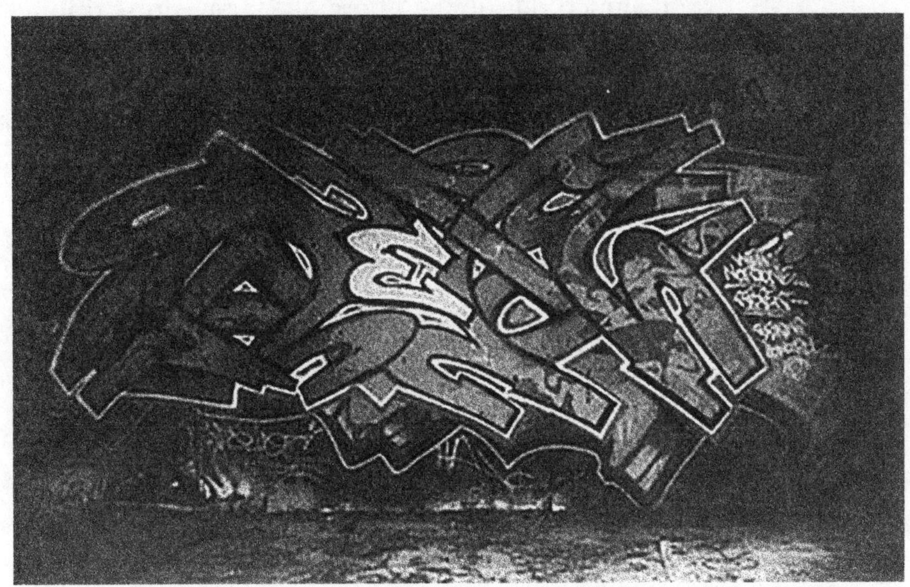

Graffiti.

Adam—a.k.a. ATOMIC—had already had my buckle made, because he showed it to me, and my heart almost exploded when I saw it. The night after I saw it, I got all of my tagging shit together, and when my mom fell asleep, I snuck out in the middle of the night on my bike. I had a sweet Diamondback, the Porsche of BMX bikes at the time. I loved that bike. It was my most prized possession, the coolest thing I had ever owned. As I slipped out of the house at 2 a.m., dressed in all black, my backpack loaded with eight cans of paint and a notebook with the drawing I was going to paint, I thought I was some kind of Navy SEAL–type gangster. I rode to the highway, dropped my bike in the grass, and walked to the base of the sign. It was made of galvanized steel, with crossbars that made it super easy for contractors to climb up when the sign needed to be cleaned or changed. It also made it easy for me.

I started climbing. My heart was pounding, and my hands were shaking. I had practiced painting the tag on a large piece of cardboard in my garage, and I knew it would take me about ten minutes. I noticed an overpass a couple hundred feet away. I hadn't seen the overpass when I got there, because I'd come in from the other side, but as I reached the top of the access ladder, I saw a cop car sitting underneath the overpass with its lights off. *Fuck.* I stood as quietly and still as I could while desperately hoping the officer was sleeping or at least not paying attention. The car was dark and still. It was too far away for me to see what was going on inside of it, but I didn't detect any movement, so I told myself, with visions of wearing my buckle to school, that everything was cool and it was probably empty and just parked there to get people to slow down. I waited a moment. But I wasn't lucky, because as soon as I took another step up and was ready to take out my drawing and my paint and get to work, he spotted me. He cranked on the lights and turned the spotlight so it was shining directly on me. I nearly shit myself. The cruiser pulled out and raced from the overpass to the access pole. I thought about running, but I wasn't sure I would get away and knew I would be in even bigger trouble if I ran and got caught.

The car stopped, and the officer got out. He was the stereotypical Miami cop, with huge, bulging arms and a furry mustache, and he looked up at me and yelled, "What the fuck do you think you're doing, you little shit?" I climbed down and tried to be cool and claim I hadn't done anything yet, but he knew I had paint in my backpack. He gave me the rundown of charges I would face if I didn't cooperate: trespassing, vandalism, attempted destruction of public property, and mischief. He asked if I wanted to keep lying. I did not. I admitted why I was there, and he drove me home. The whole time, I gave the classic sob story of *I'm a good kid and get good grades, my parents are going to be pissed and punish me forever, please let me walk home.* It didn't help. He ignored me and drove, but he was nice enough to drop me off a block from my house so I wouldn't have to explain getting out of a cop car to my parents. Before I walked away, he told me, "If I ever see you around here pulling shit like that again, ain't nobody going to rescue you, understand?" and I made sure he knew I understood him. I crept quietly back into my room. I barely slept the rest of the night. When I went back the next morning, my bike was gone.

I never got the belt buckle. I know that a couple of guys in the crew thought I punked out and didn't do the tag because I was scared, and I never told anyone what happened because I was embarrassed to admit that the cops got me and someone stole my bike. I didn't leave the crew, but eighth grade was almost over, and I was starting at a new high school in the fall. I loved the crew and the art I made as part of it, and I am still friends with some of them today, but I started to gravitate away from graffiti and focus more on creating paintings and sculptures that didn't have the potential to land me in a jail cell. By the time I entered DASH, the Design and Architecture Senior High School, in the Miami Design District, there was no doubt I wanted to be an artist. What that meant and what I wanted to create, I wasn't locked in on yet, but I knew that I wanted to create and evoke responses.

As I moved through sophomore year into junior year, I started thinking about college, and specifically about going to art school. During the summer between those years, I visited New York for the first time. I stayed in the East Village, and from the moment I arrived, I felt like I belonged, that this was my shit, the city of my dreams, where I wanted to go to school and live my life. There was graffiti everywhere. There was hip-hop music drifting through the air all over downtown. There were galleries and sneaker shops, people wearing cool brands I had never heard of, food and life and energy on every block. I remember walking into Washington Square Park and thinking it was the coolest fucking scene I'd ever seen, people doing their thing, making music and painting and playing chess and dancing and sitting in the grass and smoking weed. That trip was one of those seminal moments when you know your life is going to change, and that you've found something or someplace that is going to define it. While I was there, walking through Astor Place, I saw a school called Cooper Union. I had heard of it and knew it was an art school, but the only other things I knew were that it was in the coolest neighborhood in the world and I was going to figure out how to go there.

The Cooper Union for the Advancement of Science and Art was founded in 1859 by a wealthy industrialist named Peter Cooper. It was founded on Cooper's belief that an education "equal to the best technology schools" should be available to young people, regardless of their race, religion, sex, wealth, or social status, and should be "open and free to all." It had three schools within it: art, architecture, and engineering. It averaged ten thousand applications every year for sixty spots in each class. All of its professors were working artists, many of them famous, and a few of them artists I had already studied in high school. Though my parents had saved for college, they had told me they probably only had enough for a couple of years and that I would be responsible for the rest. Cooper was free. If you got in, you received a full scholarship. It was a dream—part of the greater dream of being an artist. And nobody from DASH had ever gotten in.

"DO NOT IGNORE YOUR OWN SELF DOUBT. THAT IS THE OLD YOU REMINDING YOU HOW MUCH YOU HAVE ACHIEVED."

MENTOR NOTE

My adviser, my college counselor, and my parents were all pessimistic about my chances of getting into Cooper. My overall grades were average, despite my art grades being stellar. I had spent much of high school working on things that interested me instead of things that might get me into college, and my transcript showed it. They suggested I look at other art schools and that I consider majoring in graphic design in case the artist gig didn't work out. DASH had a college day, but no one from Cooper came to it. There was another magnet high school for the arts in Miami called New World. A number of kids from New World had gone to Cooper, and I saw that a rep from Cooper would be at the New World college day, so I went. And though I was still shy and introverted, I knew this was my best chance to get into the school.

Richard, the rep, was cool—beyond cool. He was an artist who worked for the school to make extra cash in between his shows, and I was both thrilled to meet him and incredibly intimidated by him. I don't know if he felt sorry for me or was impressed by my determination or if he helped everyone, but he gave me his card and told me to email him once I finished my submission packet and that he'd review it for me before I officially applied. Meeting him felt like the break I needed to get me from Miami to New York. To get me to Cooper.

At the time, the application consisted of three essays and an art project. The prompt that year for the art project was to depict the passage of time. I spent the next three months in my bedroom, drafting, revising, redoing. I probably did each component five times. I'd write the essays and read them and throw them away. I'd make a painting and hate it. I'd make a drawing and feel insecure about it. I neglected my schoolwork to focus on the application, which was a risk, because it didn't help my already mediocre grades. I debated what was good and what was no good and what exactly I wanted to say and show. I thought about how I should describe myself in my application. It's not an easy answer when you want to impress people but not come off like an arrogant asshole kid. Richard had told me that Cooper looked for people they could mold, who had the ability to think but hadn't yet acquired the technical skills to make great art. He told me that if my work looked too stylistic, I wouldn't get in, that they didn't want students who worked in a singular style or had a locked-in idea of who they were as an artist. Luckily, that was who I was: seventeen and just starting to figure some shit out.

I wish I still had the piece I finally submitted. It was very simple and, in my opinion, pretty cool for a kid. In order to show the passage of time, I glued

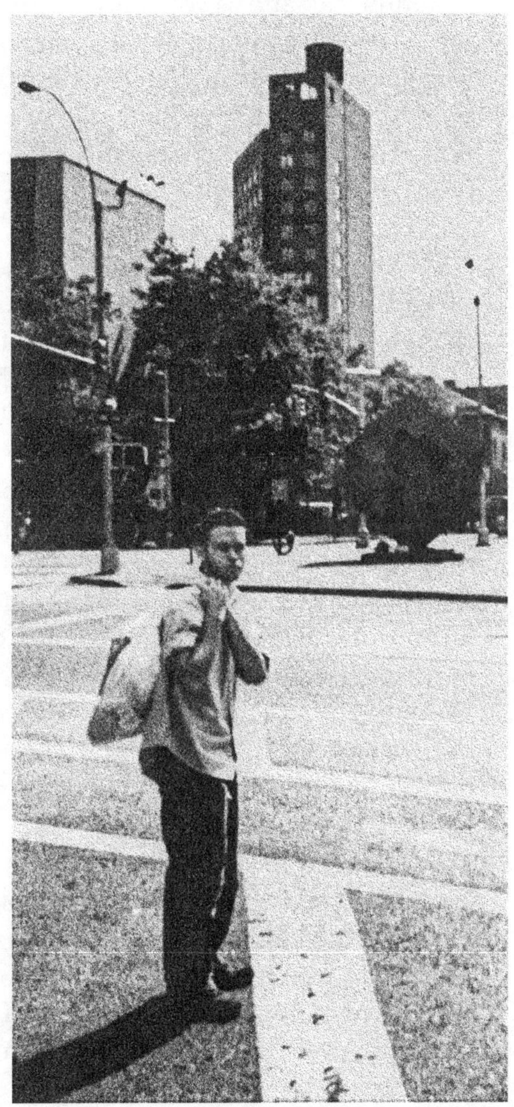

Astor Place, 1999.

a series of leaves in various states of decay to a piece of white foam board. On one side there was a perfect, beautiful leaf, and as you moved across, each leaf was more eroded, ending with the remnants of a leaf that was just a single veiny fiber. That was it—there was no description and nothing else, just a visual depiction of the passage of time through nature, a simple series of decaying leaves.

I sent in the application. I knew it was probably a long shot, but I had put everything I had into it, and if nothing else, it showed both me and the school that I could work hard and that I was serious. I had applied to a number of other schools, but Cooper was all I wanted. One day Richard called, saying he had some good news and some bad news. My hand was shaking as I held the phone. The bad news was that I had not been accepted. My heart sank. I couldn't feel my hands. My stomach immediately felt sick and heavy. I started imagining my life and my whole potential fading away. I may have even started to sob like a baby. Then Richard said, "Wait, wait—the good news is that you were put on the waiting list." Talk about a mixed bag of emotions. I was devastated, and at the same time I knew I still had a chance.

I asked him what number I was on the waiting list, and he said he couldn't tell me but that it wasn't a long list and I was on it and that was what mattered. I'd have to wait it out. There was nothing else I could do. I am not great at being patient. I thought about it all day, every day. But time kept moving. I graduated, and it was the beginning of summer. School started in September, so I had to make a decision. I decided to go to MICA, the Maryland Institute and College of Art, in Baltimore. A great school, but not what I wanted, not what I thought was the best, and definitely not the place that I believed would fulfill my dream. It wasn't *New York fucking City*. But I told myself

I would end up in New York eventually; it would just take longer. I started getting organized and preparing. I remember being in my bedroom in early August, doing some packing, when my mom called my name and said, "Richard is on the phone for you." I ran to the phone. I'm not very fast, but I would have won an Olympic sprinting medal that day. I knew this was going to be a pivotal moment in my life, whichever way it went. I thought he was calling to tell me it was over, that I didn't get in and that I could reapply next year, but a small part of me still hoped and still believed.

Richard said, "Pack your bags, Daniel. You're in." I dropped the phone, I was crying, I was screaming. I was running around the house, and my dog was chasing me and barking, and my mom was shouting after me, *"What did he say?! Daniel?!"*

"I'm going to New York!" I still get goose bumps thinking about it almost twenty-five years later. It was miraculous, and though I didn't really believe in things like manifestation, it almost felt like I willed it to happen with my intense desire to go.

Two weeks later, I was on a plane with my dad. Cooper was a 100 percent full-tuition scholarship, so it was literally my only chance of getting to New York, and it had come through. My parents had enough to cover my apartment for the first year, and after that I would be on my own. I was ready. The city was electric. The world I wanted to live in was alive all around me with art and artists, music, streetwear, freedom, ambition, and the future. I still have a picture of myself in Astor Place the day before school started. My dad took it. I'm right in front of the cube outside the old Kmart, and Cooper is in the background. I lived on St. Mark's Place, right above the St. Mark's bookshop. It was the opening page of my story in New York. Which became the opening page of the story of my life.

CHAPTER IV

HOW TO GET A GALLERY

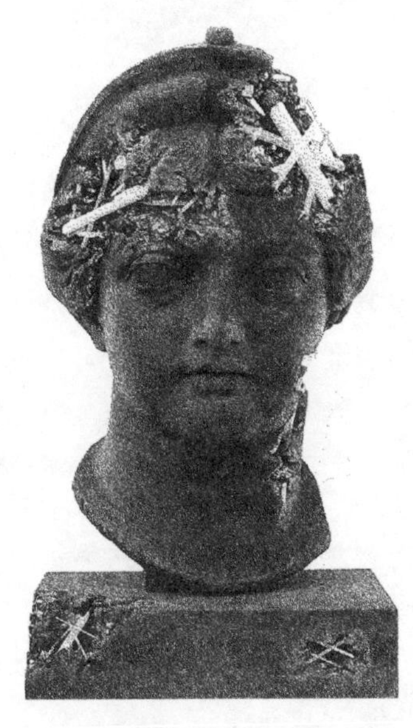

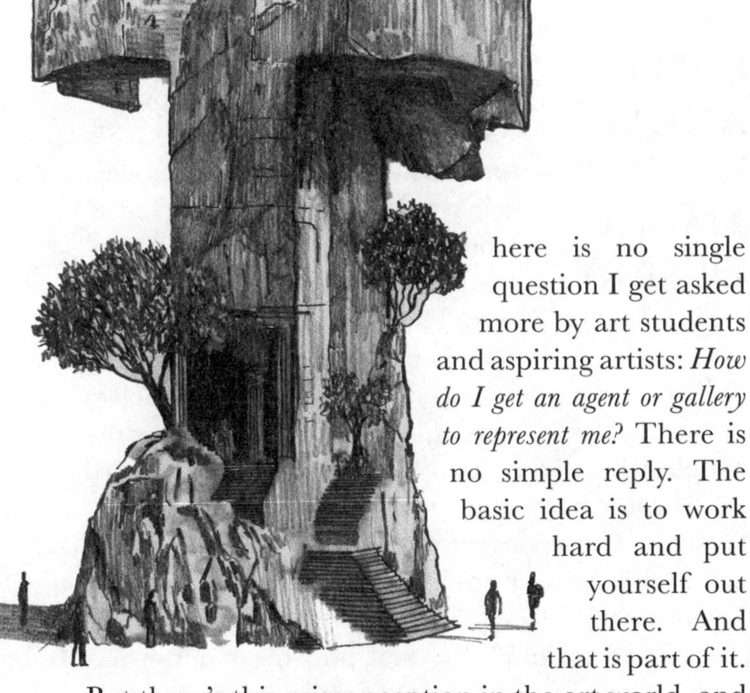

here is no single question I get asked more by art students and aspiring artists: *How do I get an agent or gallery to represent me?* There is no simple reply. The basic idea is to work hard and put yourself out there. And that is part of it. But there's this misconception in the art world, and in the wider creative world, that you just make and put out some work, and an agent or gallery will sign you and you'll be all set. The truth is, that's total bullshit.

To get to that point, you have to grind like you have no idea. Nothing will just happen, at least not for 99.9 percent of the artists in the world. The mantra I share with young artists looking for representation: Live the profession you want to be. If you want to be an artist, then *live* it. Be it. Every minute of every day. Your art comes first.

I tell young artists the truth because a lot of people won't or don't have the stomach to do it. If you want to make it as an artist, plan on working some shitty job for a couple of hours a day and spending all your money on art. Eat instant ramen. Fuck paying separate rent for an apartment; sleep in your studio. Shower with a hose or at your friend's place. Put everything on the line and risk it all. Getting representation requires an unbelievable amount of patience, hard work, and hustle. It isn't fucking rocket science, but you'd be shocked at who won't put in the work or the hustle. Those are the bullshitters. Those are the people posting hate comments on successful artists' work because they themselves never put in the time. They are the people who weren't told the truth about how hard this is and what it really takes. I don't say any of this to scare young artists. I say it because it's crucial and because I don't want to pull any punches. I want to help.

"THE TRUTH IS, MOST PEOPLE CAN'T HANDLE THE WORK IT TAKES TO MAKE EXTRAORDINARY THINGS."

MENTOR NOTE

Now you know the first and most important part. Once you are truly dedicated to and living the life, here are the other steps: (I) Identify an appropriate gallery or galleries. (II) Make yourself known to them. Show up and keep showing up. (III) Make your work known to them. Be your own best promoter.

(IV) Pursue every opportunity with and without them. And most importantly, (V) keep working.

I'm going to walk through how I worked each step and how long it took me to get full gallery representation. It didn't happen via the express lane, and I can't count how many pieces and installations I made before I finally had representation.

I

IDENTIFY AN APPROPRIATE GALLERY

I spent tons of time in art galleries while I was at Cooper Union. One of the great things about going to art school in New York is that the city is also the art capital of the world and the art market capital of the world. Any gallery of any significance has a presence in New York, as does any artist. I'd go to galleries a couple of times a week. Sometimes I would go to specific galleries to see specific shows or the work of specific artists, but often I would just go to Chelsea, the Manhattan neighborhood with blocks and blocks of the best galleries in the world, and wander around.

As I wandered, I also paid very close attention. I would look at a space and imagine my work in it. I would look at a gallery's roster of artists and imagine my name among them. I would ask around about a gallery's reputation before going home to research galleries online. Though gossip and rumors are often bullshit, and always exaggerated, there is usually some kernel of truth in there, so wherever I went, I listened to what other people were saying about galleries.

Emmanuel Perrotin is the renowned French dealer who changed the course of my career and my life. He opened his gallery in Paris in 1990, when he was just twenty-one years old, and later expanded to multiple international locations, including New York, Hong Kong, Seoul, Tokyo, Shanghai, and Dubai. He is widely celebrated for championing both emerging and established artists, including figures like Takashi Murakami, Maurizio Cattelan, Damien Hirst, and Sophie Calle, and for blending high art with playful, boundary-pushing exhibitions. He did a lot of things other art dealers were afraid of, and he made a major impact.

Long before I met Emmanuel, I admired his work. Being signed by him didn't seem realistic, but that's where the grind comes in. I decided this was my dream, I visualized it, I never stopped working toward it, and I was willing to sacrifice anything to make it happen.

II

MAKE YOURSELF KNOWN TO THEM. SHOW UP AND KEEP SHOWING UP.

I finally met Emmanuel in 2003. I was sharing a studio in Miami with a number of friends after college, and I had heard there was an art collector named George Lindemann who knew Emmanuel. I met George and asked him if he could invite Emmanuel over to the studio. He came and saw what we were all doing. Apparently it made an impression on him.

A year later he invited a few young artists to do a group exhibition at his gallery in Paris, and I was lucky enough to be included. The show went great. I had two pieces in it, and they were both purchased by Hervé Mikaeloff, who later became a very important art adviser to LVMH (more on that soon). After that first show, whenever Emmanuel was in town for the annual Art Basel Miami Beach art fair, I invited him to my studio. I also stayed in touch with people I knew at his gallery in Paris.

I made sure to send complimentary notes about their shows and send them pictures and updates of my work. His gallery was always at the top of my list of places to spend time. I never went more than a month without reaching out in some way. It was a balancing act of being persistent and making myself visible but not being a pest.

III

MAKE YOUR WORK KNOWN TO THEM. BE YOUR OWN BEST PROMOTER.

At that point in my life, I wanted a solo exhibition in Emmanuel's Paris gallery more than anything in the world. It was my sole focus. I would stay up nights or find myself zoning out over a sketchbook because I was thinking about how I could convince Emmanuel that I was ready and deserved this shot. When you're a young artist starting from nothing, it's hard for people to share the vision you have for yourself. I struggled with how to show people my potential. You have to make yourself so vulnerable by putting yourself out there, knowing you could face crushing rejection in the process. I tried to imagine, if I were Emmanuel, what could convince me to take a chance and give a young artist a show at my gallery. I needed to figure out how to show him not just my passion but also what was unique about my perspective. Why me?

I decided that the best way to get Emmanuel to pay attention to my work was to bet on my hustle. I doubled down. I was always in the studio, working from nine to nine, every day, whether I had an idea or not. My artist friends were out partying or doing other things and would stroll into the studio at three or four in the afternoon. They had their way, but that wasn't going to be my path. I sure as hell wasn't going to miss out on my chance to make it just so I could go to some parties. Many of those guys never made it past the work they did in that studio. They never had careers in art.

Meanwhile, while they had fun, I produced a whole series of drawings and sculptures. The drawings were of caverns and icebergs, with buildings growing out of the darkness among the stalactites. And the sculptures were these white iceberg-like forms with architectural constructions protruding like beams that had fallen into the snow. All the way through this stage of grinding, I was showing in other group shows and putting up my own exhibitions, and making sure Emmanuel and everyone at his gallery knew what I was doing.

"BELIEF BEGINS WITH YOU–SHOW THEM YOUR PASSION, YOUR VISION, AND YOUR UNIQUE PERSPECTIVE."

MENTOR NOTE

I started asking myself how I could show Emmanuel my vision for what an exhibition at his gallery would look like. And the answer was right there in the question. I knew he would be in Miami again for Art Basel in December of 2004, and I was going to put everything on the line to convince him. I decided to build out my studio space just like his gallery: the same layout, the same columns, the same light coming in through the windows. I set up my work just like a gallery show inside this reconstructed version of his gallery (except my version was made of cardboard and two-by-fours). I wanted him to easily understand it and see it. I called him in Paris—even though international calls were insanely expensive at the time—and invited him to come to my studio in Miami. Three months later, he was there. As he walked in, he immediately

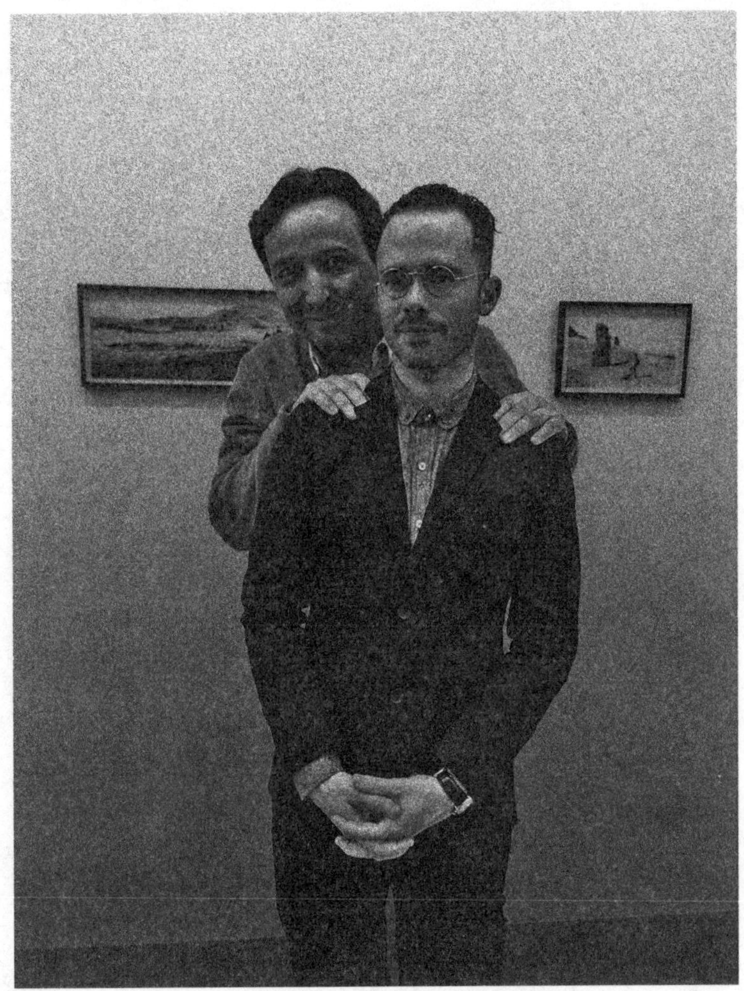

With Emmanuel Perrotin at one of my shows in Paris.

recognized his space and quickly understood how the exhibition and all the work would translate to his gallery.

It's not like a solo exhibition offer was on the table. But I remember to this day that after he had walked around the entire space, he looked back at me with a little smile, and at that moment I knew I had to push for my dream. There are these moments, these inflection points in everyone's life, where you have a chance if you're willing to take it, and I was locked in on this dream of mine and knew that this was one of those moments. I took a deep breath, tried to calm myself, even though I was nervous as hell, and decided to take my shot. I looked Emmanuel straight in the eye and said, "I would love to show this work in your gallery in Paris."

I'm sure the pause he took lasted only a second, but goddamn did it feel like an eternity. This was one of those moments when a dream could be realized or I could take a massive gut punch. But the craziest thing happened—a reaction that I didn't anticipate at all. He took that short pause, looked at me, and casually said, "Let's do it."

IV

PURSUE EVERY OPPORTUNITY WITH AND WITHOUT THEM

I had grinded for three years since college with barely a sniff at representation. I'd faced countless rejections and dead ends. Now I was going to have a show at one of the best galleries in Paris. All that nervous energy I was holding inside when I pitched Emmanuel about the show transformed into a massive shot of adrenaline when he responded. I think I could've run through a wall right then, I was so hyped.

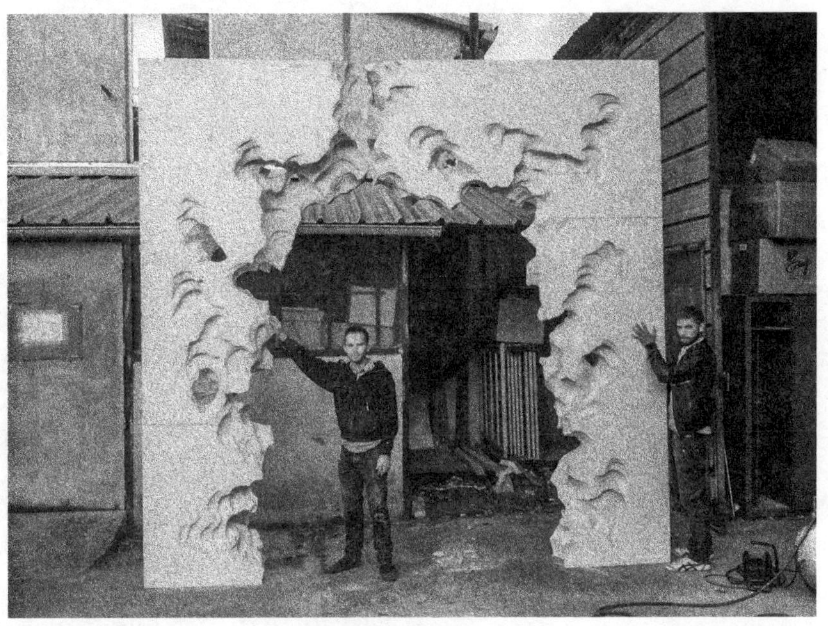

The eroded arch I made for the FIAC 2009 Art Fair in Paris.

Soon afterward, the realization of what was coming really landed. I knew I needed to get to work. As hard as I'd been working, I needed to work even harder. I needed this show to be perfect. I busted my ass for months getting that exhibition together. I don't know how much I slept or ate during those days, but it wasn't a lot. It was all work. All the time.

The show opened on my twenty-fifth birthday, in September 2005. I was vibrating. I was so excited for this moment. My family came to Paris for it—my parents and grandparents. A handful of my art friends scraped together the cash to fly to Paris as well. I don't know how they did, because none of us had any money. That type of friendship isn't typical. I was honored. The love that this group of people showed me by traveling all that way to support me was major.

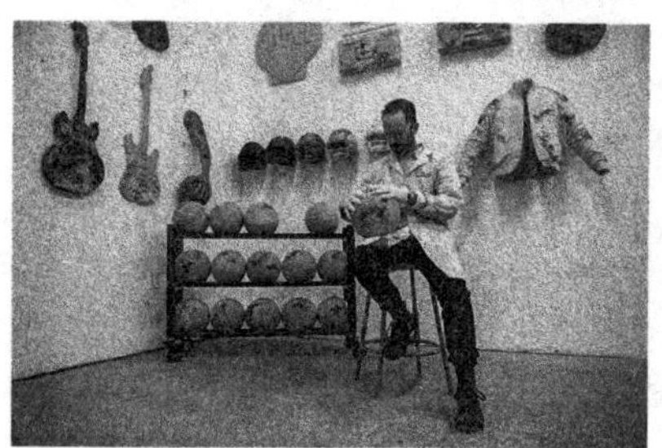

Working in my live-in studio.

It's hard to understand what it feels like to have your first solo exhibition. The nerves and the anxiety going into it are enormous. You know that you don't get another first chance like this, and to have it on the stage that I was going to be on—you can't take that for granted. Luckily, I had all of the support from my family and the guidance I needed from Emmanuel. He had this way of keeping me in check. He would keep me calm and centered. As the show approached, he talked to me about how he didn't want to put a tremendous amount of pressure on me and the show. So he decided not to put my name on the gallery's website. His reasoning was "We're going to see how it goes before I decide to represent you."

I didn't know enough about how to launch an exhibition at the time, so I went along with what he decided. And while I worked on the pieces for

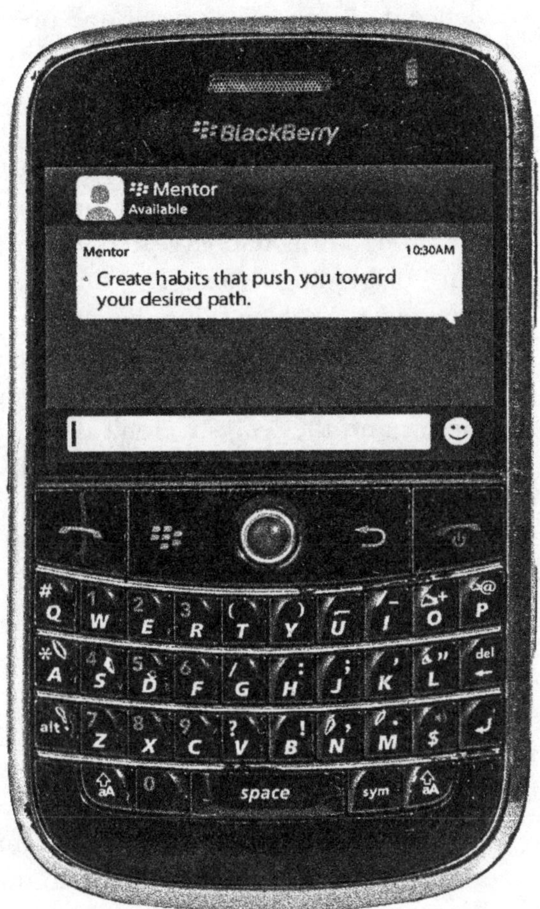

BlackBerry
Mentor
Available
Mentor
10:30AM
Create habits that push you toward your desired path.
space
sym

MENTOR NOTE

his show, I kept doing other things, making more work, showing it, selling it when I could. Though I had been given a chance and had busted my ass to get it, it was not a sure thing. I could not rely on it being a success, no matter how hard I thought about it and worked on it. So while I worked with confidence, I also checked myself and prepared to accept that the show could be a failure. What was important was that I had a shot. And I knew that if I had gotten this one, I could get another one.

The day after the show opened, I saw Peggy, the gallery director. She told me the show had sold out. *In one day.* I was flabbergasted. I couldn't believe it. I'm not kidding or exaggerating when I say it was the greatest fucking thing that ever happened to me. My years of work and study and dreaming had been validated. I didn't know who'd bought all of the pieces, and the works weren't that expensive, but it didn't matter—people had liked them enough to buy them, to add them to their collections and their lives. I walked away with around $23,000 from the sales, which was about twelve times as much as I had in my bank account at the time. And though it had taken me a year to make the pieces, and the money wasn't enough to support me for a year, I didn't care at all. It wasn't about the money. Selling those pieces was the ultimate validation that I belonged in the Art World. I was an Artist with a capital *A*.

When the show sold out, Emmanuel said, "We're going to add your name to the website now if you want. If you choose to be, you are now represented by Galerie Emmanuel Perrotin." A simple statement and change to the website that meant everything. It launched my career and led me to where I am now.

There was no contract, no paper between Emmanuel and me. It was a gentleman's agreement based on honor and respect. To this day, I still don't have a paper contract with him or any of the galleries I work with. There is an understanding about how we're going to work that goes beyond a physical contract. I'm sure every artist would be advised against that now. I'm sure if I'd had a lawyer at that point, I would've been advised against it, but it worked, and it still works. Emmanuel and I have the right understanding and a mutual admiration and respect. Not everyone is going to have that. It's a relationship unique to us. Without it, I'm sure the partnership would've crashed and burned.

V

KEEP WORKING

I recently hit my twentieth anniversary of working with Emmanuel. From that first show in 2005 until now, we've never not worked together. Twenty years of marriage is a long time, but twenty years in an artist–gallery relationship is a lifetime, and it doesn't happen often. It's a beautiful and rare thing. I'm blessed to have found this home for my art. It's crazy how fast those years go and what you create in that span of time. And in all those years, we did all of that work and transacted millions in sales without anything being papered. I still find that to be fucking unbelievable. To me, that's the definition of trust.

An example of that trust is a big exhibition at the Orange County Museum of Art in 2024 that I saw as a de facto mid-career survey, as a measuring stick of where I stood after twenty years as an artist. In preparation for that show, I cataloged a lot of my older work and brought it back out to display. I wanted people to see the journey of my work, how I've moved from one idea to the next, and how I arrived at my current subject matter. I certainly didn't want the show to be like an end-of-career thing, but twenty years is no joke. I've produced a lot of work, and reflecting on the journey is a healthy way to not forget where you've come from and where you'd still like to go.

I shared my thinking about how to put this show together when I was out to dinner with Emmanuel, and I asked for his help. I wanted to track down all the pieces from that first show in Paris back in 2005. I told him I wanted to show progress and that I'd love to have as many pieces as possible from that first exhibition in this upcoming one. I remember what happened next like it was yesterday. Emmanuel looked at me and said, "I know where everything is from that show."

And there was just something about the way he said it and the look on his face that seemed curious to me, so I asked, "What do you mean you know where everything is from that show?"

And would you believe this shit? He says all nonchalantly, while raising his fork to his mouth to take a bite of his salad, "Yeah, I bought the whole show." I was in shock, and as the realization landed, I damn near started crying. When my first exhibition sold out, it had given me so much confidence at that stage of my life. I had just turned twenty-five, and I was riding a feeling of *Wow, maybe I can make it as an artist.* Without that kind of start to my career, I don't know how things would've turned out. I couldn't believe he'd never told me, but I know it would've defeated the purpose. It was an amazing gesture that set the course for everything that followed.

As the dinner went on and we kept talking, Emmanuel told me that he doesn't pick artists for their work; he represents them for what he sees in their *future* work. He saw the potential I had to build a career. But he needed to also see that I could put in the hours and the effort, the sweat and the tears.

He needed to see that I could be patient. And he needed to see that I could act like a professional. Because I'd had no other choice, I'd become what I'd needed to become to secure representation. This story applies to any creative field: music, fashion, design, etc.

If I can do it, so can you.

CHAPTER V

WHY YOU SHOULD ALWAYS SURROUND YOURSELF WITH

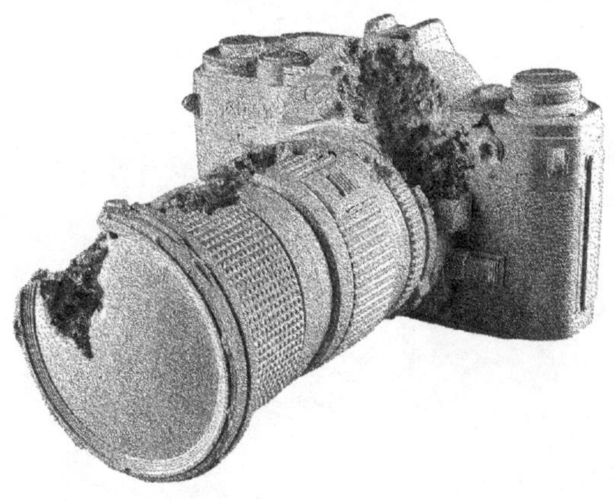

HIGHLY SUCCESSFUL, COMPETITIVE PEOPLE

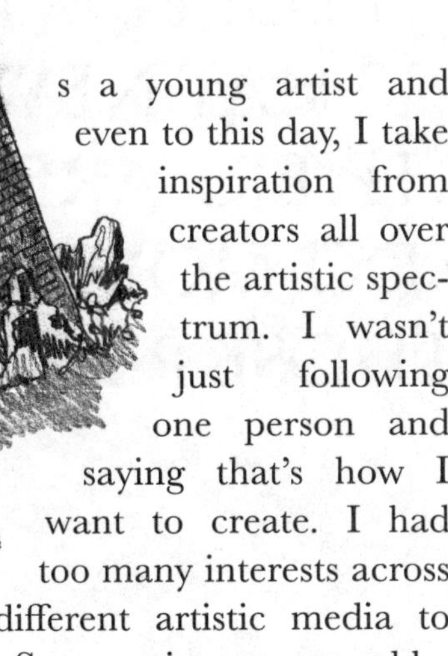s a young artist and even to this day, I take inspiration from creators all over the artistic spectrum. I wasn't just following one person and saying that's how I want to create. I had too many interests across different artistic media to lock in on only one area. Some artists are moved by certain things, but I get inspiration from so many places that I'm never going to say *This is what I want to do* and focus on a single medium. My perspective comes from Marcel Duchamp, A Tribe Called

"MOST PEOPLE ACCEPT THE WORLD AS A FIXED REALITY. AS AN ARTIST, YOU CAN CREATE A SPACE THAT IS JUST BEYOND IT, THAT REVEALS NEW WAYS OF SEEING AND EXPERIENCING LIFE. SOME PEOPLE WILL NOT ACCEPT THAT NEW REALITY. BUT THERE ARE THOSE WHO DO. MOVE TOWARD THOSE PEOPLE."

MENTOR NOTE

Quest, Robert Smithson, Metallica, René Magritte, and countless others.

Like every artist, I push boundaries. That's not saying anything revolutionary, but it still needs to be said. I always want to make sure I'm blurring the line between art and nonart. To make people ask themselves *What is art?* over and over again. To make them uncomfortable. I wanted to rip away the traditional context of objects and architecture and show those things in a totally different way. Have other artists before me attempted that? Yes, but not in the exact style I've done it or with the materials, both physical and cultural, that I've used. And that is how I've continued to push boundaries and to make art that is new and different.

I'm a student of life, so I devour pop culture and I track what's current both in the art world and outside of it. Not with some special intention; it's just my nature. I have a handful of special people in my life who have influenced my work, and you can see them in what I create, but most of them are not Artists. I hate Art as some elitist circle. If your idea of being an artist is sitting around telling each other how great you are, then fuck off with that. I was never interested in the cliques of artists who jerk each other off about how brilliant they are. To me, that means you've had a small moment of success and now you are going to just milk it. Now you are about bullshit and people telling you how good you are. There is a lot of that in the Art World, unfortunately. There is a lot of that in many creative fields, unfortunately.

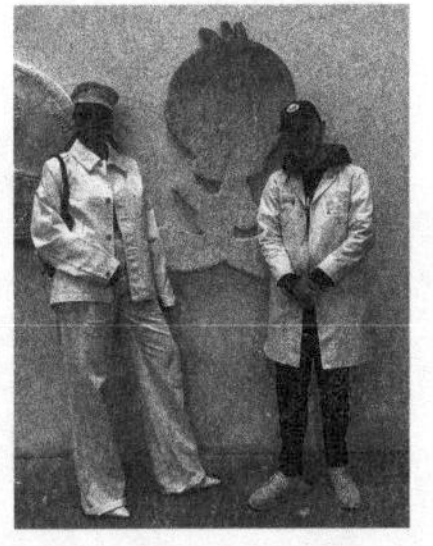

With Rihanna.

You have to prove yourself over and over in this world. There were artists who came out of school at the same time I did and blew up right away. They were more successful than me right out of the gate, and they were creating works that seemed more inaccessible or even ungenerous to their audience. Their art was more difficult to understand, and they were rewarded for it. But making difficult art didn't interest me.

In college I had a core group of friends. Some were artists, but I was also friends with musicians and dancers, fashion designers and jewelry makers, and one of my closest friends worked in an ad agency. I was friends with all of them because they were interesting and I liked them as people. Socially, I always felt like an outsider at Cooper. And the way that I created and wanted to create only heightened that feeling. Either I wasn't part of "the group" or there was always this thing in school where a lot of people, including professors, thought that the work I made was too generous, too broad. But I always made things that I wanted to make, and I wanted as many people as possible to see them, and through a broad approach, I hoped huge numbers of people would enjoy my art.

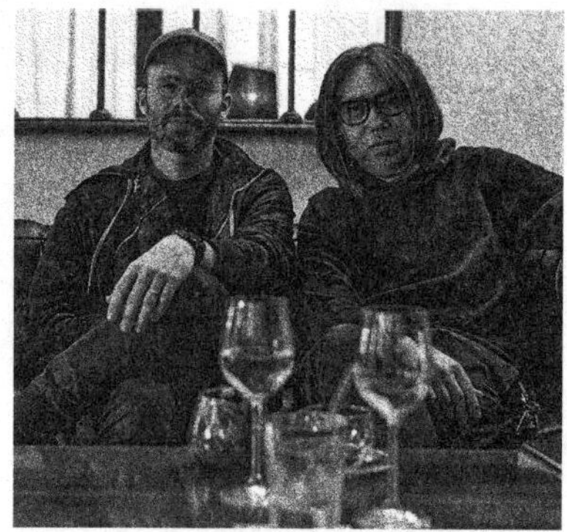

With Hiroshi Fujiwara, Tokyo.

Because of that belief, I was often more drawn to people in fashion and music. Their world felt more magical to me. I was awed by the size of the audience they reached, and it felt like there was this massive potential to do interesting things in their world. While the art world felt confined and guarded, fashion and music were open, and I wanted to bring pieces and inspiration from those worlds into what I did. I wanted to create work that would resonate across society.

Before my first exhibition in Miami, Emmanuel invited me to Pharrell Williams's house for dinner. Pharrell lived in this penthouse apartment that took up the top two floors of a skyscraper, a commercial office building, in the Miami neighborhood of Brickell. It was the kind of place where you'd expect to find a Bond villain or a playboy. When we got there, Pharrell was still out, so we waited. An hour later, he strolled in with his whole squad. He was still killing it as a producer at the time. In 2003, he produced nearly 43 percent of all the music on top 100 radio; he was working with Beyoncé, Britney Spears, Justin Timberlake—all the biggest pop stars. He was famous, but not like *your parents know who he is* famous. I knew his clothing line, Billionaire Boys Club, and I had seen him outside his Miami store a couple of times. But I was surprised when we started talking and he knew my work. We didn't eat until after midnight. Helen, then his girlfriend, now his wife, cooked the whole meal.

At some point during dinner, Pharrell asked me to pull up my work on the internet so we could look at it together. He did it casually, like we were old friends. We were in the kitchen on a Mac that was set up with production equipment. He started firing questions. He's one of the most curious people I've ever met. Anyone who enters his space, he's going to ask them a million questions, but not the dumb kind where somebody's just filling space. He'll take time and think about what he wants to talk about. He wants details. *What's this about? Why'd you do that? How did you make this?*

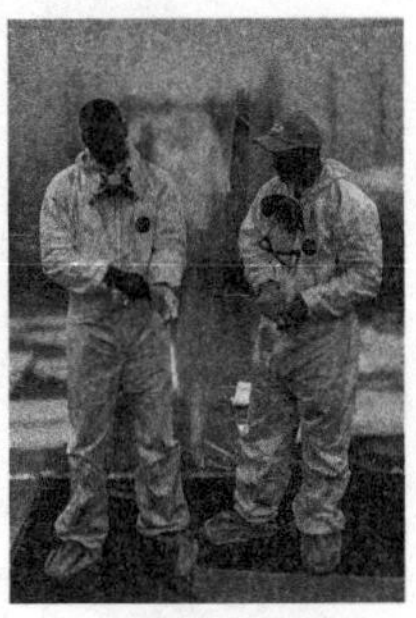

Collaborating with Samuel Ross.

Pharrell asked his security guard, the same one he's had for years, to grab a case from another room. It was a giant Louis Vuitton trunk, with one of these incredible pieces of jewelry he'd made with Jacob the Jeweler inside. It was a giant necklace, the famous N.E.R.D. necklace. He took it out and hung it around my neck. I couldn't believe how heavy it was—it probably weighed ten pounds. We talked about his creative process making jewelry with Jacob, which is so different from working as a producer.

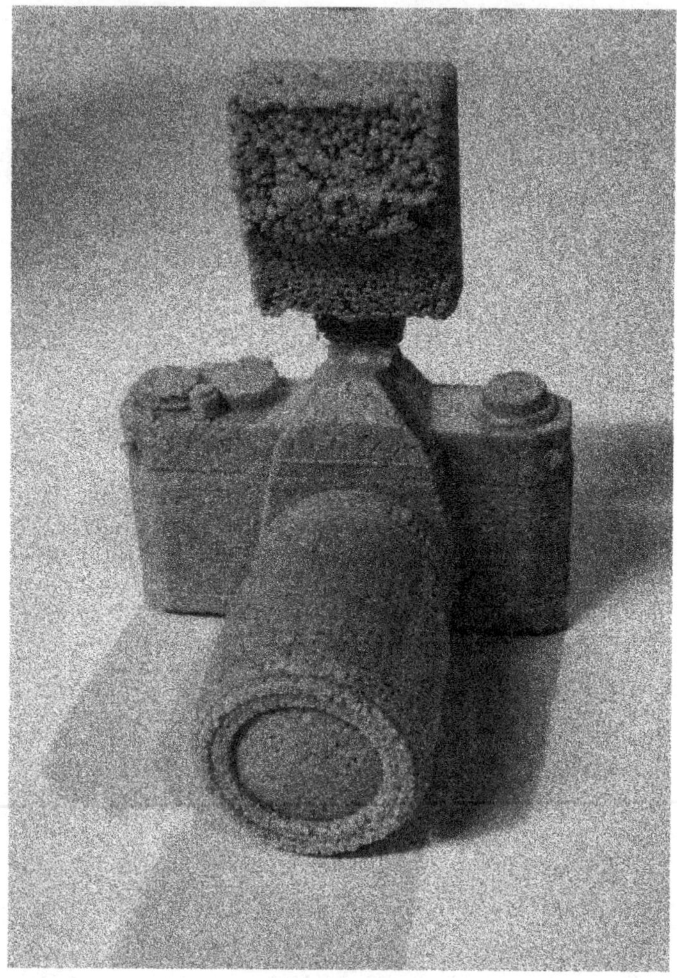

Cast of first camera.

It's one of my favorite things to do, being around people who can do amazing things and push themselves to be the best at it. Whether it's making music or playing basketball, talking with elite-level achievers is an amazing way to improve your own process, especially when it's something you have no skill at whatsoever. I don't read music. I can't play the piano. And I think watching and listening to someone play the piano at an elite level is mind-boggling. I don't have any concept of how to do it. Listening to Pharrell speak about his musical process is incredible. Being surrounded by and interacting with people who are great at what they do—that's why I do a lot of my collaborative projects.

We exchanged numbers at that dinner, and Pharrell reached out to me a couple of months later. He came to my studio and we spent a few hours talking about art and our favorite artists. He ended the visit by asking me if I would ever want to do some kind of project with him. He wasn't sure what it would be, but we'd figure it out. I tried to play it cool, but I couldn't say yes fast enough.

My process isn't scripted, but when you put it next to Pharrell's creative process, the way he makes music feels so much wilder to me than the way I make art. As we started talking about what to do together, he said he thought we should work on something in the music space. I had just finished the first and initial piece in what would become my Future Relics series. It was a cast of my original Pentax K1000, the one my grandfather gave me for my eleventh birthday. The one I shot the doors series on. I thought about how musical instruments throughout history are usually associated with a particular time period, whether it's harpsichords in the sixteenth century or electric guitars in the rock-and-roll era. I asked Pharrell what the first important device was that he'd made music on—an instrument or computer or whatever. He said

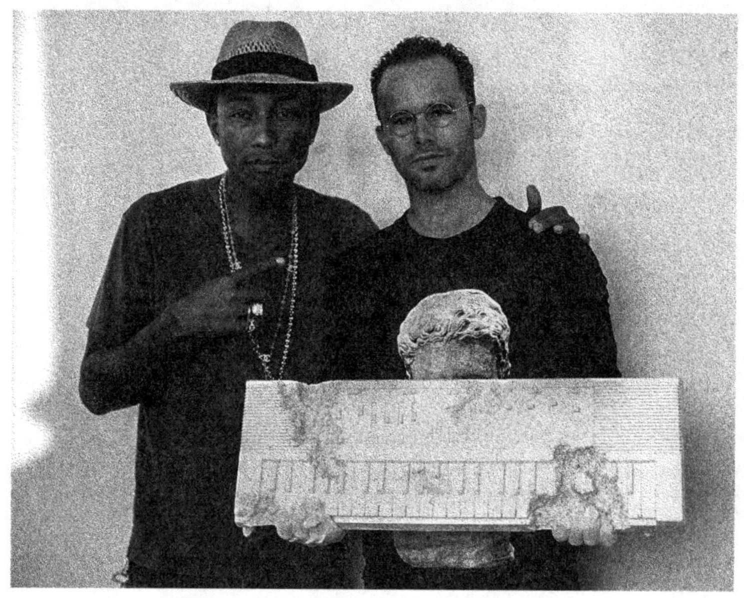

Pharrell's Casio.

it was a Casio MT-500 keyboard with drum pads. It was the first keyboard Casio sold that had an audio-out port so you could make a four- or eight-track recording. He was in high school in Virginia Beach, and he would make recordings by layering sets of four different tracks over and over again. It was also the first time that he'd made his own beats. I asked if he still had the keyboard, and he did, somewhere. We had to find it. I told him I wanted to make a sculpture out of it and that if he could get it to me, I would cast it as a Future Relic. It was not just an object that was important to him and related to his music, but it was also linked to a moment in time.

When it was done, I took it over to his place, and he loved it. He loved the idea that the Casio keyboard that had changed his life could be made into a sculpture that might someday end up in a museum. Pharrell wanted to do an exhibition, but one keyboard wasn't enough to mount a successful show. So I gave Pharrell the original and made three more using the most interesting materials I had at my disposal at the time—volcanic ash, white quartz, and pink crystal. When I finished, Pharrell walked into the space and just smiled and nodded.

This was in 2013, and the new Standard Hotel was about to open in the East Village. Pharrell called and asked if we could host a party there during Fashion Week, with the plan being to use the party to unveil my work to the world. He was starting to move further into fashion and was convinced that this event would be a big moment. He was right. It ended up being not only the biggest party and exhibition of the week but the biggest of the year, and it was a pivotal inflection point for my work and my life.

Watching Pharrell and listening to him work and operate had an immense impact on me. He was thinking and working twenty-four hours a day. He kept himself in great shape and had a huge amount of energy. He chased whatever piqued his curiosity. He was warm, friendly, optimistic, collaborative, and kind, despite his immense success. He was willing to try anything, take any shot, make any call. He had, and still has, a relentless drive to make great things and make an impact on our culture, and he wanted to be the best at whatever he did. I decided that I wanted to meet more people like him and that the best way for me to be the best version of myself, as a man and an artist, was to surround myself with the most ambitious and accomplished people I could find and learn as much as I could from them and do as many things as possible with them.

The evening we had the party at the Standard for the Future Relics, followed by a dinner at the Bowery Hotel, was life-changing because of the people I met. The Bowery is two blocks south of Cooper Union, where my life in New York had started. A full-circle moment. Because I tend to work up until the last possible minute perfecting everything before a show, I'm usually exhausted at the openings and don't go to the after-parties, but despite my exhaustion, there was no way I was going home. The event was by far the biggest I had ever been involved in, with as many people seeing my work in that one night as had seen it in my entire career. Jay-Z and Beyoncé showed up. I managed to get a few minutes with Jay and showed him my work. It took another decade, but I ended up working with him on a major sculpture of his hands in the Roc formation. I also later designed the cover for his definitive book, unveiled at another massive event in Brooklyn years later.

"SHOW ME YOUR FRIENDS AND I'LL SHOW YOU YOUR FUTURE."

MENTOR NOTE

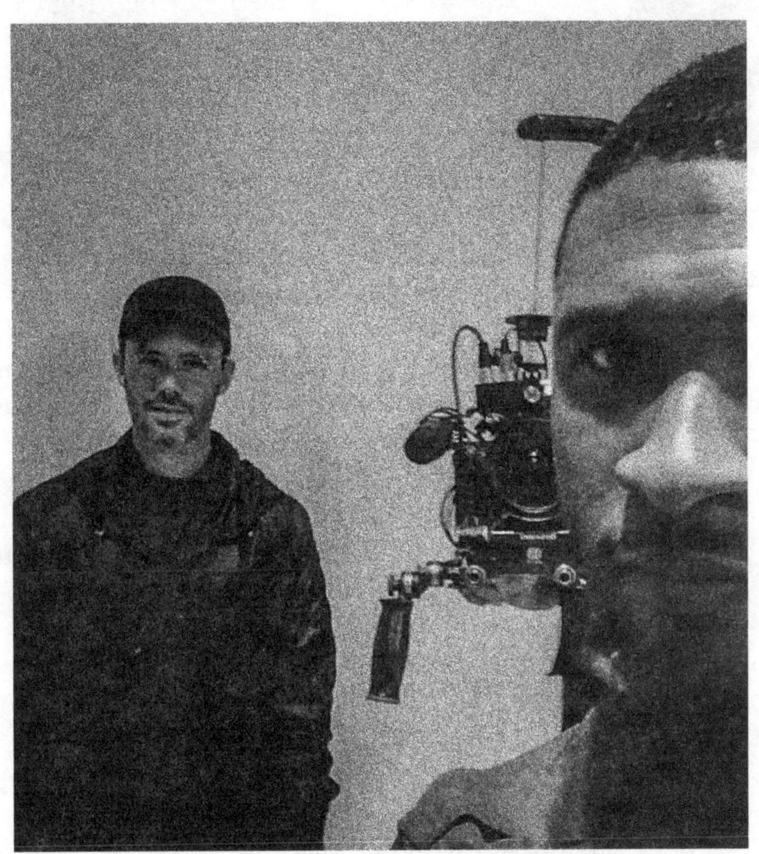

With Usher when I directed his music video.

Pharrell had deemed my work important, and the people in his world picked up on it. It was a lucky break, but in reality I felt as if I had made that luck by working as hard as I had to get Emmanuel invested in me to begin with. Luck is out there floating around, but you have to put yourself in positions where it can find you.

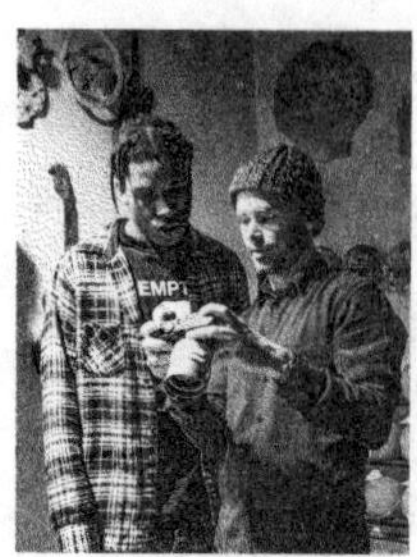

With ASAP Rocky in my studio.

Virgil Abloh was one of the people I met that night. He was similar to Pharrell in that he was in constant motion, constantly thinking, constantly taking action. He had a particular way of viewing the art world. His eye was sharp, and he had impeccable taste. Though he worked in fashion and music, he had a degree in architecture and a deep knowledge of art history, and he wanted to get more involved in the art world. I was working in art and coming from the opposite direction, wanting to get more into fashion and music. At the time, Virgil was Kanye West's creative director, on tour and traveling everywhere with him, so after that night I'd only see him when they were in New York for an event. But we wanted to learn from each other and help each other, and this drove hours and hours of conversations and a steady stream of text messages and DMs between us.

Like Pharrell, Virgil had what seemed like unlimited energy and drive. He thought of everything he did, whether it was in music or fashion or art or design, as part of a greater creative practice. He had a working idea that if you take any existing work of art, architecture, design, or fashion, any piece in any medium, and alter it by 3 percent, you'll have made something new—a version of Picasso's famous quote "Great artists don't borrow, they steal." And like Picasso, Virgil was one of the most productive artists of his time. The amount of work he did between the time I met him and the time he passed away, in 2021—in the music world, with his fashion brand Off-White, at Louis Vuitton, and with all of his various collabs, including with painter Takashi Murakami—was just astounding. I miss him. He was one of the smartest, most genuine, most interesting, most ambitious, most creative, and most capable people I have ever known, and I believe he will go down in history as one of the most significant artists of my generation. In many ways, despite people like me and Pharrell who were working with the same ideas, nobody did more to break down the walls between fashion, music, art, and streetwear than Virgil. If you're into any of those things, you owe him a debt. The time I spent with him was a great gift. He died at the age of forty-one. Hope to see you on the other side, V.

I also met Ronnie Fieg that night. Ronnie founded a brand called Kith, a streetwear/lifestyle brand. He started out at David Z., an iconic chain of footwear stores in New York. He came up as a stock boy and worked his way onto the sales floor. Ronnie has pictures of himself selling Timberlands to Jay-Z, the Notorious B.I.G., and many other iconic New York rappers. He was moonlighting on a project with Asics and placed an order of his own design with Asics through the David Z. account. When his boss found out, he got fired for it, but the entire design run sold out. Feeling confident, Ronnie started Kith, which was originally a sneaker store in the back of a shop called Atrium, on Broadway. He was there every day, and I started hanging with him a couple of times a week. As the shop became more successful, Ronnie started talking about expanding Kith and was looking for a new space. I had just started an architecture studio called Snarkitecture with Alex Mustonen, a friend I had gone to school with, and though we hadn't done any real designs yet, I told Ronnie I wanted to design his store. He was meeting with more experienced architects and designers, but I kept telling him he was going to end up hiring me.

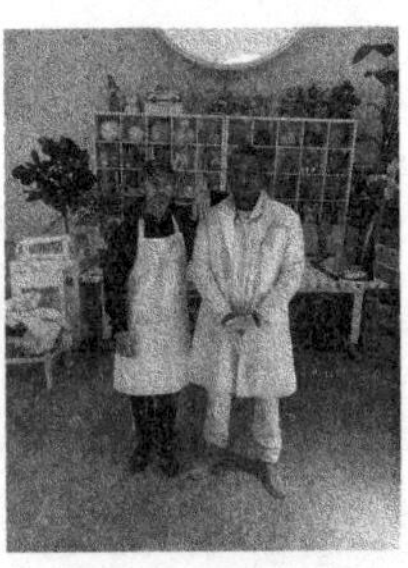

Working with Nas on the cover of his album.

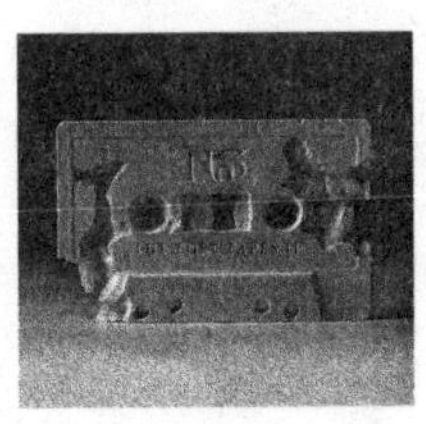

The album cover I made for Nas.

My pitch was completely antithetical to the way other shops in New York were designed. Because real estate is so expensive, when they lay out a Nike store, for example, they're thinking about product SKUs versus square footage. They have to calculate how to sell enough shoes and clothes to make the store profitable. My idea was to make the entrance to the space an experience that would be so out of the ordinary and inspiring, it would motivate people to buy things. I proposed a concave, church-like structure composed of Jordan 1s cast in plaster that would hang at different heights to create a Fibonacci series dome. The rest of the store was treated very minimally. Ronnie loved it. And though he had to stretch every dollar he had to make it work, we did it anyway. His view was that he'd rather go out of business having done something spectacular than stay in business and be lame. So we did it, to great stress and anxiety.

It was a huge success. The store was flooded with customers, many of whom first came for the experience but ended up loyal customers. And the lesson for me was: *Take the risk.* Be bold. The work is most important. If the work is great, money and customers—or in my case, collectors—will follow. Kith has become one of the most prestigious streetwear and clothing brands in the world, and after New York I designed the stores in Los Angeles, Miami, Tokyo, and Paris, as well as a kids' store in New York. In every single location, we followed the same model: Create the best and most unique experience possible. If you do, the money will follow.

Being around people like Pharrell, Virgil, and Ronnie drives me to be the best I can be in every way. The same is true of being around competitive and successful people of any kind. They make you think, *I can do that. How difficult can this be? I see how hard that person works—maybe I should step up my game. If they can do it, I can do it. If they're making their dreams come true, so can I.* And as simple as these statements and ideas may be, they can make the difference between success and failure. You need to be careful and aware, because the inverse is also true. If you look around and your friends aren't doing much with their lives, that too is infectious. Get away from people who don't inspire you, don't push you. Run. Watching your friends succeed drives you to succeed as well. And if they're true friends, as mine have been, they will be there not only to cheer you on but to work with you, exchange ideas, help you, grow together, succeed together.

CHAPTER VI

MY YEARS WITH MERCE CUNNINGHAM

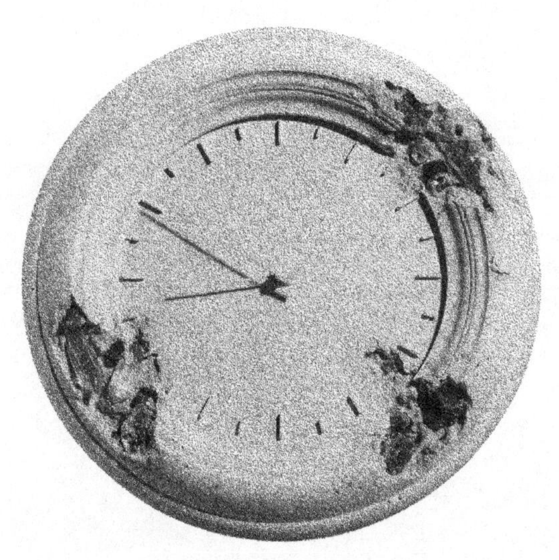

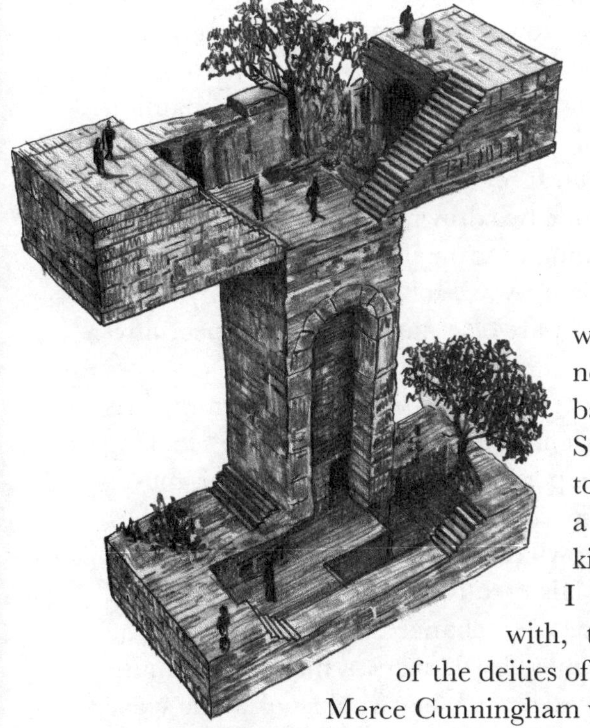

want to rewind now, a decade back before the Standard party, to tell you about a very different kind of legend I got to work with, this time one of the deities of the art world. Merce Cunningham was a pioneering American dancer and choreographer who profoundly influenced modern dance. Born in 1919 in Centralia, Washington, he began studying dance at the Cornish School, in Seattle. He later went to Black Mountain College, where he met the composer

John Cage. Merce danced with Martha Graham's company in New York before founding the Merce Cunningham Dance Company in 1953. Throughout his career, Merce collaborated with artists like Robert Rauschenberg and Andy Warhol, continually pushing the boundaries of dance and interdisciplinary art. He was a hugely influential figure, but I hadn't paid much attention to dance, so I had only known of him because I studied his work with Marcel Duchamp in the 1960s.

I met Merce in 2004. I was a year out of Cooper and living in Miami. It was an odd period in my life, kind of an in-between time. I was in touch with Emmanuel, but he wasn't representing me yet, and I hadn't had my show in Paris yet. While I was courting him to make it official, continuing to work and make art, I was in a group exhibition in Miami at the Museum of Contemporary Art. This was my first museum project. It revolved around the idea of environments. I made two drawings of large caverns with buildings seeming to grow inside them. It was a big show, and though I was excited to be in it, my pieces weren't a huge part of it, and I didn't expect anything to come out of it.

Miami had just built a big new performing arts center, the Adrienne Arsht Center, which was looking for high-profile performance pieces—theater, music, and dance—that could bring attention and audiences. Merce was in town discussing a potential commission at the center. His creative process revolved around John Cage's ideas of chance. He would arrive at a space accompanied by dancers, a musician or musicians, and a visual artist. They would look at the space together, then they would separate, and Merce would create the dance, the musician would create the score, and the artist would make the stage designs and the costumes, all independently. None of them would know what any of the others were doing, bringing the elements together only in the performance. It could create chaos or it could create beauty, or both.

While Merce was in town, he visited the group show at the MOCA and saw my drawings. He asked the museum director for my phone number. The director called me, and the conversation was a *holy shit* moment. An artist at Merce's level had seen my work and wanted to speak with me.

He called the next day. I didn't really know what to say or what to expect or why he wanted to talk, and I was nervous. We spoke for a minute about my drawings, and he said, "I've been commissioned for this new dance, and I was thinking you could create a stage design for me. What do you think?" While I was processing, Merce asked if I was still there, and I said, "Yes, I'm here. And I'd love to do it, but I don't know anything about stage design. I've never even been on a stage. I wouldn't know where to start." He laughed and said, "That's perfect—even better! Come to New York, come to my studio. Part of the point, and the experience, is to see what artists from outside my world will create."

His studio was on the roof of a legendary, incredible building in the West Village called Westbeth. It's a huge warehouse that was converted into artists' live-work studios in the sixties. You had to be an artist to live there. A board interviewed and approved all of the residents. There were dancers, painters, composers, sculptors—every medium was represented. When I arrived, Merce had a season of performances underway at the Joyce Theater, in Chelsea, so I went to the shows, and that was my first real exposure to his work. Afterward, I would spend time at the studio and just watch performances or rehearsals. I spent time with his stage manager and the executive director of the company, trying to understand how Merce thought about design and how it worked on the stage. It was an amazing place to learn. There were so many knowledgeable, talented people in one place that you had to be an idiot not to want to use them as resources to improve your craft. If you ever have the opportunity to learn from a talented and experienced creator, do it. Don't think you're too good for it or you know how to do something already.

Going into my work with Merce, I wanted to have a grasp of how he worked and how to be successful when designing sets for him. Once he had engaged me to do the set design, he didn't want to know anything else. He basically said, "You make what you want, and I'll see you at the premiere." His only direction was not to put anything in the space that could injure the dancers in any way. That was the only direction and the only rule. It's unbelievable that he'd trust a twenty-four-year-old who'd never designed a set before with that kind of creative autonomy. But that was how Merce worked. He was a genius.

Meeting Merce and working with him is a large part of why I got attention early in my career. Reflecting back on the pieces that inspired him to reach out to me, I'm still amazed that he saw enough in them to give me the opportunity he did. He saw my potential and wanted to help me realize it. I owe him so much. Never turn down an opportunity, especially early on in your career, even if it's completely outside of your comfort zone. I didn't ever imagine that one of my biggest breaks would be designing a dance stage. But I was open to the idea, and working with someone like Merce was a chance I could not pass up. I would just have to fucking figure it out.

Designing that initial set was intense. I had so many anxiety dreams about it. This was a make-or-break job, so far beyond a small group show in Miami. It would put me in front of big-name people who had power, influence, and money in the art world. The process was a beast. It was going to be a live performance. The set would be in an opera hall with five thousand seats. Once the work went on tour, museum directors from all over the world would see this performance and the set. Merce putting a spotlight on me and my work broke me out of the pack.

Over the years, I've often wondered what it was about those pieces in Miami that drew Merce to me. Sometimes I asked him, and he always simply said, "I thought it might be interesting to work with you." So simple that it just raised more questions in my mind. What did he see in those drawings? They were these cavern drawings, nothing that related to set design. I finally came to the conclusion that Merce actually thought it was more interesting to work with artists who didn't actually know about theater. And maybe, because he was at the back end of his life, he wanted to return to where he'd started in the 1950s, when it seemed anything was possible. I worked with him for the next five years after that first collaboration. He later told me that part of his intention in collaborating with younger artists was that it allowed him to find things that he wouldn't otherwise choose to do. If he put his own taste into everything, he would start to direct things in a way that would avoid possibilities he hadn't considered. Bringing me on from an outside perspective opened up different possibilities. And he knew that not all collaborations worked. You know, you're putting different art forms and ideas and people together. Sometimes it's awesome and sometimes people don't vibe and it doesn't work. That was probably the thrill of it for him, or at least in part.

I had a little over a year to create the stage design, and I went to a lot of Merce's shows and started to think about the difference between creating something for the stage and creating something for the gallery or museum. The most obvious difference is that the audience is fixed. If you go to a gallery or museum, you can walk around the sculpture. You can get up close to it or stay back. You have a completely different experience when you can also walk away. There's a duration control. For me, working on the stage design was about the visual quality of the audience being able to look at something only from a particular viewpoint. It allowed me to play all these games with forced perspective. Merce employs this thing called a crossover, where the dancers would exit on stage right, walk behind the curtain, and then reenter, and he would do something involving a continual stream of people. Because everything that's outside of the box of the stage just doesn't exist. And the audience accepts it in a weird way. They don't think about these exits and reentrances.

I employed that strategy in my set design, but from a vertical perspective. I created a building that looked like it was falling onto the stage floor. It came down from the ceiling, and part of it, the part the audience couldn't see, appeared as if it were under the surface of the ceiling. It was like an old television, when the vertical hold would slip and the image would be split so that the top was on the bottom. That was the very simple idea behind it. The building looked huge, but only because I was using forced perspective, like the set designers at Disney World do to make buildings look bigger on the rides. The windows get smaller as you go up the floors. I designed the building to look like a vintage movie theater. The joists had a marquee on the outside and had all these receding lines and lights, including the marquee itself. It allowed these forms to be thicker toward the front and thinner as they go back. In photos it looks quite large. And the building seems almost like a spaceship that comes alive throughout the performance, because I also designed the lighting inside it and the costumes. Everything was black and white or shades of gray.

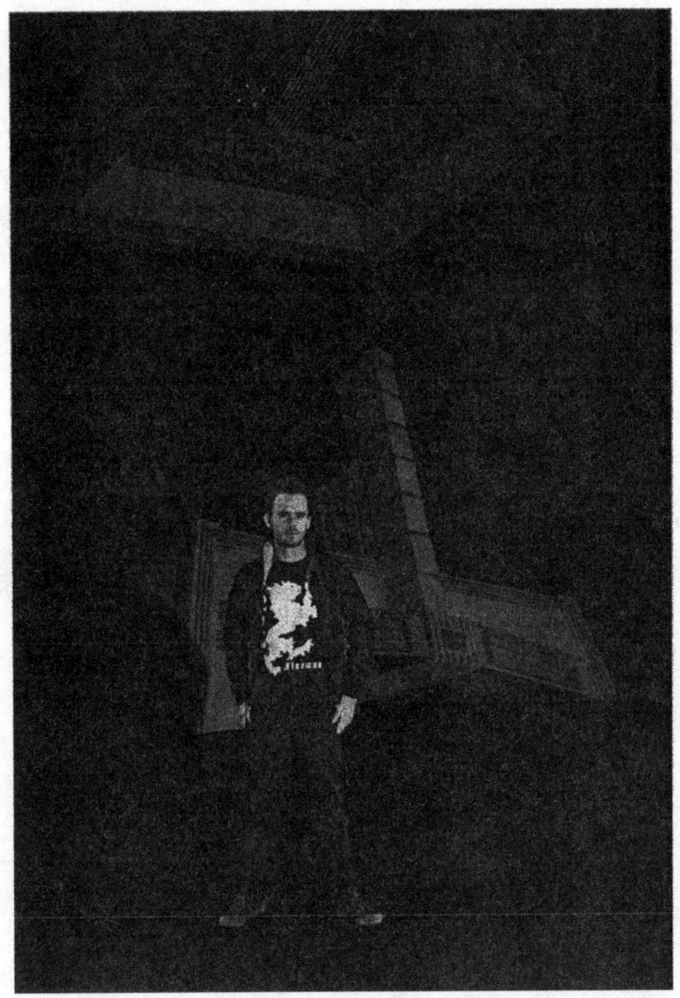

The set for the Merce Cunningham performance.

Like I said before, Westbeth was a character all on its own. You couldn't spend a minute there without inspiration from the place or the people. The costumes that I designed were actually based on something I saw in the basement of the building. There were costumes and pieces of sets, props going back to the 1950s. I went down there one time with the stage director for the show, and we found this costume that looked like a bear. I picked it up and I was like, "What is this?" And he said, "Oh, Bob Rauschenberg made that in 1972." My response was "Why the fuck is it sitting on this shelf gathering dust?" He laughed and said, "I don't know, where else would we put it?" It was still a living thing for them. They used it in restaging some of those performances. That's the kind of crazy shit you'd find in Westbeth. There were other costumes that Rauschenberg had made. There were bags of the Silver Clouds that Warhol made for Merce, there were notes tacked to the walls from Duchamp and Cage. That storage area in the basement was a treasure trove.

Bob and Merce had an interesting history, and part of my journey with Merce was understanding Bob's place in his life. For Merce and John Cage, Bob was always the kid—he was at least a decade younger than them. Then, in 1964, Bob was in the Venice Biennale and won the Gran Premio award as the best international artist, the first American ever to win. The award was a huge coming-out moment for Bob, and his star surpassed all of theirs. While they were all there, Merce decided to stage a performance at a theater in Venice called La Fenice, which was Duchamp's favorite, during the Venice Biennale. Everyone in the art world was there: Peggy Guggenheim, Andy Warhol, Jasper Johns . . . Name a big-time artist at that time and they were there. Except for Bob; he didn't show up. He had won the big prize the day before and was partying

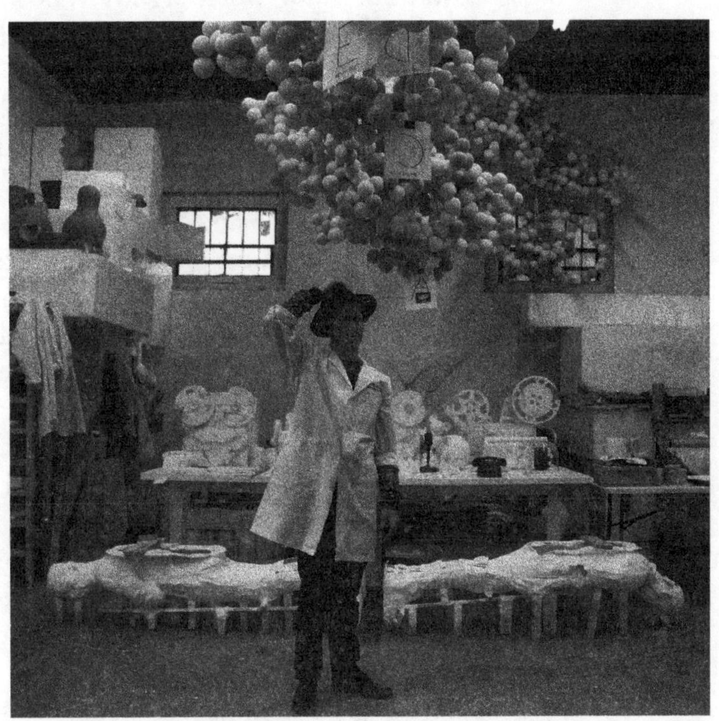

With "Clouds" designed for final performance.

in St. Mark's Square. Merce felt slighted by Bob, and they had a big falling-out because Bob didn't show. Thankfully, they reconciled later on in life.

I was down in the Westbeth basement looking at some archive images and found some silver costumes Bob had made for Merce. Although Bob and Merce had a history, Bob's genius could be seen in those costumes. They were slightly reflective, and I thought they might glimmer in the light of the stage. I decided to reinvent them. I knew that Merce wouldn't care—he'd want what was best for the show. I used reflective fabric, making costumes that looked like silvery fish. They were great.

When the show was finally ready, I was twenty-six and had been working on the stage design for nearly two years. I'd had my debut exhibition at Emmanuel's gallery in Paris the year before. The past six months I'd spent working only on the lighting. I think some of the people involved were afraid I was going to fail. I had spent every penny of what they'd given me and more. And it was the biggest budget I'd ever had, over $20,000.

The stage was this living object that's going to get touched all the time. People were going to kick it, walk on it, jump on it. So it had to be very durable, and that isn't typically a consideration with artwork in a gallery. I built the stage with a metal armature that I had welded, with the front of the building adhering to the armature. Originally, I designed the building to have its own lighting. The stage crew rightly pointed out that that lighting setup wouldn't work when we toured to other places with different voltages and plugs. We had to adjust the design so that lights from the grid could get dropped down into the building and be plugged into the existing lighting. There're a lot of variations in that—the lighting possibilities were incredible. Obviously, on stage all the shit that you can use really helps. We used fog for one part where a spaceship-like object lands and the dancers recede into the background. Working with the crew and figuring out all the wrinkles to make the stage as successful as possible was difficult but rewarding. It was one of my favorite works because of the boundaries I was pushing creatively and personally.

Before the premiere, there were two or three months of rehearsals at Westbeth. That was the first time I actually saw what the dance was going to be. If I had to describe it, I would call it movement potential more than dance. Some of the movements were super fucking weird. If you were looking at them, you'd be like, *What is that?* It's not trying to achieve something beautiful. It's not trying to evoke anything. It's exploring possibilities. One of the special things that I learned from Merce later, after having been on tour with the company and watching so many dances, is that most of the ways that he used movement had to do with either expanding or compressing your experience of time. Sometimes you'd watch a forty-five-minute dance performance and it felt like it went by really quickly. Other times, a performance that was twenty minutes felt like it lasted a year. He intentionally pushed and pulled on people's understanding of time. There were periods of rest when almost nothing happened. One finger moving on the entire stage, with five thousand people focused on it. The rhythm of the performance was almost as important as the movement. He used the intricacy and amount of movement on stage to completely control the audience.

The show premiered in Miami in early 2007, and I wanted to be in the audience. I have a photo with Merce backstage right beforehand. He never watched from the audience in the whole history of his career. He would sit either at the front of the stage or backstage. During these performances, he always sat stage right, so I went back there with him before curtain.

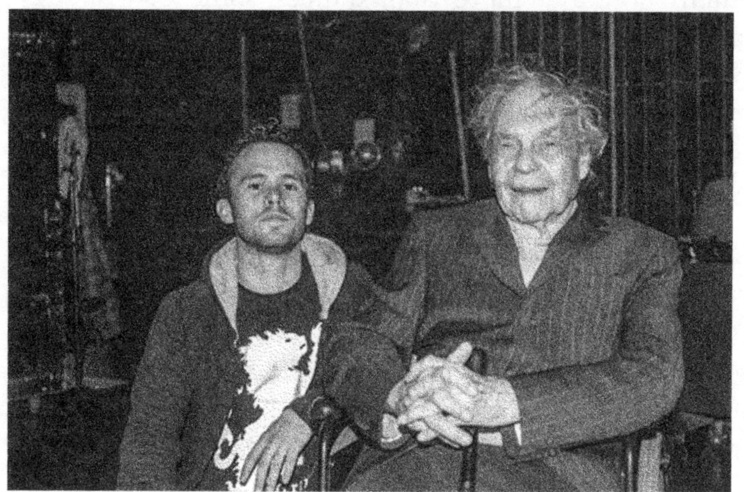

With Merce, right before the premiere.

I told him I wanted to be out in the audience to watch, so he said to come backstage right afterward. I didn't know it, but he wanted me to take a bow, something he could no longer do himself because he was in a wheelchair.

What I witnessed was incredible. Seeing the whole thing come together, the costumes shining on an almost all-black stage, the complete attention of the audience. It was a feeling I will never forget. And then it was over. For a moment: silence. It was complicated to get backstage from the audience seats. You had to go through all these different doors. I ran as fast as I could from my seat. By the time I got there, I could hear the applause: Five thousand people were giving a standing ovation. Merce was in his wheelchair, and as I approached, he waved me past. "Get out on the stage!" As I walked out on stage, I realized that you couldn't see anything. The lights were so bright. All I heard was the roar of all those people clapping and yelling. I bowed down and looked at my black sneakers and thought, *This is one of the most important moments of my life.* As I stood up, Merce was being pushed on stage. As he took his place next to me, the lights were raised in the theater so Merce could see everyone. Because of my connections to the art community there in Miami, starting in middle school, almost all my friends had been able to make it. For a brief moment almost everyone important in my life was in one room. It was a moment I'll remember for the rest of my life.

Once we got off stage, Merce asked if I'd like to come on tour with him and his company. He was going to Australia and Europe, where he was thinking of doing a tour of small five-hundred-seat theaters in France. I was still creating art and still showing it and still on my hustle to become part of the Art World, but this was a huge opportunity. Despite dance and stage design not being my media, getting to work and tour with someone of Merce's stature would give me great experience and exposure. And I could draw and make small paintings the entire time.

After that initial performance in Miami and before we left for the tour, Merce said he wanted to take the whole company out to Captiva Island, where Bob Rauschenberg had had a studio since the seventies. As far back as high school, Rauschenberg had been like a god to me, one of the most important artists of the twentieth century. Off we went. Everyone else had known him for a while, so it was less of a thing for them, but I was super hyped. I didn't know what to expect. His house was two blocks from the beach. It was this pyramid structure with a giant staircase on either side. The staircase led up to a massive ten-thousand-square-foot studio that looked like an art gallery or a museum. It was pure Rauschenberg. By the time he died, he was probably a billionaire. Definitely one of the wealthiest artists ever, and he spent the better part of the second half of his life on Captiva, just living quietly and making art.

When I met him, he had had a stroke and was in a wheelchair, but he was totally coherent. Merce took me over, and before he could make the introduction, Bob said, "Oh, Daniel, so great to meet you. I love what you did on that stage. Wonderful!" I was floored. Robert Rauschenberg knew who I was. He'd said my name to my face before even being introduced. I couldn't believe he had just told me that he loved my work. It was a profound moment. We started talking about art, and I started asking him questions. There was no way I was letting go of an opportunity to learn from one of the great masters. Some of the works that fascinated me most were his very famous chairs cast in solid bronze, from a mold made from an old wicker chair. I had seen many pictures of the chairs but never imagined I would see them in real life. They were so impossible-looking.

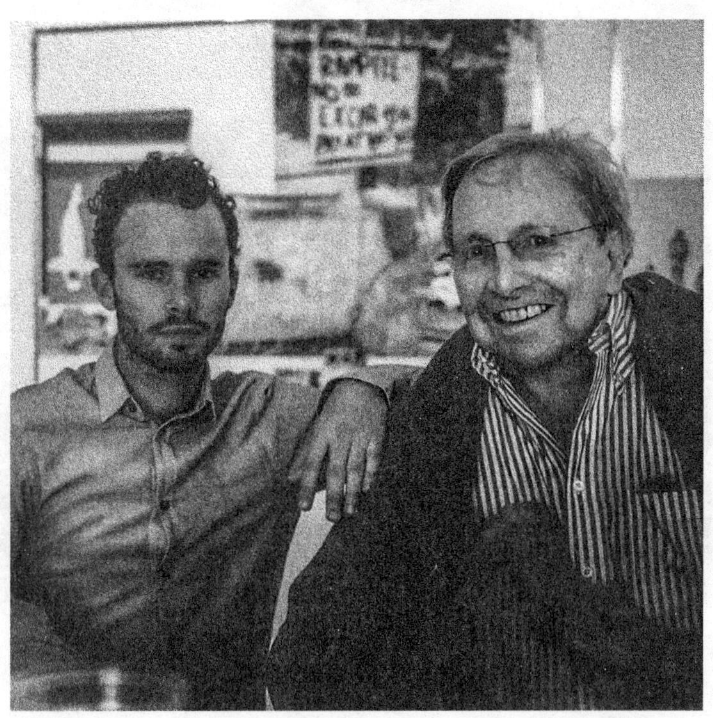

With Robert Rauschenberg.

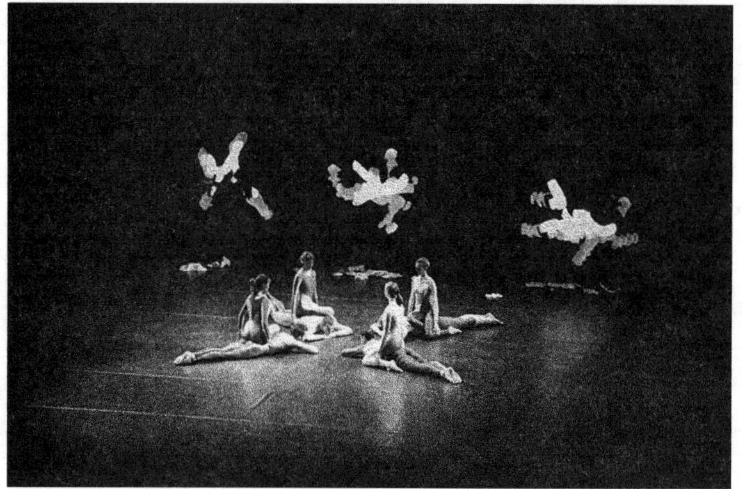

European tour with Merce.

There was a magic to them, and despite having a pretty deep knowledge of sculptural processes, I had no idea how they were made. We spent two days on Captiva, and I spent the entire second day moving around the studio with Bob and talking about art. I felt like a little kid, filled with wonder and delight and awe. I was a total fan, and I'll never forget it. At the end of that day, he told me how he made the chairs. I remember thinking, *I want to be able to make work this magical one day.*

It was a dazzlingly surreal visit. At the end of the second day, Bob said he wanted to make rings for everyone. I didn't know what he was talking about, but everyone was really excited and went downstairs to his foundry. There, an artisan was making titanium frames for his paintings, which made them incredibly light and easy to move. The artisan measured all of our ring fingers and made the rings from a single piece of titanium with one weld. Everyone on the visit got one, and I have never taken mine off. For twenty years, whenever I see my right ring finger with Bob's ring on it, I am reminded of that day and inspired to be the best I can be.

As I toured with Merce throughout 2007 and 2008, I was committed to honoring the legacy of Rauschenberg's stage design work. Nobody but Merce and I knew I was doing it, but I often made sets with materials or color themes or structures similar to those Rauschenberg had used. At the beginning of 2009, Merce's health started to betray him. He began to fade. I went to New York and spent a day with him, half of it at Westbeth and half at his townhouse on Eighteenth Street, where he'd lived in since the seventies. We reminisced about our time and work together, talked about art and dance. He told me stories from his incredible career and showed me some of his own art collection. Duchamp had given him a stack of amazing note cards and airline tickets covered with little drawings. I mean, Duchamp! I had never seen a Duchamp outside of a museum, much less a stack of them. There were small paintings by Rauschenberg, Johns, Warhol, Cy Twombly. The paintings and art were worth tens of millions of dollars, but Merce didn't care. To him, they were gifts from cherished friends. They were memories. They were a history of his most important relationships. It was a great day, though sad. As I was leaving, he gave me a hug at the door and told me to keep making great things, to keep being myself, and to keep being open and collaborative and bold.

Merce passed away in his sleep in July 2009. I found out from the front page of *The New York Times*, and I broke down and wept for a long time—a long, long time. It felt less like losing a friend and more like losing a family member, an influential uncle or grandfather. However I define him—friend, mentor, partner, collaborator, wizard, or fairy godfather—he was a massively influential and important person in my life. My career and the work I've done and how I do it certainly wouldn't be what it is today if I hadn't met him, worked with him, been mentored by him. Every part of my life as an artist was impacted by Merce.

His death didn't end our collaboration. He dictated that there should be one final group of performances and a massive party, both to take place at the Park Avenue Armory, in New York.

Because it was Merce's final show, it was high-profile and was covered by media from around the world. He had given thought to the dance, but he knew he wouldn't be able to do the staging. His instructions were that there were to be three stages of particular size and position in the venue. And he wanted me to design them.

The shows were on three consecutive nights, December 29, 30, and 31, 2011, with the last night on New Year's Eve, running into 2012. Per Merce's wishes, the final night was an immense party. The dancers performed four hours of various types of his work from the 1950s through to what he was creating just before he died. John Cage music accompanied the dancers. I did the lighting, stages, and costumes. The show was set up so the audience could move around the stages and the dancers. Before I made the design, I went through a collection of photos I had of Merce on tour and a second collection of photos from Captiva. Almost all of my pictures of him, from everywhere we went together, seemed to include the ocean and the sky, and that felt appropriate to the occasion. I made huge cloud sculptures that floated over the stages while the dancers performed. It was a magical three days that punctuated and ended one of the biggest artistic and personal relationships of my life. Fittingly, it was also one of the biggest parties I've ever seen in my life. Thank you, Merce, for everything. Hopefully we'll meet again someday, maybe in the clouds.

CHAPTER VII

A WORK OF ART:

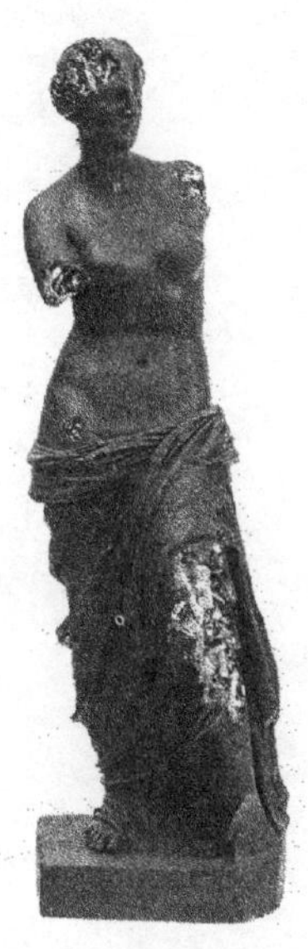

ORIGIN TO COMPLETION

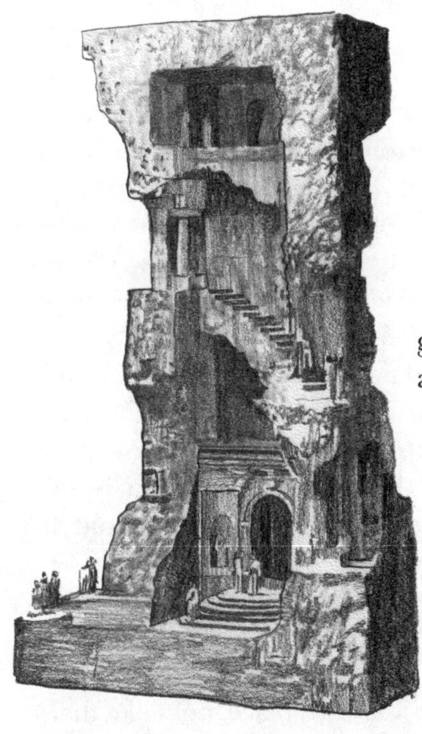

get asked a lot to talk about how I work and what my creative process looks like. It comes up over and over. But the challenge is that it's really hard for me to trace the origin of an idea. Obviously, every work starts with some kind of idea. As you're working, the ideas kind of snowball on top of one another. The work begins to take on a gravity of its own and draws inspiration and ideas toward it. That's why it's hard to find the origin of any particular work.

To dive into it the best I can, I'll use an example that was an enormous undertaking and installation, the *Unearthed Bronze Eroded Melpomene*. The piece is a massive bronze face that's sunken into the ground and tilted to the side, so it looks like it fell. There's a suggestion that the remainder of the piece goes on forever underground, having been buried over time. It is currently at Yorkshire Sculpture Park, in Northern England, and it's also been shown in Regent's Park in London.

The idea started with pieces I had been making based on classical antiquity. I had been invited to do an exhibition at the Musée Guimet, the Asian antiquities museum in Paris. In 2014, during a trip to Paris in the planning stage for the show, I made a first visit to the artistic archive of the Louvre. In the nineteenth century, the government began a major undertaking, making molds of every stone statue in their possession. Part of their motivation was that they wanted to ship plaster copies of many of the most iconic works to all the colonies, basically exporting French culture to places like North Africa. Among the copies they shipped was the *Venus de Milo*, actually a Greek sculpture from antiquity and now one of the most famous sculptures in the world. Shortly before World War II, the French ramped up their efforts, because they were trying to protect the works from the Nazis—if the originals somehow got destroyed, they would at least have these copies.

There's a famous scene at the end of *Indiana Jones and the Raiders of the Lost Ark* where there are just artifacts as far as the eye can see in a massive warehouse. No fucking joke, this place looks like that. There are Home Depot–sized racks in a cavernous space full of just molds, and they're all numbered. I was like, *What the fuck is this?* There's literally one person in the entire warehouse with access to it, and there is a mold of every single stone sculpture in France, and many others in Europe, including works at Versailles and others like *The Gates of Hell*, *The Thinker*, *David*—everything.

In 2017 I returned to the museum warehouse, and I was even more awed. My description of what's there doesn't do it justice: You can't comprehend the scale without seeing it in person. The type of mold that the French used is the exact same kind I make in my studio—same plaster mother molds, same silicone undermold. I asked the curator if I could use these molds to make sculptures for my show. "Unfortunately," she said, "probably not." They are owned by the French government, and there are multiple levels of bureaucracy to go through to even see them. They're cultural patrimony, protected by the French state.

I knew Ludovic Laugier, the head curator of the Greek and Roman wing at the Louvre. I called him and said, "Why did you never tell me about this before? This is crazy. Can I use these?" And he said, "Listen, we've tried to do other things with them before. It's really complicated." He told me that if I wrote a thesis stating why I wanted to do this and why the government should approve my use of the molds, he'd support me. Ludovic told me to supplement my application with a letter of support from Emmanuel. I did all of it and heard nothing for two years. One day at the studio, entirely out of the blue, I got an email. It said, "I got a call from the Culture Ministry, and they approved your request to use the molds." I started jumping up and down and yelling like I had won the lotto, which in a way I had.

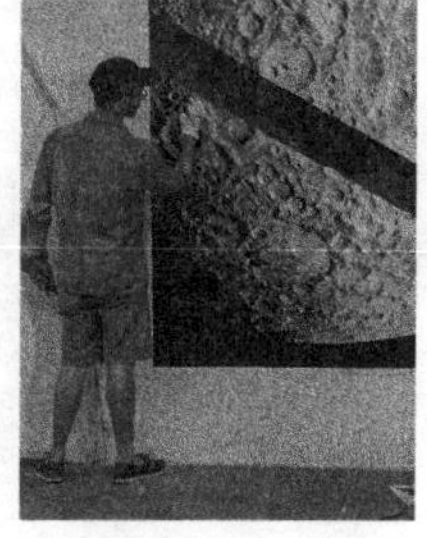

Working in the studio.

When I returned to the warehouse after receiving the approval from the Culture Ministry, I again asked if I could use the molds. This time I was told yes—whatever I wanted. The only caveat was that I had to make the work there; I couldn't take any of the molds out of the space. They have a couple of

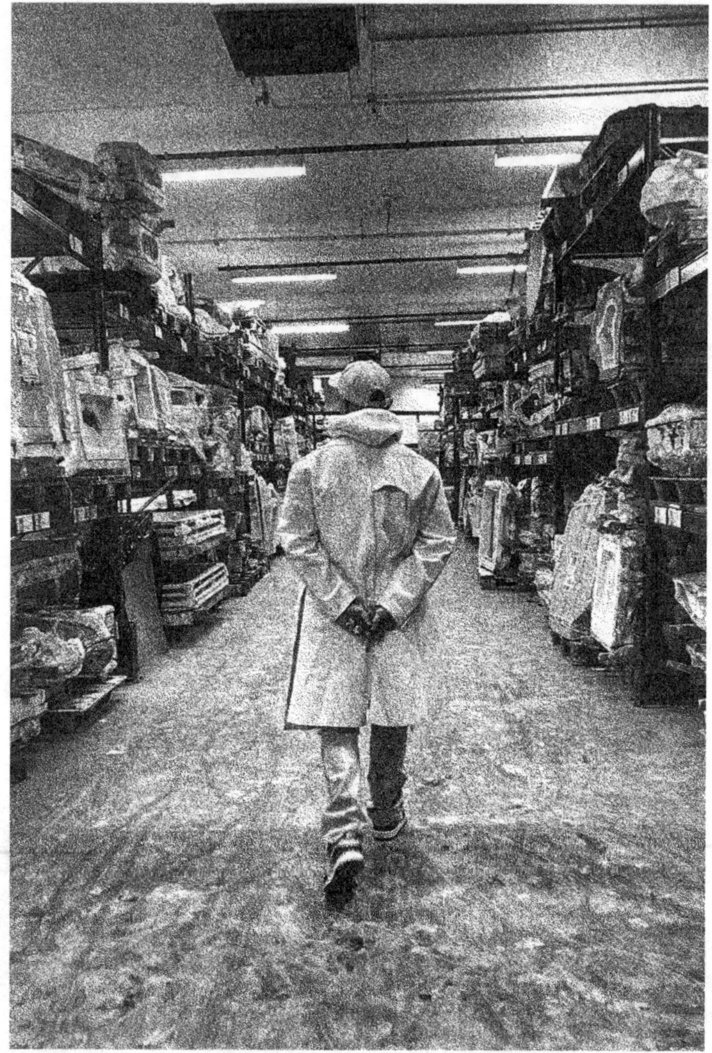

At the Louvre warehouse.

artisans they work with at the facility, and I basically trained them to work with me to create casts of the sculptures I wanted to make. The first one I made was the Zeus that is in the Louvre. It somehow felt appropriate. Since then we've made a ton of work from the casts and continue to make them to this day. Any work of mine that's based on Roman or Greek antiquities, which is a significant amount, comes from my access to those molds.

Part of my thesis on creating a series of Fictional Archaeology pieces involved the idea of confusing time. It was an area of play and exploration that was appealing to me and provided real creative excitement. The first pieces I created in this style were the cell phones and technological objects from more modern times. Once I was able to successfully fabricate those items, I had the idea of playing with pop culture objects: cars, basketball sneakers, things that we immediately know are from modern times. If I can take those objects and put them next to a cast from antiquity and they're made of the same materials, it becomes an even more impactful blurring of time, because viewers see something they associate with modernity and another object they associate with the long-ago past. Now both objects look old, and people are forced to ask what's happening. There's a time slip that's happening for the audience. Creating that pressure on people with regard to time was exactly the goal of the project.

From an art history context, the pieces would push the idea that contemporary sculpture is as relevant as ancient sculpture. I loved that I could do that by collapsing time. The objects are married in their materiality. It's simply confusing, which is what so much of the best art is, right? It creates this conflict for the viewer where they are not able to reconcile things, and they start wondering, *Oh, what is this, and what could this mean?*

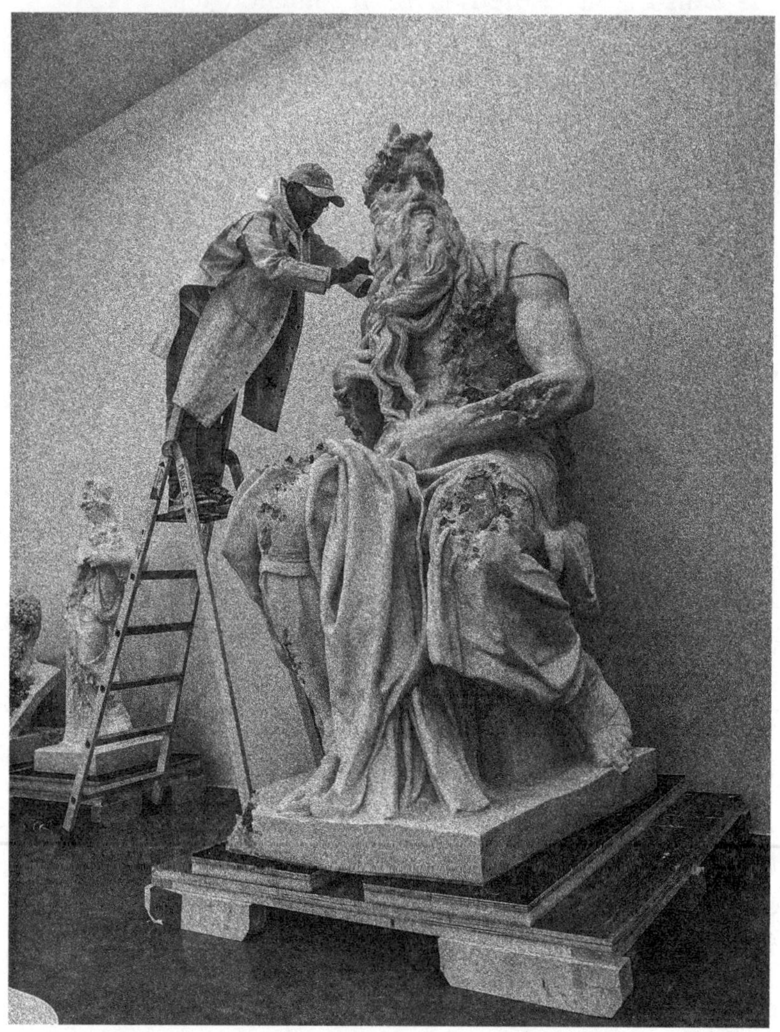

With work adapted from cast of Michelangelo's MOSES.

In the exhibitions where I showed the works I'd made from the French antiquity casts, I would never show them by themselves as classical works. They were always combined with contemporary objects: sometimes objects related to music, sometimes cars, sometimes sports. If you jump to the future and you think about archaeologists looking back at this moment in time, what are they going to study? The most historically relevant cultural icons in a thousand years will be the things that for now feel very rooted in mass consumer culture. So I'm trying to link those two things—the classical sculptures that shape our concept of the distant past and the mass consumer objects that will shape how the future understands our culture today.

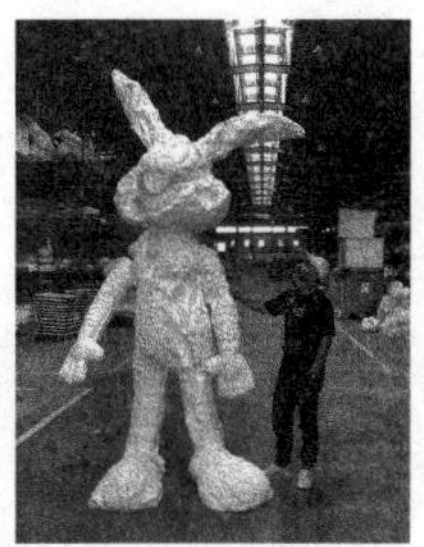

At the foundry outside Shanghai.

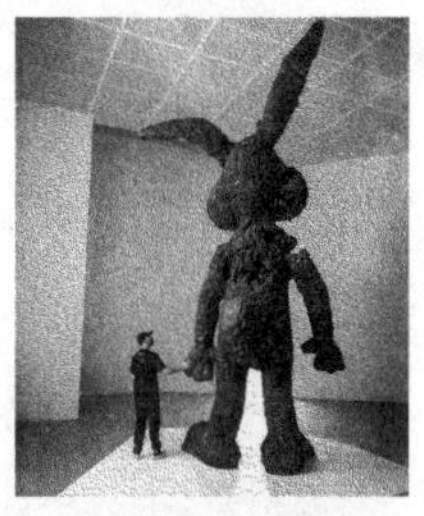

At the exhibition, Shanghai.

Some people in the capital-*A* Art World misunderstand (and I think intentionally misunderstand) what I'm doing. They assume I'm all about the commercial value of the objects I'm representing. That's not it. I'm interested in the larger audience that this subject matter affords me. It's about their relevance in the culture.

The first work I created from the French antiquity molds was in plaster, and the final version of it was in bronze. I loved it, but it looked brand new. It would take centuries for the bronze to age, and I wanted this body of work to look old and feel old. I wanted people who saw it to believe it was old. I started thinking about how to simulate the green patina that's on ancient bronze works. I tried some synthetic patina, but it felt and looked tacky and fake. So I cast a small bronze version of Melpomene and put it outside my house on Long Island, which is near the ocean and has heavy amounts of salt in the air. My plan was to simply observe it and see what happened. The sculpture started aging rapidly, oxidizing and becoming discolored in certain places. A patina developed, and it started to really look old in a way that surpassed my expectations. While I was experimenting with these techniques, I was invited by curator Clare Lilley to do a big exhibition at Yorkshire Sculpture Park. This is a five-hundred-acre estate in the northern English countryside near West Bretton, Wakefield, with rolling hills and actual sheep walking around it. It's filled with some of the most monumental sculptures ever made, pieces by Tony Smith and James Turrell, Richard Serra and Ai Weiwei, giants of art whose work I deeply admire and respect. It was both thrilling and intimidating. I knew I needed to make something that could stand side by side with the other work at the park. My own version of monumental. Something as good as the work that would surround it.

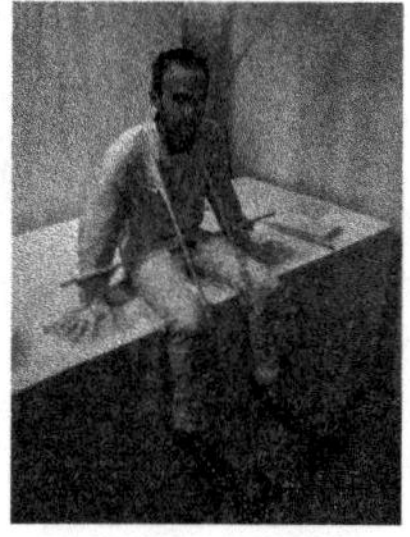

Using myself as a mold because I had to sit for hours inside of this to make the piece.

I began to lock in on scale as a major focus. I went to the park and walked around the fields for hours thinking about what I could make that would capitalize on the space, the views from different perspectives, and the area they had given me. Within the space is a huge elevated promenade next to a garden that gently slopes down to a lake at the bottom. There was a perspective in my space where, as you walked through, if I put a large sculpture in it, you would be looking both up at it and down at it, which I thought was really incredible. The entire time I was walking around, I was drawing and sketching ideas. And I kept coming back to *scale, scale, scale.* I started thinking about doing a gigantic sculpture, but the logistics of something the size I wanted to make, maybe a hundred feet tall, would be a nightmare, if not impossible. I thought of Melpomene and drew a giant head sitting in the space, with the idea that the rest of the piece recedes into the ground.

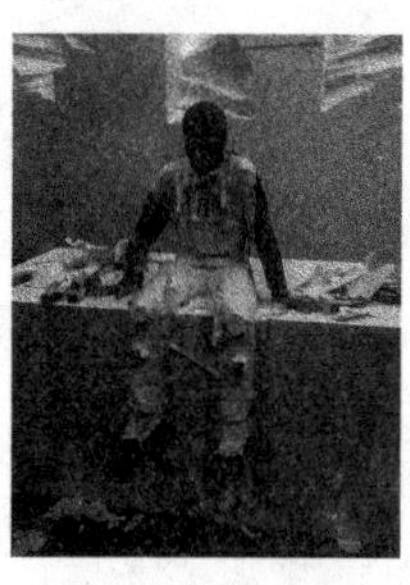

The final piece.

The actual construction of the Melpomene was fascinating. The first step was working with the foundry to figure out how to build it. We had to figure out how to isolate the part of the figure we'd see coming out of the ground. There were multiple conversations about the materials to use and how to stabilize it. We decided on a stainless steel structure inside of it, and it was the first time I'd combined these materials with bronze.

In thinking about the material in the work, I always want it to act as a storyteller, just as the design does. When you look at my work, the visual quality of it tells you one thing, but when you understand what it's made out of, it tells you another story. Here I was using a steel structure to hold together bronze and crystalline forms. The bronze would be slightly eroded and have the stainless steel "crystals" growing out of it, and the crystals would be polished, in contrast to the decaying bronze. The real technical challenge was figuring out how to make the disparate materials join together. Through a lot of work and experimentation, we devised a way to slot the crystals into the steel frame, like a mechanical joint. It would allow me to make the sculpture I envisioned while keeping the mechanics of it invisible to viewers.

Figuring out that process wasn't easy, and I am lucky to have a great team of people who help me. We first scanned the original sculpture, blew that up to scale on the computer, and used 3D software to figure out where to divide it and how to build the structure. Once we had a digital prototype, we made a couple of the Melpomenes at a smaller scale to test our thesis and structural plan. We 3D-printed the pieces in plastic and put the sculpture together, and it worked. Plastic, though, is a very different material from steel and bronze, so we moved to making a real prototype with those materials, and it also worked. We had spent about six months experimenting and were ready to make the sculpture for real.

There are a couple of different foundries that I work with when I make bronze sculpture. One is in upstate New York and one is in China, and I work with them because both are down to really experiment and will try just about anything. The Melpomene was made at the foundry in Asia, about two hours outside of Shanghai. It was originally built to create giant sculptures of Mao. The building is humongous: It's got a massive gantry crane, and you probably could fit four 747s inside of it. I started working with them on some smaller-scale work, and after being impressed by the results, I went and visited and saw how much they could actually do. When I first sent them the design of the Melpomene, I expected some pushback, maybe a back-and-forth conversation about how exactly they were going to get this piece done, but none of that happened. They simply said, "Yes, we can make this," and sent me a production schedule. The Melpomene is a large piece, but it's smaller than most of the things they've made in that foundry—some of the Maos were multiple stories tall. They understood scale and could handle it far beyond what I was asking them to do. I was thrilled.

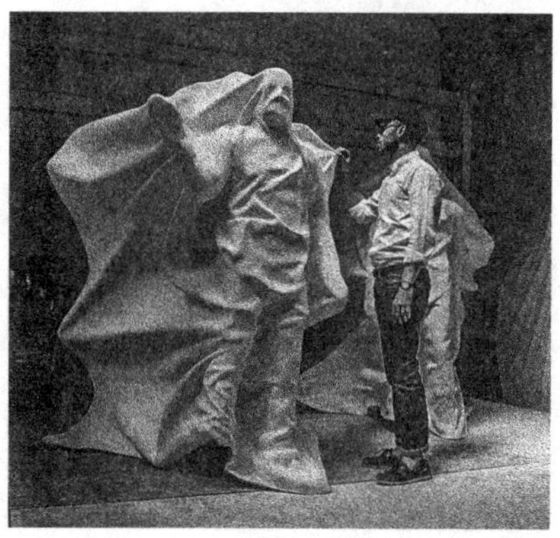

In the studio.

I love making things at large scale. I always loved Richard Serra's work. I got to meet him once when I was in school, at an event for the Matthew Barney exhibition at the Guggenheim. He used to say that he made things the way he did, out of the materials and at the scale he did, so that in ten thousand years they'd still be there no matter what happened in the world. Unless his pieces take a direct strike from a nuclear weapon, nothing can harm them. It's virtually impossible to make something that will last ten thousand years. The thing I make that has the highest likelihood of lasting that long is bronze. And even the bronze would be challenged to survive that long, because of the way it's cast. Though the bronze pieces have a half-inch-thick shell with a steel-frame core inside, eventually the weather and seasons will break them down. Mine might not have ten thousand years of life like Serra's, but they stand a good chance of making it half that long.

It took the foundry about eight months to make the sculpture. They built it in multiple stages, making each of the major pieces individually before putting them all together. I visited after each major piece was finished, and again when the entire thing was done. One of the challenges we started dealing with as the sculpture was being finished was how to move it. We knew it was going to weigh about ten tons, or twenty thousand pounds. Normally any large bronze sculpture that I make has a slight elevation beneath it so that a forklift can get under it to get it off the ground and move it. Because of the environment where the Melpomene was going to be displayed and because of the suggestion that the sculpture continued deep beneath the ground, I couldn't have a normal base or elevation. The foundry came up with the idea of casting a hook in the top of the structure and having all its weight lead to this one point. The hook could be recessed so nobody would see it, and that would allow us to move it while keeping the perception that it was immovable. We tested it at a smaller scale, and it worked. And though I was somewhat concerned that the hook would be visible to viewers, it wasn't. We had figured out one of the toughest issues.

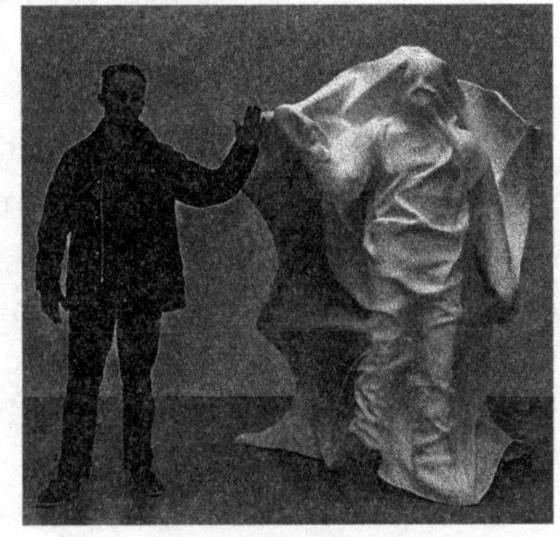

On display, Paris, 2013.

When the sculpture was finished and the opening scheduled, we moved it from Shanghai to England via ship. In England, it got loaded onto a train and then a large, covered flatbed truck, and then it was placed into the ground with a crane. I moved it multiple times to get it in the perfect position. Once it was exactly how I wanted it, I just stood there staring at it. It was beautiful. It was imposing. The idea of perspective had worked exactly the way I had imagined it would, and as I stood there looking at it, I was overtaken with emotion. It's a unique feeling when you see a final work of art in its exhibition space—part pride, part accomplishment, mostly just joy at seeing your vision fully realized. And that particular moment is one of the most joyous of my career.

For the opening, I rented an entire vintage luxury train car from London and brought a bunch of friends and journalists, about a hundred people, up to Yorkshire for the day. Hundreds more showed up for the event. The sunken Melpomene is one of my most visible pieces, both in scale and in terms of the number of people who have seen it. The exhibition was supposed to be on for just a year, but it was so popular that the park asked if they could keep the sculpture for a while longer. It was a fairly simple answer—I said yes, because I like the idea that it could be there for the next fifty centuries.

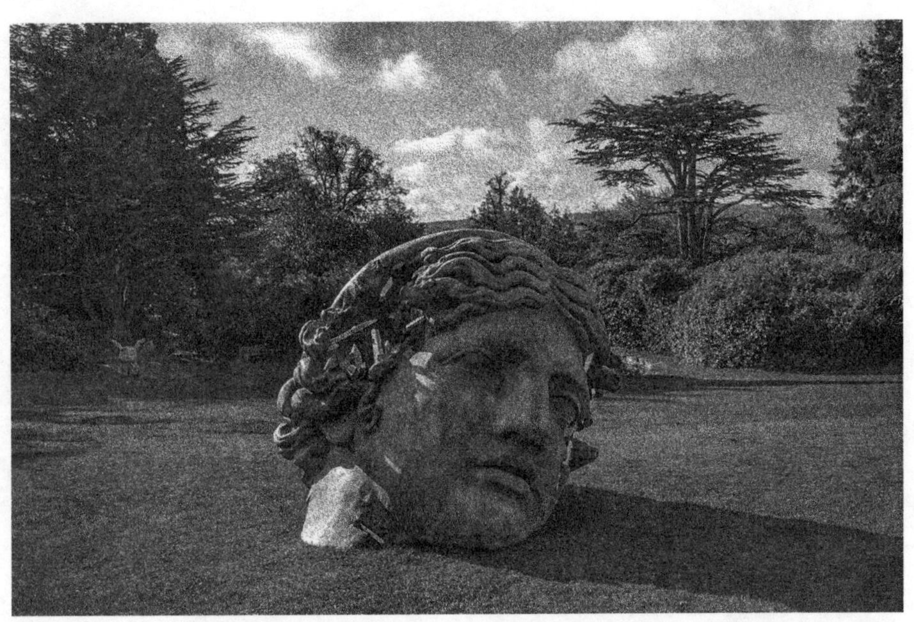

UNEARTHED MELPOMENE on view at the Yorkshire sculpture park.

CHAPTER VIII

WHY FAILURE AND REJECTION ARE IMPORTANT

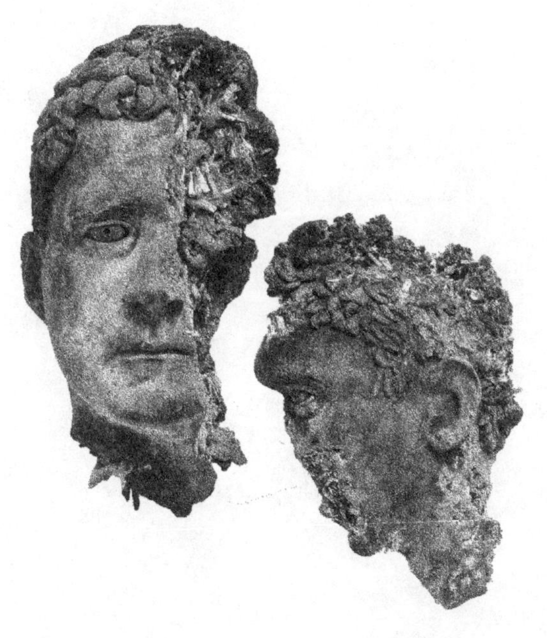

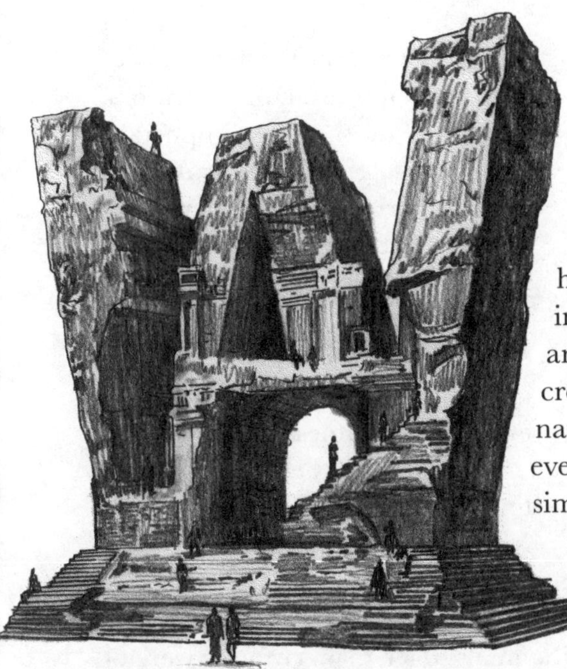

hen you're starting out as an artist, or in any creative space, it's natural to want everything to feel simple and easy, for the work to flow out of you—that you shouldn't have to force creativity. It's completely unrealistic and delusional. You're going to fail far more than you succeed. Failure and rejection, and your ability to learn and grow from them, can be fundamental to developing to the next level.

In 2006, the Whitney Biennial was the most important exhibition you could be in as a young artist. First organized in 1932, the Biennial became widely regarded as the most significant survey of contemporary American art. For generations it served as a barometer of the cultural and artistic moment, often introducing the world to artists who would go on to define entire eras. To be included was not just to exhibit but to be formally acknowledged as part of the narrative of contemporary art history. To be included meant that your work was guaranteed to be featured in *Artforum*, *Flash Art*, and every other major art magazine that I obsessed over during and after art school. The exposure wasn't just about ego; it put your work in front of collectors, museum directors, curators, and—for me the most important audience at that time—galleries. The galleries that I dreamt of working with were looking at this show, and every artist I knew was also watching to see who would make it. At the time, I wanted it more than anything I had ever wanted professionally.

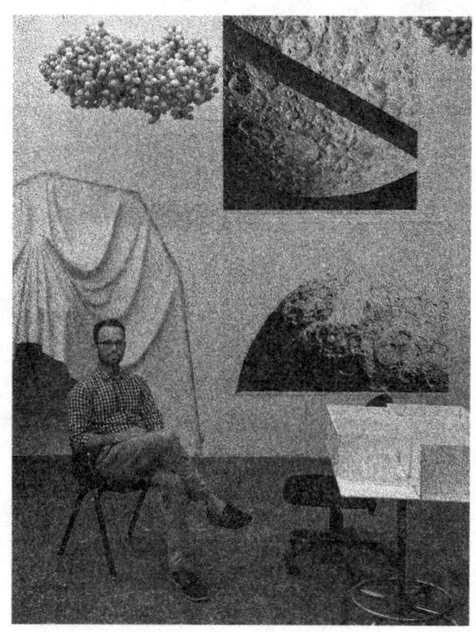

Planning an exhibit by starting with a model of the gallery.

I met Chrissie Iles, the curator for the 2006 Biennial, through friends of mine from Miami. Chrissie had been the curator of film and video at the museum since 1997, and she co-curated both the 2004 and 2006 Biennials. Back then, curators weren't scrolling Instagram or looking at JPEGs on their phones to find artists. They were still physically traveling, getting on planes, knocking on studio doors, sitting in artists' spaces, and talking face-to-face. When Chrissie visited my studio, she spent about an hour with me. We talked about my work, how I was just starting to figure out a language combining architecture with natural processes, confusing the two, making things that looked like they were crumbling or eroding, but with intention, with poetry. She asked me about the materials, about the meaning, about where I saw myself in the moment. Artists are always a kind of living documentary of their times—we're capturing the zeitgeist, whether we know it or not—and Chrissie was trying to understand where I fit into that zeitgeist.

After she left, I felt good. Actually, I felt better than good—I felt confident. I'd spoken well about my work. I wasn't pretending to be something or someone I wasn't. I was part of a community of young artists, and it felt like we were building something together, like there was a real movement happening. A few days later, she emailed to thank me for the visit and asked if we could meet again. I was hyped. This wasn't just a "nice to meet you" follow-up. She wanted to meet again. The Whitney fucking Biennial. The thing I had dreamed about and wanted since I first knew of its existence, which was when I was about fourteen. I had a chance. It felt close and attainable. I believed.

I was scheduled to be in New York a few months later. I emailed her when I arrived, and she immediately invited me to the museum to sit down and have another discussion. At the time, the Whitney was on the Upper East Side in the famous Marcel Breuer brutalist masterpiece. As I walked through the building, I was imagining my work in it. The entrance alone, with those beautiful round lights in a perfect grid, felt like the kind of stage every young artist fantasized about in quiet moments. Given how our first meeting went and how quickly Chrissie had invited me over, I could already picture myself walking into the opening, surrounded by the gallerists I hoped would pay attention, and the collectors who might finally understand what I was doing. I imagined walking through those doors alongside artists who were defining the era: Maurizio Cattelan, known for his satirical sculptures; Wolfgang Tillmans, whose photography captured the essence of contemporary life; Tracey Emin, with her confessional installations; and Kara Walker, whose silhouettes confronted themes of race and identity. These were the figures setting the tone for contemporary art at that moment, and I envisioned myself among them.

That second meeting went well. Really well. Chrissie was engaged, asked direct questions, and I gave her honest answers. Nothing felt forced. Nothing felt like I was trying too hard. It just clicked. When I got back to my studio, I did what I always do: I got to work. Just as I had done when preparing for my first show with Emmanuel, I built a scale model. I actually built out a section of the Whitney based on images I found online. In it, I imagined an entire room: all white, all calcified, but crumbling, the walls decaying, a desk in the center with one leg broken, barely holding itself up, a framed painting sliding off the wall like it was melting. The whole space looked like it was collapsing under the weight of time. I thought it was one of the most poetic and consistent works I had designed up to that point, and it was a big gesture, bigger than anything I had ever made.

A couple of months later I hadn't heard anything, so I emailed Chrissie again. She wrote back telling me that letters would be going out the following week and asked for my mailing address. *Holy fucking shit! That must mean I'm in!* I was sure of it. The letter was in the mail. I started thinking about the show and imagining how I might build the room. I literally checked my mailbox every couple of hours for the next week like a lunatic. Finally it came: a thick envelope with the Whitney logo printed on the back. I stood there holding it, hands shaking, heart fluttering, lips quivering. The Whitney fucking

Biennial. This was the moment. This show was going to change everything for me.

I opened the envelope. Hands shaking, heart fluttering, lips quivering.

"Dear Daniel, I regret to inform you that your work was not selected for this edition of the Whitney Biennial."

I read it again. And again. I think I actually sank to my knees as I read the rest. It was as generic as it gets, something about how it had nothing to do with the quality of my work but that it didn't fit the curatorial viewpoint she was presenting. The envelope also included an invitation to the opening and a one-year museum membership. A consolation prize.

I was crushed. Completely. I had built this moment up in my mind, standing in that museum with my community—the artists I looked up to, the collectors, the curators, the gallerists. I saw it all before it even happened. And now it wasn't going to happen at all.

Over the years I've kept a list of what I have learned and gained from failure.

FAILURE ENCOURAGES GROWTH, LEARNING, AND INNOVATION. Every failure provides an opportunity to learn and improve. Mistakes often lead to unexpected discoveries, pushing you to experiment and evolve your style. When you want to make something but you can't because you lack the skills, that pushes you to develop them.

FAILURE BUILDS RESILIENCE. Rejection and setbacks are part of the creative journey. Learning to handle them strengthens your perseverance and determination.

FAILURE DEEPENS EMOTIONAL EXPRESSION AND INSPIRES AUTHENTICITY. Personal setbacks add depth to your work and often lead to raw, genuine work that resonates deeply with audiences.

FAILURE TEACHES PROBLEM-SOLVING. Facing obstacles encourages creative thinking and adaptability, which are essential for artistic success.

FAILURE ALLOWS YOU TO LET GO OF PERFECTIONISM. When you fail and later succeed, you learn that perfection is not necessary for progress and can be a barrier to it. Understanding this allows you to take more risks, and the more risks you're willing to take, the greater the chance that you will make something great. And there's real beauty and freedom in imperfection—your own and that of your art.

FAILURE CREATES A UNIQUE ARTISTIC IDENTITY. Repeated failures and lessons learned from them shape your personal style and voice. You learn who you are by making and remaking things that matter to you.

FAILURE MOTIVATES HARD WORK. Failure can be a wake-up call, pushing you to refine your craft and put in more effort.

FAILURE SEPARATES PASSION FROM INTEREST. If you keep going despite repeated failures, it confirms your deep passion for making work and your drive to succeed as an artist. If you give up, you're not an artist, at least not one who will make a living at it.

FAILURE DEVELOPS PATIENCE. Artistic mastery takes time, and failure is a reminder that your progress is a long-term process.

FAILURE STRENGTHENS ARTISTIC PURPOSE. Failure forces you to reflect on why you create, reinforcing your dedication and mission.

FAILURE HELPS YOU HANDLE CRITICISM. Repeated setbacks make it easier to accept constructive criticism and use it to grow. Whether you like it or not, as an artist you are going to be criticized. Accept it. Learn from it if you can. Even if you don't think the criticism is well founded, that doesn't mean you can't learn something from it.

FAILURE BREAKS COMFORT ZONES. Artists who experience failure are more likely to push boundaries and explore new artistic directions.

FAILURE PROVIDES STORIES TO SHARE. Struggles make for great narratives, whether in the artwork itself or when engaging with an audience.

In 2013, I decided I wanted to try to be a film director. Many artists have gone down that path. Some have been incredibly successful at it. A couple of them, Julian Schnabel and Steve McQueen, turned out to be better filmmakers than artists. My journey didn't go as well.

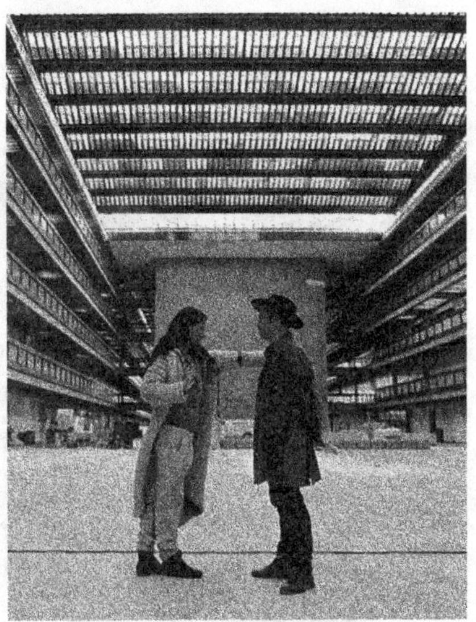

With Juliette Lewis during the filming of FUTURE RELIC.

I met Jane Rosenthal, who was Bob De Niro's partner at Tribeca Film Center, through some mutual friends. We talked about an idea I had for a short film in the world of the Future Relic sculptures. When people were writing about them, they'd always ask, "What is the world that this exists in?" My mind kept coming back to that question, and as I considered how I could answer it, I thought a film would be the cool way to depict that world.

Jane asked how much I thought it would cost to make the film. I didn't have a fucking clue. I'd never done anything in film, so she connected me with a producer and a cinematographer. The producer put the budget around $100,000. Jane kindly helped me secure about $25,000 of funding; I would need to find the rest. If the film was good enough and it was accepted by the committee of judges, it would premiere at the Tribeca Film Festival. It all started pretty

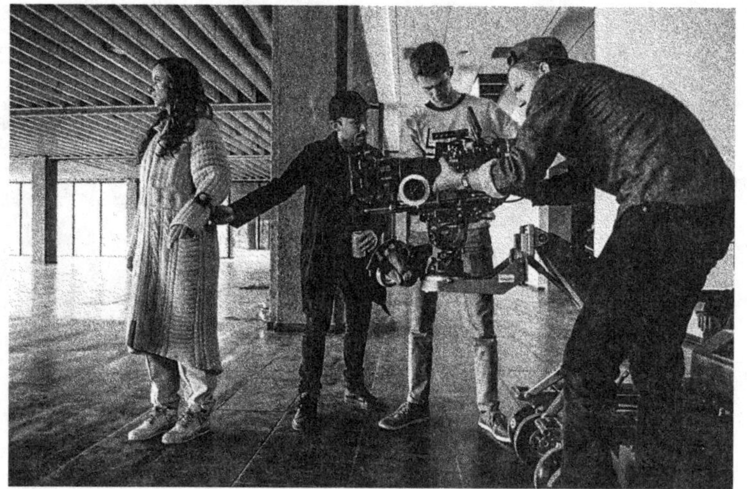

On the set of FUTURE RELIC.

quickly, but then the hard work began. I had little if any idea what I was doing.

The process was challenging but fun. Because of my profile and the fact that Jane and her friends were connected to the project, I was able to get some crazy talented actors to agree to be in it: Academy Award nominee Juliette Lewis and Mahershala Ali, who would soon win not one but two Best Actor Oscars. I enjoyed writing the script, but I was more obsessed with the visual aspect of the scenography, the costumes, the lighting, the set design, with creating this incredible world. Those areas were my main focus throughout because they're what I know and where I felt I could excel. A big part of the film was shot in New Jersey at the original Bell Laboratories building designed by Eero Saarinen, an incredible, mammoth building. Now it's a huge apartment complex and business center, best known as the place where they shoot the show *Severance*.

Juliette and Mahershala were both kind enough to basically work for free. We paid them scale, and I gave them some artwork. At the time, Mahershala was filming *Moonlight*, so he would shoot in Miami one day, fly up and spend a day on set with us, and fly back. It was an insane schedule, which I was told was pretty normal in the movie business. Juliette is brilliant and full of enormous amounts of creative energy, always there with an idea; she helped me understand certain parts of filmmaking that I didn't know. In what was a really hard experience, they, along with Jane, were real highlights. The rest was extremely difficult. Everything was very expensive, and I ended up having to come up with about $50,000 myself to finish the project. The film was as good as I could have made it, but it wasn't amazing. Something was missing—a clear narrative, a structure, I don't know. I definitely ran out of the time I would have needed to make it better.

The premiere was at Tribeca in 2015. I remember opening night and seeing my name on the big marquee out front: DANIEL ARSHAM'S *FUTURE RELIC* PRESENTED BY TRIBECA FILM FESTIVAL. It was a legit thrill. They had set up a full red carpet, and many of the actors and directors appearing at the festival attended. My film was shown in a relatively small screening space, which is usually indicative of what the organizers think of it. I was nervous. A few hundred people attended the premiere, many of whom had worked on it. A lot of my friends were there. I did a little talk afterward. Julian Schnabel came to see it, stopping by to shake my hand before the screening. Afterward he was overheard saying, "That was the worst fucking thing I've ever seen."

I didn't know how to react when I heard that. I'm an artist, and I've had exhibitions all over the world, so I know the deal. Going into the film, I was following my normal rule of never taking anything said about my work too much to heart, but this one hurt, coming from another artist. I was already nervous doing this new thing, and all the more nervous sharing it with other people. There's always a hesitancy for anyone moving into a new medium, but I'm also never comfortable staying in the same lane—I have to push or my creativity dies. I usually keep my opinions to myself when it comes to judging other artists' work. I'm not going to lie and say it didn't disappoint me, that I wouldn't have preferred a different reaction from him.

Originally planned as a nine-part series, the whole project petered out. Mahershala and I talked about it a couple of years later. He said, "What happened? I was ready to jump into it with you." And I was able to reply, "I'm not sure making film is what I should be doing."

It hurt to admit it, but I had learned a ton via the failure of making that film. In many ways, it was one

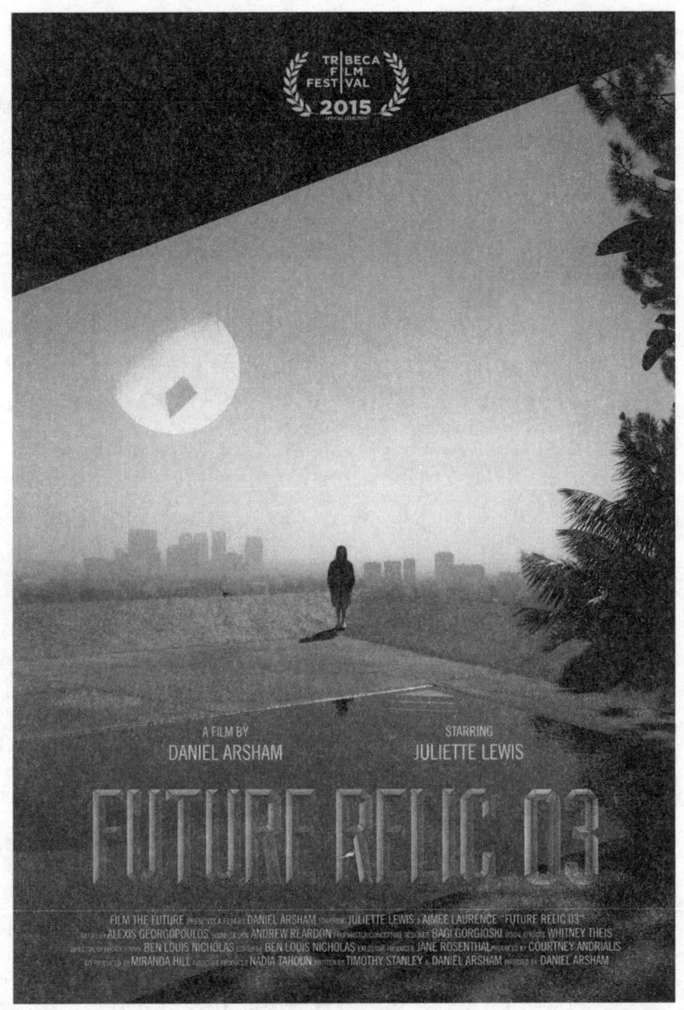

The poster for FUTURE RELIC.

of the most difficult things I've ever done as an artist. There are so many simultaneously moving pieces, so many things that have to work in sync, and the line between something being great and something being terrible is so thin and sometimes hard to see at all. There are clearly people who are extremely talented and can do all of that at the highest level, but it wasn't for me, at least not that time. Looking back, I got overly obsessed with the visual aspect of the film. The dialogue and all the other storytelling went to the back burner. That was a mistake on my part. But failure isn't something to be ashamed of or to run away from. I'm happy I did it. I value the experience I had. I'm happy to have made the friends I made. I may try it again one day. If you fail, try again.

Back in 2006, after being rejected by the Biennial, it took a couple of weeks for me to pick up the pieces, but, as I had done every other time I felt let down—not getting into Cooper on the first try, failed experiments in the studio, entire bodies of work that went unseen—I eventually got back to work. At first I couldn't even look at the model I had built as my imagination ran wild. It just sat there on my desk like a reminder of what wasn't going to be. But little by little, the work pulled me back in.

And the model—the room with the crumbling walls, the broken desk, and the white picture frame sliding down the wall—stayed in the studio for years. It collected dust, almost like it was waiting. More than a decade later, when I began working with Kim Jones on the Christian Dior project, I finally realized that space. Not at the Whitney, but on a different stage, with a different audience, yet somehow with all of the poetry, decay, and tension I had imagined all those years earlier.

The truth is, that room, that idea, never left. It just waited for its time. Like so many things in this strange journey, it took the long way to get there. It took patience. It definitely strengthened my vision.

I wouldn't be the artist I am today, with the degree of success I once thought I could only dream of, without the failures along the way.

CHAPTER IX
THE MOST MONUMENTAL SHOW OF MY LIFE

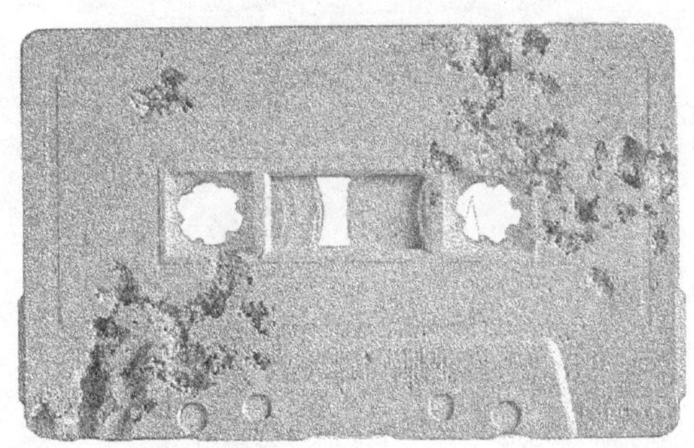

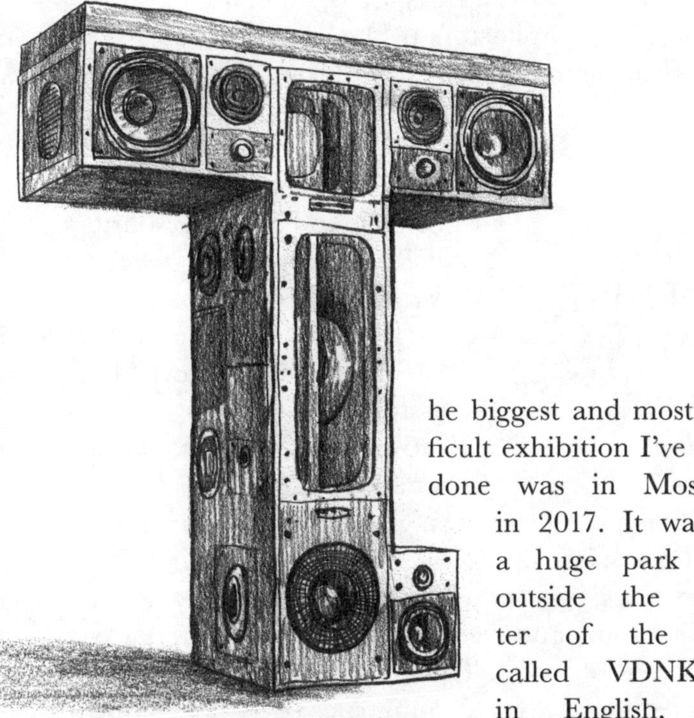

he biggest and most difficult exhibition I've ever done was in Moscow in 2017. It was in a huge park just outside the center of the city called VDNKh—in English, the Exhibition of Achievements of National Economy. Built from the remnants brought back from Stalin's Soviet Pavilion at the 1937 Paris Exposition, the original construct had pavilions dedicated to different industries, with the most massive reserved for celebrating the Communist Party. The park suffered from years of neglect until Putin decided to resuscitate the VDNKh as a cultural destination. They built a beautiful movie theater and a Russian cinema museum. They built shops and restaurants. They redid all of the sidewalks and trails. It was huge, like some kind of Russian Disneyland that lived in its own invented time period, half old Soviet, half contemporary Russia. There was one pavilion dedicated specifically to international exhibitions of art. I was the first person they invited to do an exhibition there.

At the time, the art world in Russia was booming. Money had flowed into the country after the rise of Putin, and Russian oligarchs suddenly became the biggest art collectors in the world. It was as if, after being starved of culture during communism, they suddenly wanted to catch up. American and European galleries were opening spaces in Moscow and St. Petersburg. New Russian galleries were everywhere. Young Russians were starting to make art without having to get it approved by the state. I was thrilled by the invitation and went over in the summer of 2016.

> "MAKE THE THINGS YOU WANT TO SEE EXIST IN THE WORLD."
>
> MENTOR NOTE

The space I had been given to use was an entire building originally dedicated to celebrating the Siberian logging industry. The facade was a giant Soviet propaganda–era sculpture of lumberjacks carved out of wood. The architecture and art were designed to express the dominance of Soviet culture and to project power and influence both externally and internally. It is an intense in-person experience: You realize how effective art can be when wielded to make people feel very specific emotions.

When I went there for the first time, I realized immediately that they were prepared to approve anything. Every crazy idea I gave them was met with "Oh, yeah, no problem. We're just gonna get like fifty guys in here to do it." I was kind of speechless when they said that and again when I asked, "What about lifting and moving heavy, heavy sculpture?" One of the men laughed, pointed to a hundred-foot-tall sculpture of a Russian man at the end of the park, and said, "We built and moved that thing; we can figure out anything you want to do." Knowing I could make whatever I wanted and had the resources and staff to actually get it made was incredibly exciting. It was the first and only time in my career that has happened.

I wanted to turn the interior of the building into an experiential space—to paint the entire place white and use sculpture to make the walls and ceiling look like they were being stretched and pulled and melted and folded. I wanted to embed clocks in the surfaces so they'd look like they were melting and being absorbed by the walls. I designed a huge piece to fill the largest room in the building, a space the size of a basketball court but with fifty-foot ceilings. The idea of the piece was to make the room look as if a giant had walked into it, grabbed each of the walls, pulled them toward the center of the room, and tied them together with a bow. It was a monumental undertaking.

While I was there, I provided them with highly detailed designs they could use to build all of the large-scale works. Back in New York, I started conceiving the architecture. The only thing that I left original was the floors, which were this chopped-up marble, this broken-up old stone that was all compounded together and tiled. I worked on the designs with John Bianchi, an architectural and design wizard who went to Cooper with me and who still works in my studio. After the designs were ready, John went to Russia to supervise the construction. During the whole of the installation, he stayed on-site while I went back and forth. Over the entire construction period, I probably spent three or four months

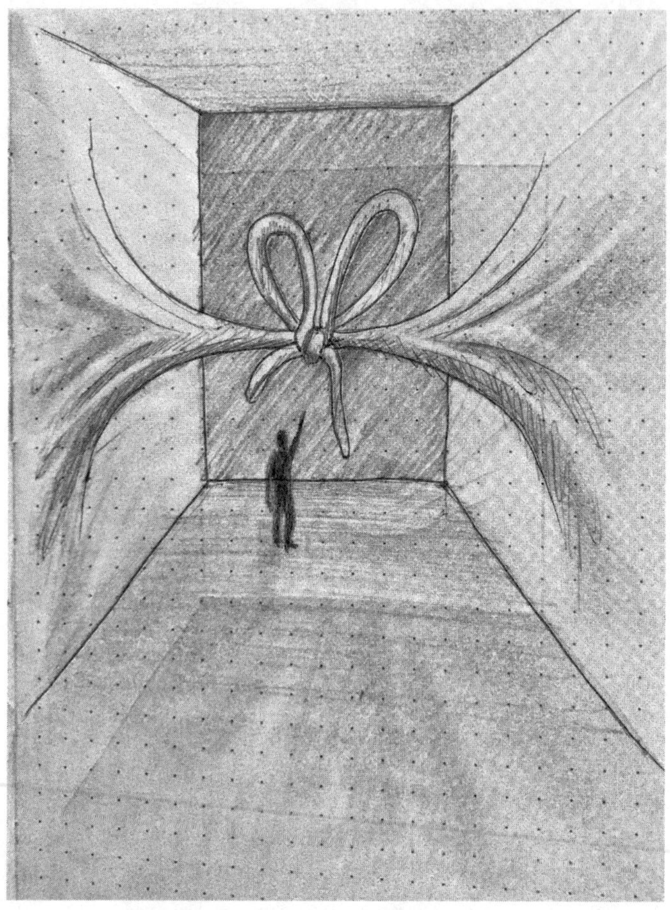

A drawing study of the work I ended up making for the exhibition in Moscow.

in Moscow. It was a wild experience. I stayed at the Metropol Hotel, right off Red Square, and I was keenly aware of being an American. I don't know how else to describe what it was like except that it felt very Russian. Everything was overly done in a specific kind of Russian way, both classic and beautiful but also kind of tacky and gaudy. There were always troops marching in Red Square around Lenin's Tomb. It felt foreign and familiar in a way that I hadn't experienced with other cultures. The scale of the architecture is striking: Everything is big, especially the doors. It makes you feel small. The weight of the architecture and the art and the government and the military history—all of it is constantly on display everywhere you go. It's incredible, and it can be overwhelming.

I worked on the show for almost two years. I spent six months conceiving it and making sketches, we spent six months on the designs and architectural drawings, and it took about a year to actually build it. I was fortunate to be the first artist to hold a show in the space. It meant we didn't have deadlines or timelines. The Russian organizers wanted to make a huge splash and gave huge amounts of freedom and endless amounts of support. And the construction crews were deeply committed. Russian people are not afraid of working hard and getting their hands dirty, and they know how to build things. Since the building itself was a historic Soviet landmark, one of the caveats was that anything original in the building could not be altered in any way. So the first thing we had to do was build a giant scaffolding system to cover the interior. We basically built walls just inside of the original walls that functioned like a shell. Once the scaffolding was up, we redid the ceilings and put in a thin, bright white scrim with a system of lighting behind it. The idea was to create a radical and dramatic contrast between the exterior of the building and the interior. Outside was a huge Soviet-era building with giant columns that had been carved with images of Russian lumberjacks. It was dark and heavy and imposing. Inside, it was bright, white, ultramodern, with melting walls and surreal figures and objects.

One of my favorite moments was when we needed to lift the main piece of the central knot and bow that were theoretically holding the room together. It weighed about a thousand pounds. I told them we were going to need a gantry crane. The site foreman laughed and said, "No, we're not." Then he left for a little while and came back with about twenty humongous Russian workers. They built a giant staircase of scaffolding instead of getting a gantry. They were insistent that it would be faster. They were going to lift it and lift it again and lift it again until they got up to the top, about thirty feet in the air. It was a very different way of thinking about materials and physical strength, the way you move things around, the fastest ways to get things done. It was so enlightening, something I still think about all these years later.

The organizers covered all of the costs. It would cost several million dollars to build the same thing in the United States today. It probably cost one-tenth of that using the Russian system and laborers. The organizers also did all of the marketing. They created and ran digital ads all over the internet, especially on art sites. They took out ads in *Artforum* and all the other major art publications. There were posters and billboards all over Moscow. The mayor of the city and the cultural attaché from the US embassy were going to open the show.

The day of the opening was a whirlwind. Everything was structured down to the minute. I did press for probably five or six hours, some one-on-one interviews, and a big press conference for a couple of

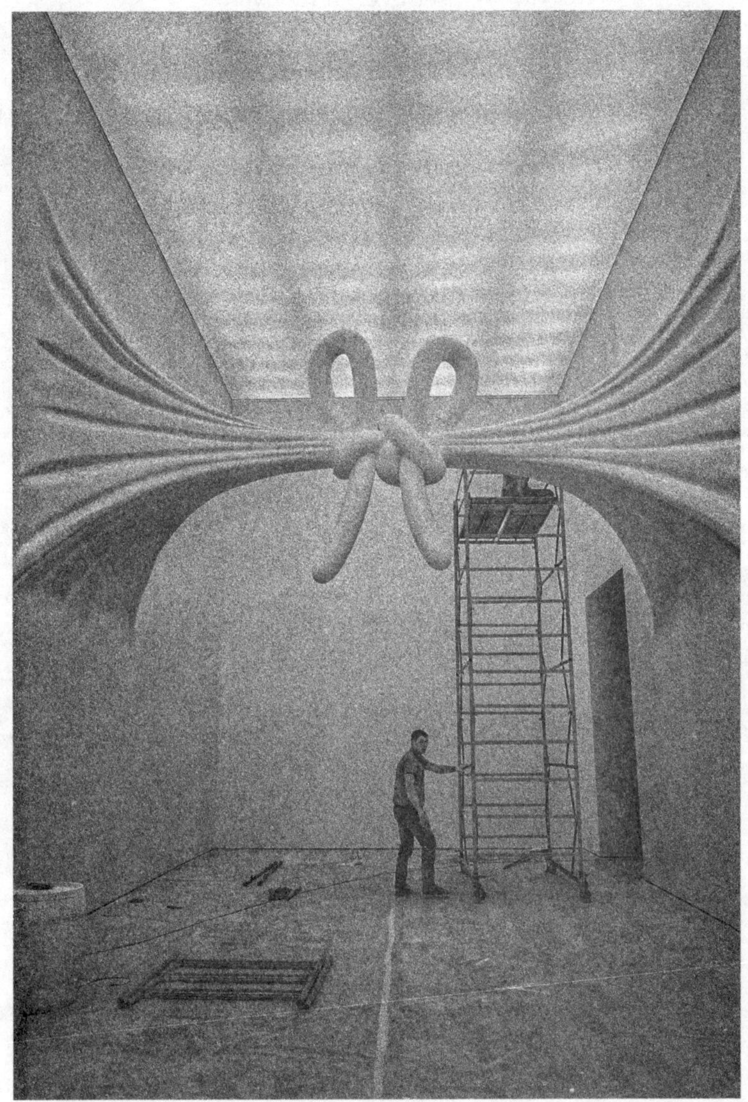

Installing the giant knot sculpture.

hours in the afternoon. By the time I got back to the Metropol Hotel to change, I was exhausted, and the day wasn't even half over.

Back at the hotel, I got dressed quickly and had a quick bite and headed back to the exhibition. Going into any show, I reach a point where the opening event feels weird. This was especially true for this one, the biggest installation I'd ever done. I wouldn't say it's a letdown, but it's kind of the end of the process, not the beginning. For everyone else, it's the opening of a show. For me, it's the end of a journey. And I always feel super depressed the day after an exhibition opening.

"THIS IS ONE OF THE MORE IMPORTANT THINGS I CAN SAY TO YOU. WHAT YOU MAKE IS NOT FOR EVERYONE. THE PEOPLE WHO APPRECIATE YOUR HALLUCINATIONS WILL FIND YOU."

MENTOR NOTE

When we pulled up, there was a huge crowd outside, a few thousand people. I was shocked and definitely thrilled. *Fuck, all these people are here to see your work; it better be good.* From the moment I stepped out of the car, everything was a blur. Everywhere I went, there was a crowd yelling my name and taking my picture. I was surrounded by patrons and Russian officials and all of their security. The exhibition was so crowded, it was hard to move, much less talk to anyone or see anything. I was in the exhibition hall for two hours, but it felt like five minutes, and most of my memories come from photographs. It was amazing, and the Russian people were amazing. It is my sincere hope that someday I'll get to go back. I am, if you remember, of Ukrainian descent, so I don't know when that will be. I hope for peace soon.

After the opening, there was dinner in the park, in what was once a residence for visiting high-ranking communist officials. The house was beautiful, like something from the Gilded Age, and there was an after-party on a boat on the Moskva River that went till dawn. It was a once-in-a-lifetime kind of night, though the whole thing is a bright blur. When I got back to the hotel, I slept for twenty-four hours.

I stayed in Moscow for a few more days. I had to wind down my presence in the exhibition and prepare and instruct the curators on how to eventually take the entire installation down. It remained up for a year. When it came down, two of the pieces stayed in a private collection in Russia. The giant knot piece was destroyed, because there was nowhere to put it. Some of the rest—probably six pieces in total—were destroyed. I still own the clocks and two other pieces. In terms of scale, it was my biggest show and the most complicated. Two years of work and my first massive international exhibition. I got back from Moscow and fought my typical postshow depression by going back to work. It's the best medicine. The cycle of creativity never ends.

CHAPTER X

WHY YOU NEED A GREAT LAWYER

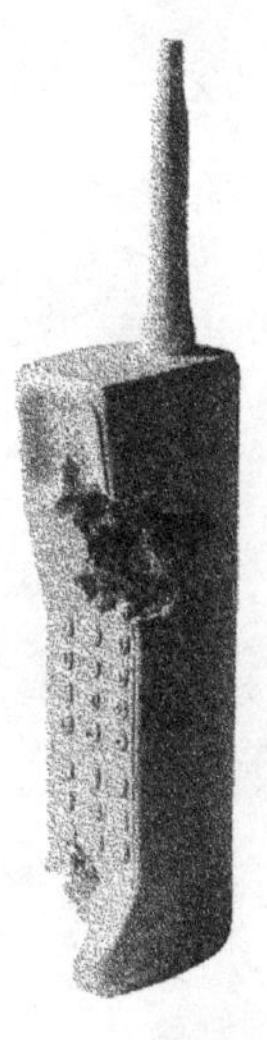

(AND WHEN YOU DON'T)

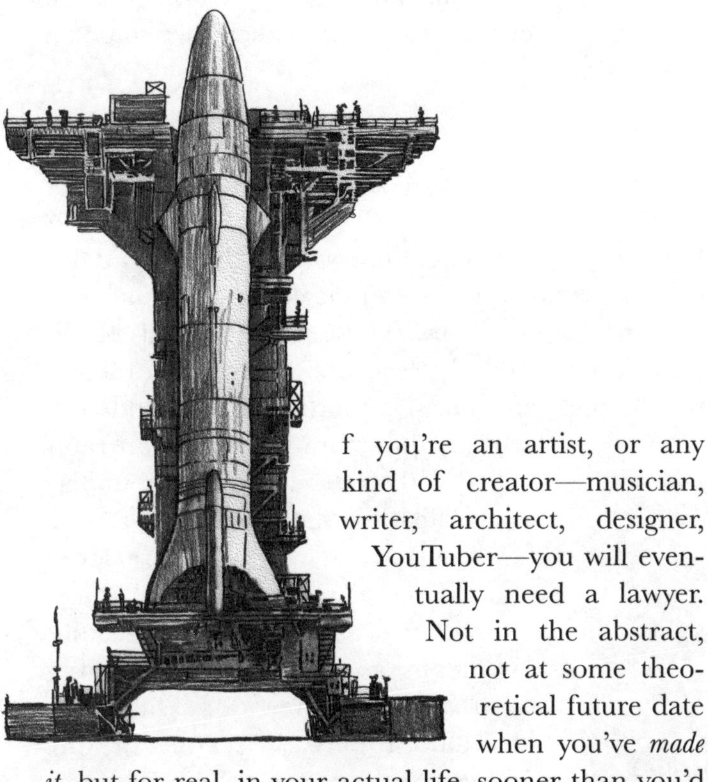

f you're an artist, or any kind of creator—musician, writer, architect, designer, YouTuber—you will eventually need a lawyer. Not in the abstract, not at some theoretical future date when you've *made it*, but for real, in your actual life, sooner than you'd probably expect. When I was starting out, I didn't know that artists even needed lawyers. I thought it was just about making good work. And that *is* the hard part, but it's not the whole thing. Nobody teaches you about contracts or licensing or intellectual property when you're in art school. I left Cooper with a degree, but, like most of my peers, I had no clue how to register a copyright, form an LLC, negotiate a contract, or even find a gallery. I had to learn all of it in real time, mostly by screwing things up. The one thing that went right: I got lucky and found a great lawyer early on. I met Vivek Jayaram through a family connection. He was a young lawyer at the time, and when I told him I needed help figuring out how to navigate the art world, he just said, "Sure, I'll be your lawyer." We've worked together since that day. Hundreds of art deals and business contracts later, I realize how crucial it was that I didn't try to do all of this alone.

NEVER GIVE AWAY YOUR WORK

Early on, I started getting approached by luxury brands, fashion houses, and sneaker brands that were excited about my work. These were the kinds of clients I'd dreamed about as a student. They offered real budgets and massive platforms. But hidden in those opportunities were contracts filled with terms I didn't fully understand, like "work for hire."

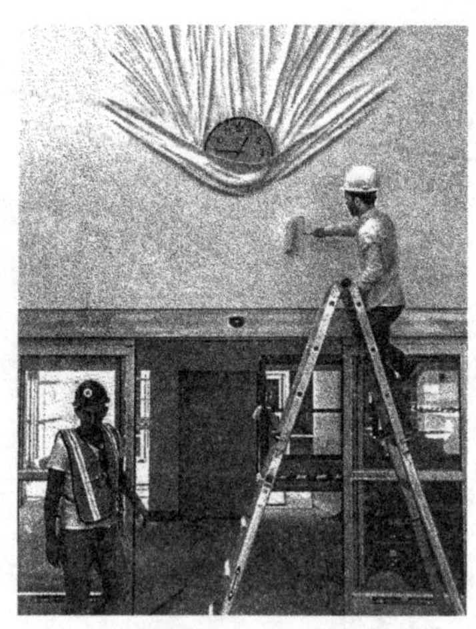

Installing a work.

On paper, work for hire looks fine: They pay you, you make something, everyone's happy. But legally, it means you don't own the thing you created—they do. The intellectual property, the concept, the design, the creative DNA—all gone. Forever. You can't reuse it, rework it, or even claim it's yours beyond an image in your portfolio or Instagram page. Whatever you do, the company you're working for owns it, and they own it forever. Not often the best deal for an artist. Because of this, from day one, Vivek and I decided, *No work for hire.* Instead, we would only agree to a license for my work. I'd create something rooted in the language I was already developing, and the company would get the right to use it for a specific project and a specific amount of time. After that, the work and all of the associated rights came back to me.

Early on in my career, this decision cost me projects. Some companies simply wouldn't go for it. But Vivek, who had seen artists give away their best ideas for a quick paycheck only to regret it for the rest of their careers, was adamant. And he was right. Years later, when some of those companies wanted to continue using my work, we had the leverage to renegotiate, and I was still in control.

It was one of the best decisions I ever made.

Here are some more examples of how I work with my lawyer. How you do will depend on what you create and how you want to make money from it.

FAIR USE ISN'T A FREE PASS

Another thing no one told me, and something I had to really work through with Vivek, was how to navigate fair use. I often use existing objects and images in my work: basketballs, cars, sneakers, film characters, branded materials. Anytime you do that, you are stepping into the complex world of copyright law. In the United States, there's a clause that gives artists a kind of protection called fair use, which basically says you can incorporate copyrighted material if your work is "transformative"—if you change it significantly, add meaning, or make something new out of it. But it's not a blank check. Just because you call something art doesn't mean you're safe. You can still get sued. You can still lose.

I spent hours—years—with my attorney making sure that what I was doing was not only creatively defensible but also legally sound. That the work wasn't just referencing something but truly transforming it. More often than not, the companies whose products or logos I've used haven't come after me. They call me to collaborate. Some of the best projects I've done came from companies that first noticed me because I was using their imagery, not to steal but to reframe it into something entirely different. It's one of those rare cases where the legal conversations actually led to new creative opportunities.

THEY'RE ALREADY USING YOUR WORK

As my career grew, a different problem started showing up. My work, without my permission, began appearing in other people's work. Companies used it in ad campaigns. Designers referenced it too closely. Fashion brands built entire elements of shows around ideas I had already explored and exhibited. Sometimes it was subtle, sometimes it wasn't. I've seen it all, from other artists to Fortune 500 companies to major recording artists using my work on stage or in videos. Vivek handled these situations with total calm. He'd send a letter. More often than not, the company's lawyer would call back and say something like "We don't know who your client is. He's not that famous." And every time, Vivek would reply, "Go back into your internal server, search his name, call me back." And sure enough, they'd find it. My work was almost always sitting right there in someone's mood board, internal presentation, or reference deck. After that, it was just a matter of how we wanted to proceed. In some cases, if I liked the people involved, I turned it into a collaboration. In others, we held the line and settled. Either way, I was never starting from scratch, because I had the structure and the legal foundation to stand on.

WHEN NOT TO USE A LAWYER

Here's the thing, and this is important: Sometimes you have to know when not to use a lawyer. When I first started working with Emmanuel Perrotin, there was no contract. No paperwork. It was a handshake, an understanding, and mutual respect. I'm sure any lawyer, including mine, would have told me I was insane. And maybe I was. But sometimes relationships are more important than signatures. Emmanuel and I just had the right chemistry, a shared trust that has lasted for years.

> "YOU CAN'T JUST THROW DARTS AT THE BOARD BLINDLY.
>
> IF YOU CAN'T SEE THE GOAL, AND I MEAN THE ENTIRE PLAN, YOU CAN'T REACH THE FINISH."
>
> MENTOR NOTE

That's not to say you shouldn't protect yourself when agreeing to gallery representation. In most cases, you absolutely should. But you also have to know when you're entering something where the real value is the relationship, not the cash. That was the case with Emmanuel. It worked because we respected each other. It wouldn't have worked otherwise.

When I went back to Cooper to teach, I actually brought Vivek into my classroom to talk to the students about all of this—about contracts, intellectual property, licensing. I realized, standing in front of them, that no one else was going to tell them this stuff. They were going to leave school just like I did:

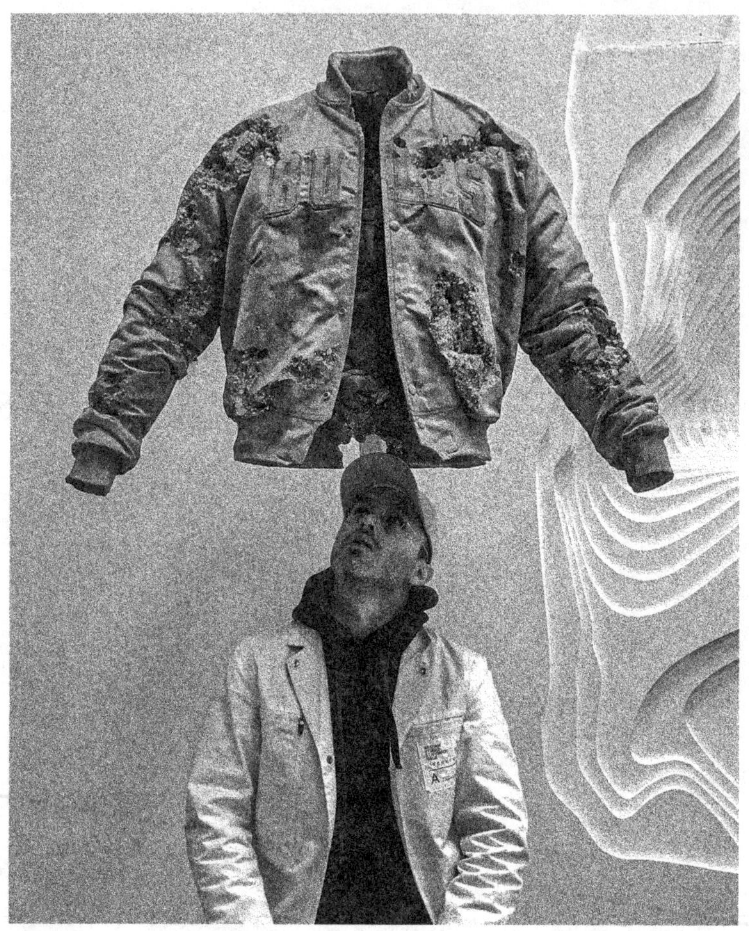

With a very complex cast work.

talented, motivated, and totally unprepared for the business side of being an artist.

I've had friends tell me they *don't want to get lawyers involved*, because it complicates things. But if you're doing this seriously, if you're really going to live off your work, you're already in business, whether you admit it or not. The question is whether you're going to be smart about it.

I wouldn't have made it this far without Vivek. He wasn't just my attorney. He was, and still is, part of my studio, part of the practice itself. Make an attorney part of yours as well. You won't regret it.

CHAPTER XI

THE HURRICANE

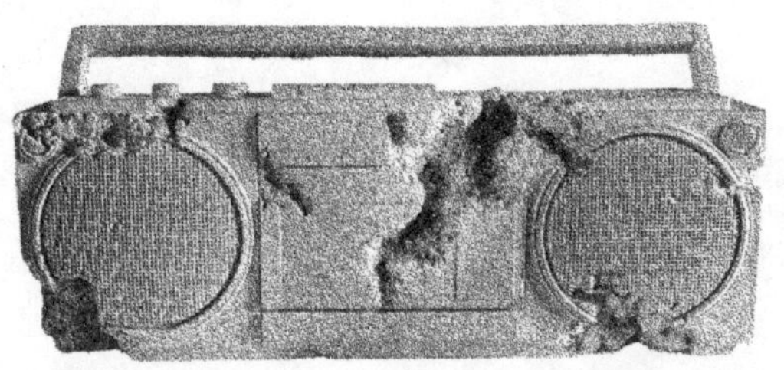

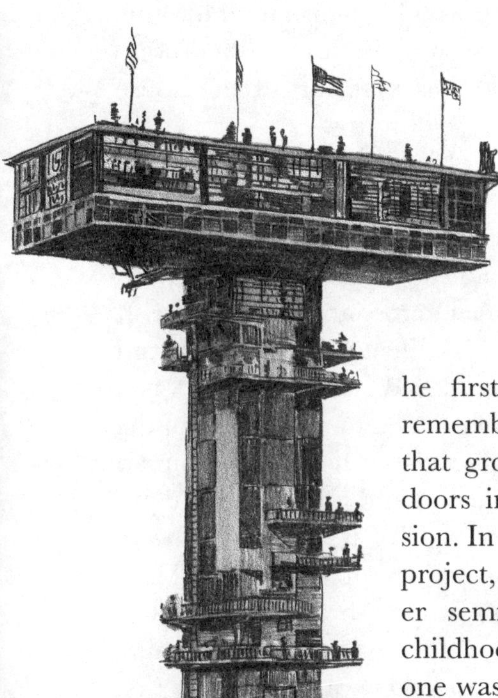

he first art series I vividly remember completing was that group of photos of the doors in my Miami subdivision. In addition to that photo project, there was another seminal moment in my childhood in Florida. This one was far more sinister and destructive: Hurricane Andrew, which made landfall on Monday, August 24, 1992. This event would shape my life and my art forever.

The Saturday before landfall, I heard about the pending storm from my friend John. He said it was going to be bad, really bad. I asked my mother if she'd heard about it. My parents had separated about a year before, and my father didn't live with us anymore, but she told me he was coming back to help prepare and to stay with us during the storm.

That afternoon, we went to the local Publix supermarket and stocked up on food, canned goods, batteries, candles, and bottled water. It was packed with people with carts overflowing with all they could grab, with the shelves damn near empty. We went to Home Depot to get plywood for the windows, and it was a zoo. Hour-long lines just to check out. My dad couldn't get enough wood to board up the whole house, so he decided to just do the master bedroom. He felt that if he could lock that part of the house down, we would be safe.

As I helped my dad, I could see my favorite tree in the background: a forty-foot-tall ficus that supported an amazing tree house my friends and their dads had helped us build. It was a really solid structure, fifteen by fifteen feet across and built to last. It had a floor made of thick, heavy-duty beams, and the walls were substantial and sturdy. There was a rope ladder underneath that led to a trapdoor in the floor. Helping to build that tree house gave me an early glimpse at construction and how things are put together, and I liked the logic of it. The beams were laid down, plywood was put on top and screwed into the beams. Everything was cross-braced for stability, and then the vertical walls were set in place. I think seeing all of that come together was one of my first real experiences with sculpture.

As my dad was screwing the boards over the sliding door, I wondered if the tree house I loved so much would be strong enough to withstand the coming storm.

After many hours of prep, day turned into night, and I went to bed like I would on any typical Sunday. Around 1 a.m., my mom woke me up and said, "Everyone is going to sleep in the master bedroom." My father, my mother, my sister, our dog Shane, and I all assembled and waited.

I couldn't fall asleep. The wind was howling so loud, it sounded like a freight train rolling right outside our house. There were huge, booming thunderclaps that would shake the entire house. I could hear the framed photos on the wall rattling. I could see lightning constantly flashing between the windows and the boards we'd put over them. I was thinking about my tree house. I was really into skating at the time, and the previous Christmas Santa had given me a Tony Hawk Skull deck, by far the coolest thing I'd ever owned. It had come with a pack of these fantastic graphic stickers and small postcard-sized images of Tony Hawk skating on the same deck. I had stapled a bunch of them to the walls on the inside of the tree house. I was kicking myself for not retrieving them.

"IT'S VERY RARE AND DIFFICULT TO HAVE EVERY ASPECT OF YOUR LIFE IN PERFECT HARMONY.

WORK, FAMILY, ROMANCE, HEALTH...

TAKE CARE OF YOUR MENTAL STATE FIRST AND REMEMBER THAT NOTHING IS PERMANENT."

MENTOR NOTE

The power went out a few minutes later, and we sat in the dark. As the sound of the storm was getting even more intense, I was trying to distract myself by playing around with the flashlight. I shone it up at the ceiling. As I moved the beam around, I could see water trickling along the inside edges of the beams and dripping down the walls. I pointed it out to my dad, but he kept saying, "We're safe here, we'll be okay."

We had a battery-powered radio and turned it on. Every channel was the same: reporters tracking the path and the severity. Andrew had dramatically strengthened as it hit land. After it hit Miami, it became a Category 5 hurricane, the most dangerous type, with sustained winds of more than 157 miles per hour and gusts up to 200. This storm was an absolute monster, a killer. As the reporters talked about the eye of the storm and where it was going to go, we realized it was headed right for us.

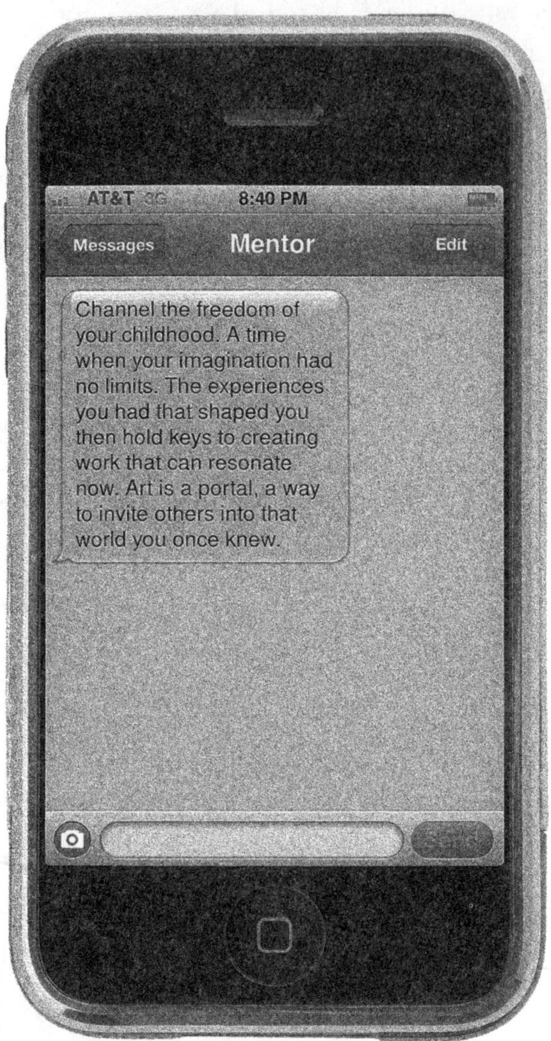
AT&T 3G
8:40 PM
Messages
Mentor
Edit
Channel the freedom of your childhood. A time when your imagination had no limits. The experiences you had that shaped you then hold keys to creating work that can resonate now. Art is a portal, a way to invite others into that world you once knew.

MENTOR NOTE

There was nothing to do and nowhere to go. We started hearing these crazy, loud crashing sounds, getting louder and coming closer, louder and closer. And then a massive explosion. My ears popped and started ringing and kept ringing. Everything was still for a moment, and I felt the pain inside my head growing. The dog was barking nonstop, and my sister started screaming. We could hear glass shattering in other parts of the house, things flying around and hitting the walls. It sounded like fucking mayhem. It *was* fucking mayhem.

My dad decided we needed to go into the closet. In there, we could hear the house disintegrating around us. I imagined my bed flying away, like Dorothy in *The Wizard of Oz*. It was so loud that we had to scream when talking to each other. I said to my dad, "The walls are moving." He quickly replied, "No, they're not." But the whole family looked up at the wall, and we all saw it: The entire wall was bulging like a lung filling with air.

There was another explosion. Another. Another. The water was starting to build up in the closet. It was so cold, just freezing cold. I wasn't sure if we were going to survive. The looks on my parents' faces terrified me.

The bedroom door blew open, and more water started pouring in. My dad ran out of the closet and tried to close the door. I couldn't see him, but I could hear the door smashing and slapping against the wall and the doorframe in the wind. It was quiet for a moment, then the quiet was shattered by a horrible scream. He ran back in, his hand dripping with blood. The door had smashed his hand against the now shattered walls. He tied one of his socks around his hand to stop the bleeding, crept back out into the bedroom, and pulled the mattress against the closet opening as best he could. At that point, I was pretty sure we were going to die. My twelfth birthday was only a couple of weeks away. I remember thinking, *Fuck, I'm never going to kiss a girl.* Crazy. Standing in knee-deep water, with the train whistle, the wind outside, my dog howling, my sister crying, my parents scared and fighting again, I wondered if it would be painful to die. I didn't think I'd have to wait long. At least then it would be quiet.

We stayed there in that tiny closet for six hours, with the continual soundtrack of all hell breaking loose outside. No one spoke for the last few hours. Finally, the noise outside started to die down. Just as it started to actually feel quiet, there was a very loud and violent snapping and breaking sound, followed by an earthshaking thud: a massive tree narrowly missing our little closet. A branch created a massive hole in the corner of the ceiling. Light blasted through the opening, and when we saw blue sky we finally knew it was morning and that the storm was past us.

We walked out of what remained of the bedroom. It was like nothing I've ever seen or experienced, before or since, and I hope I never do again. Most of the house was gone. Most of every house around us was gone. What was left of ours was covered with pink insulation foam that had blown out of someone else's roof. There were tree branches and leaves and roof tiles and shingles and fragments of wood and dishes and furniture and paintings and all kinds of detritus stuck in the foam. In every direction we looked, all we saw was destruction and wreckage. Water rushing everywhere. Wreckage. Everywhere.

I heard my mom yelling my name. She was standing where our kitchen table had been, over what looked like a piece of a building—strong beams with a plywood surface attached to them and the remnants of a wall. It was broken at the edges, and parts of it had obviously snapped in the wind. As I walked toward her, she was pointing down at something.

I came closer and I could see it: a postcard of Tony Hawk skating on the Skull deck, stapled to a piece of wood. My favorite tree, and my tree house with it, was the one that had crashed through our roof.

As insane as it was to make it through the storm, the aftermath was a bizarre, postapocalyptic time. It was an incredible experience to have as a child, being exposed to the fragility of life and really feeling for the first time that nothing was solid or firm. Normalcy that disappeared in a matter of minutes.

Our neighborhood had been decimated. Trees and wooden structures annihilated. Palm trees obliterated. My house was eight or nine miles inland from the coast, but an immense amount of water—brackish, almost salt water—had washed up into our house. Yards were just full of junk. Shit was everywhere. People's belongings, roof tiles, and rubble were everywhere. I found family photographs blocks from home.

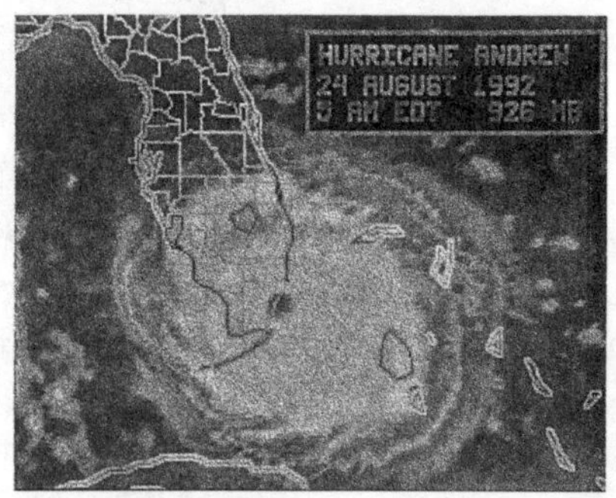

In the eye of the hurricane.

A family friend named Bill Mills asked me and all the other neighborhood kids to help clean up. One of the kids said, "We'll do it for twenty dollars a man." Bill pulled me aside and said, "Daniel, you and I are friends. I have always found you to be a very upstanding and honorable kid. In times like this, we all need to pull together and work together as a team. If you decide not to help out with this, we're not going to be friends anymore."

It was a shocking thing to say to a kid, and it stuck—this kind of life lesson coming from a parent's friend. Bill was an important presence in my childhood. He showed me how to use power tools and make things with my hands. Before the storm, he'd had a woodshop in his garage, and I used to go over there and make things with him. We'd create skate ramps and boxes. He made his own furniture and made a toy chest for my bedroom. My parents were not people who made things in that way. I'll never forget what Bill said. I helped everyone clean up, and I was glad I did. Our neighborhood felt like a real community. Everyone was kind to everyone. Everyone needed help. Everyone helped.

There was a food and water shortage, and there was nowhere to take a shower. We had enough food to get by for a short time, but with no electricity, we couldn't cook, so we made fires outside in the backyard. For us kids, there was something crazy and magical about being in your backyard and having a bonfire to cook your food. It was some of the most delicious food I have ever eaten.

We slept inside what remained of the house. There was nowhere else to go. I could see the sky at night through the hole in the roof. It didn't rain for days after the storm, and with all the electricity out you could see the stars. Seeing all of those stars at night in a suburban neighborhood was awe-inspiring.

I particularly remember trying to find a way to shower. Getting the water running again took a long time. I went over to the house of a friend who had a pool in his backyard. The pool had a screen enclosure that had collapsed into the water. The couch from his living room had also ended up in the pool. But we figured a way to get wet in the pool, stand on the couch while we soaped up, and then rinse off by falling back into the water.

Many years later, when I was in college studying art, so much of the experience of the storm and the aftermath came back to me. Like all young artists, I was looking for subject matter. What are the unique experiences that make me who I am? What has been imprinted in my soul in a way that only I can express?

Andrew was a traumatic experience for me but also a strangely magical one, especially its aftermath.

So much of what I do in my work is about deconstruction and reconstruction, about decay and erosion. The experience of watching the building I had grown up in being physically torn apart, seeing the insides of the walls, seeing how weirdly fragile the structure was—all of those things have been integrated into the conceptual framework of my art practice ever since.

CHAPTER XII

WHY GO TO ART SCHOOL

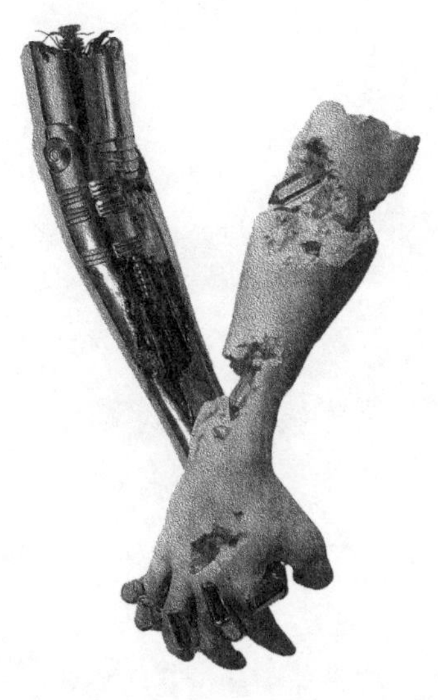

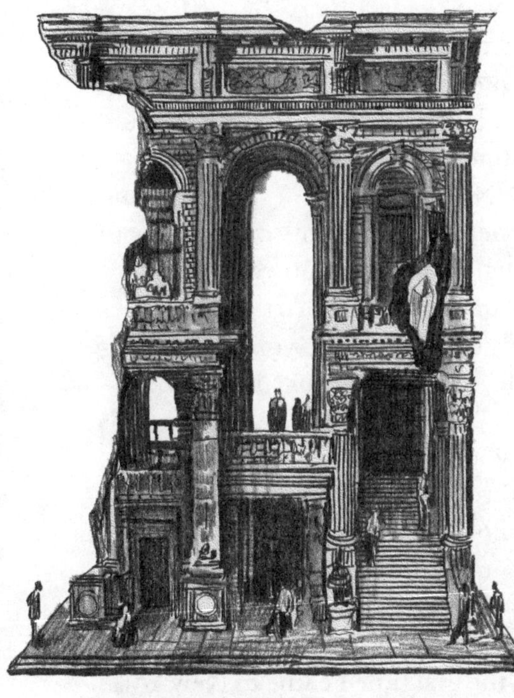

knew at an early age that I wanted to make a career out of being an artist. It was the only choice. I couldn't imagine another path for my life. My art education began in middle school and continued in high school, and as high school wound down, for me it was either art school or bust.

Whether it's the right choice for you depends on you and your goals. If you want to be an Artist in the Art World, I would absolutely recommend it. If you want to work in architecture or design, I would absolutely recommend it (though there are also other places to study those disciplines). I think of art school in a really basic way: People who want to go into business, as broad as that term is, go to business school; people who want to go into creative fields, as broad as that term is, should go to school for it. Here's why.

EXPOSURE TO DIFFERENT MEDIA. You'll experiment with painting, sculpture, printmaking, digital art, photography, and more. This hands-on experience helps you discover what truly excites you.

STRUCTURED LEARNING. The curriculum forces you to master foundational techniques before specializing, giving you a solid base that will serve you throughout your career.

CRITICAL FEEDBACK. You'll get critiques from professors and peers, learning how to take constructive criticism and refine your work.

INDUSTRY CONNECTIONS. Professors, visiting artists, alumni, and networking events open doors to opportunities you might never find on your own.

DEDICATED TIME TO CREATE. Art school gives you a unique period of focus where your only job is to experiment, create, and refine your artistic voice.

ACCESS TO FACILITIES. You'll have access to tools and materials that would be prohibitively expensive on your own—darkrooms, print shops, sculpture labs, and digital studios.

COMMUNITY. Surrounding yourself with other artists fosters inspiration, collaboration, and motivation to push your work further.

I was seventeen the first time I came to New York, on my official visit to Cooper. It was dazzling. New York was huge and busy and full of a kind of beauty and energy that only exists there. I was recently reminded of that first trip when I was driving into Manhattan with my two sons right before dusk. The sun had just set, and it was the golden hour.

Do not try to create and analyze at the same time. Those are separate processes. Just create and think later.

MENTOR NOTE

We were crossing the Williamsburg Bridge, and the lights of the city were sparkling against the sunlit background. It was that magical time when everything looks so big and almost unreal. My son Casper noticed it too. I told him about that first trip and how I had decided that this was where I wanted to live and make my dream come true. Like most kids, he thought his dad was babbling a bit, and when I finished he asked, "Did you do it?"

"Did I do what?"

"Did you make your dream come true?"

I smiled. It was a proud moment to be able to truthfully tell him, "Yes, I did."

My parents were skeptical of my dream, and rightfully so. My father wanted me to study graphic design, because it had a practical application—I'd have a skill that could be applied to many more areas. Even when I was in school, I didn't fucking know what I was going to do afterward. Although I wanted to be an artist, it seemed very daunting. I thought long and hard about whether I should follow my father's advice.

Thankfully, I had some time to make the decision. The way that most art education is structured comes from the Bauhaus school of art. In the first year, you study drawing and two-dimensional design; the second year, you study three-dimensional design and color theory. After the first two years, you specialize. Though I didn't entirely like or agree with all that structure at the time, it's one of the reasons to go. Whether it's drawing, painting, digital art, or sculpture, formal training helps refine techniques that might take years to master independently. It felt like drudgery at the time, but in retrospect it was incredibly important to the development of my career. Part of the reason I am able to work in multiple media is that I learned all of the skills to do so when I was there. I didn't enjoy

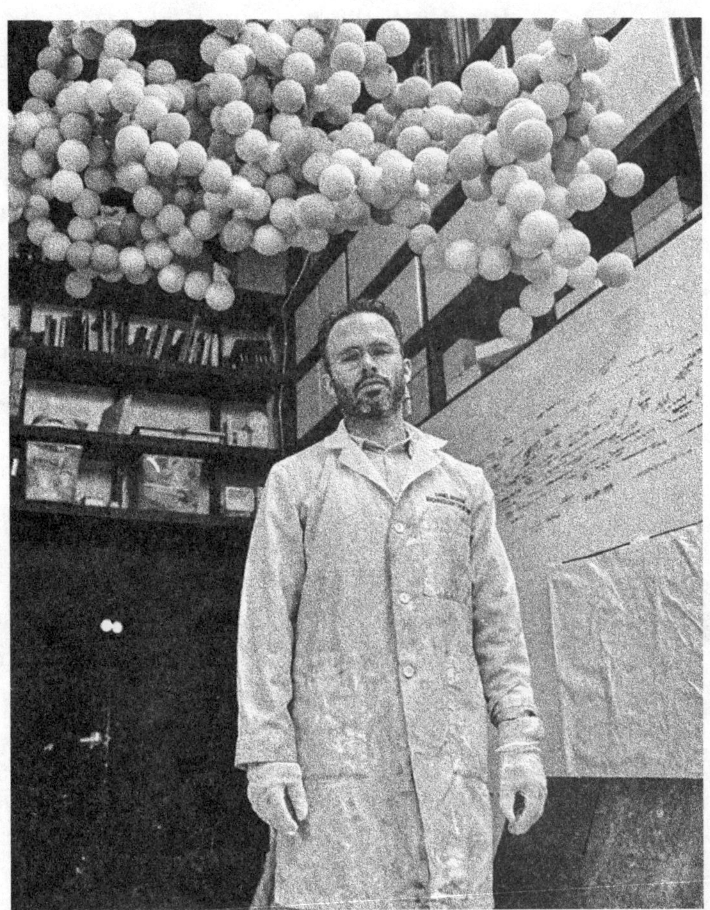

In the studio.

it at the time, but it has proved invaluable. You never know where your instincts or opportunities will take you, and the more you know how to do and the more technical skills you have, the more you can take advantage of those opportunities.

I had a really hard time my first year, at least in school. I loved being in New York. The city was electric, gritty, dirty, and dangerous, which it really isn't anymore. I loved St. Mark's Place, which was filled with punks and weirdos. I spent a ton of time in Washington Square Park, which was filled with people playing chess, skaters working on tricks, people swimming in the fountain, dudes selling weed, and people doing drugs in the middle of the park. It was all on display, and I loved it. But while I certainly was happy to be in the city and wanted to stay, I was also still a young, awkward kid who had grown up in a very safe environment, literally and figuratively. After every project, there are formal critiques where both the professors and the other students in the class comment on your work. Every single time that first fall, and most of my first year, my work just got brutalized.

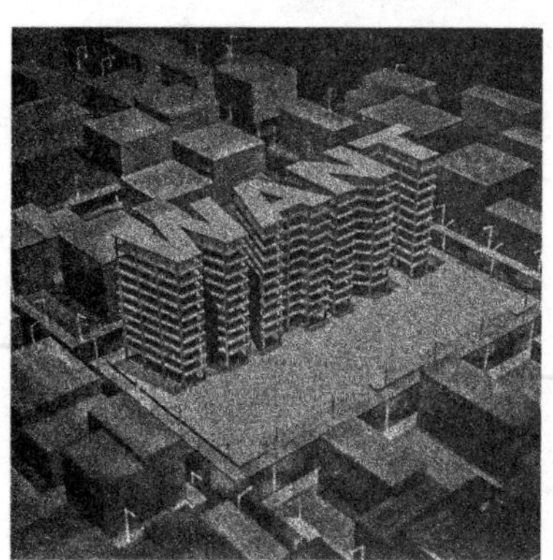

An early painting.

I knew it wasn't personal, that it was about trying to form our own language as artists, but it still stung when every single week something you made was torn apart by other students or your professor. It made me lose my confidence. It made me want to quit. It made me want to go home, even though I loved New York so much. It made me hate school and dread the critiques. But by the end of the first semester, I understood the point. My work was getting much better, largely because of the critiques, and I was learning to be able to take what helped and apply it and let go of what didn't without it hurting my feelings. I'm happy I went through it. Getting feedback from experienced professors and peers helps artists improve, and learning to handle constructive criticism is an essential skill for a professional creative career.

At Cooper, those first two years were like boot camp. The classes focused on making things and learning basic skills, physically crafting and conveying ideas through form. As much as I had drawn and painted before, I'd never really made sculpture before Cooper. Sculpture was intimidating. But one of my favorite classes was with Doug Ashford, who became one of my favorite professors. He taught 3D design using only cardboard—flat cardboard. He made it cool and taught us it was possible to make sculpture out of anything. We'd get prompts like "Make a sculpture that describes gravity." We had massive sheets of cardboard and had to just figure it out. It was hard and incredibly fun, and I felt like a kid again, just starting to play around with materials. And there was a valuable lesson that if you could use materials in unexpected ways, or make them look like something else, there was a kind of magic in it. This was an invaluable skill for an artist, and I still carry that lesson with me today.

"WRITE YOUR DREAMS DOWN. THAT WAY YOU REMEMBER WHEN YOU REACH THEM."

MENTOR NOTE

Color theory was another eye-opening experience, especially because I'm color-blind. On the first day, the professor asked if anyone in the class was color-blind. Two of us raised our hands. He pulled us aside and said, "There will be things in this class that you literally won't be able to see." He was right.

Color theory teaches how colors interact. It's a mix of art and science, understanding how a color appears alone versus how it changes in relation to others. One of the key figures in this field was Josef Albers, who studied at the Bauhaus and later formalized his color theory curriculum at Black Mountain College. The professor would show us color phenomena—how colors influence perception, how they appear lighter or darker depending on their surroundings—and challenge us to create works employing those effects. It was mind-blowing.

The following years at Cooper were about finding my voice as an artist. I studied with professors like Ashford and Hans Haacke, both of whom had profound influences on me. Haacke's work was highly conceptual, focusing on the weight of history in objects and architecture. One of his most famous pieces involved jackhammering the floor of the German pavilion at the Venice Biennale, leaving it shattered. Walking into that space was a visceral experience: It forced you to confront the broken foundation of history itself. And while my art is quite different from his, I always aspire to have the same kind of impact on a viewer that he had on me.

There are no discipline-specific majors at Cooper Union, which is unusual for an art school. You graduate with a bachelor of fine arts, which enables you to take courses in any subject that interests you. I took a lot of painting classes. I took a few sculpture courses. I studied basic architecture. I made all kinds of work, some of it okay and most of it not very good. I failed again and again, but that's part of finding your voice, trying everything and seeing what you love and what your skills and talents lead you to make. I struggled with what my viewpoint was going to be, what my art was going to say, and what my perspective was, and I kept coming back to my being a kid from the suburbs. I didn't want to be an asshole with some pretentious bullshit art style that everyone laughed at or shat on or that had nothing to do with my life.

Eventually I stopped worrying about grand artistic statements and focused on what I loved: cars, film, pop culture, music, architecture. I started making art related to those things, my favorite things. I made architectural models of buildings with hidden text in their floor plans. If you were inside, you'd never know that the structure spelled out a word when viewed from above, and the words were things I loved. It was a turning point for me: I wasn't just making things; I was creating meaning, even if it was only meaningful to me. At first I got crushed in my critiques, but I also started finding other students who were into the same things and making art about them. It was great to have this community, one I could have only found in art school. Surrounding myself with other artists fostered inspiration, collaboration, and motivation to push further.

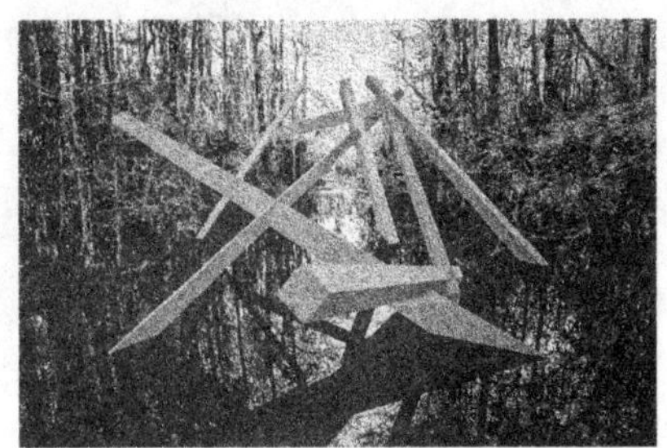

An early painting.

By the time I finished Cooper, I was making deeply mediocre versions of works I would later make into presentable, exhibition-quality pieces. But the ideas were there. I was at the start of what would later become important bodies of work for me, things like the Future Relic series. Even though I hadn't fully fleshed out the ideas, I had all the technical skills I needed to really get started as an artist, and all of the conceptual training to make valid work. I was also ready to be criticized and to learn from it. Most importantly, I understood what it meant to work, to make schedules and meet deadlines.

People will always bring up talent, but I don't think I had much natural skill. I don't even really believe in talent. I believe in work. I believe in putting in the hours. I have earned every single thing that I have done through thousands of hours of work. My grind and focus have become second nature. That's my talent. Art school forces you to embody that strangely productive kind of myopia. If that work ethic doesn't come out for someone during school, it probably doesn't exist in them and they aren't cut out to be an artist. The creative life isn't easy. The stress, pushing yourself to an uncomfortable place—that type of dedication isn't for everybody. Art school helped me figure it out. Maybe it will also help you.

Years after I graduated, I returned to Cooper to teach for a semester. I structured my class as an interdisciplinary seminar, bringing in guests like my attorney, Vivek Jayaram, to discuss intellectual property, Matthew Ammirati to talk about Porsche design, and Pharrell to explore his creative process. The students were blown away. I tried to teach them a mix of practical information about being an artist and technical training for making art. I loved it. I had a ton of fun and met a ton of cool students, some of whom have gone on to start great careers of their own. What I found interesting was that I could tell in the classroom and studio visits who was going to make it and who wasn't, and I have been almost entirely right. The ones who make it are the ones who understand it's going to be a grind. They're the ones who have the most trials and failures and experiments lying around their studios.

Most of the students bought what I was selling, but some didn't.

One asked, "How much money do you make?"

I told her, "A lot. Probably more than you can imagine."

She replied, "It seems easy."

That caught me off guard, so I asked, "What seems easy?"

"What you do. You seem so relaxed. I want to skip the early part and just start showing and selling. Can you introduce me to a gallery?"

I thought about it and told her, "It might not seem like it, but the struggle is the best part. If you skip the struggle, you won't make it. The struggle is the whole point."

Art school isn't a golden ticket, but it gives you the tools to succeed. If you get in, you haven't "made it"—you've just earned the chance to put in the work. The creative life is difficult. The stress, the pressure, the self-doubt—it isn't for everyone. But for those who commit, art school can be the foundation of something incredible. It was for me.

CHAPTER XIII

INSPIRATION: THEN AND NOW

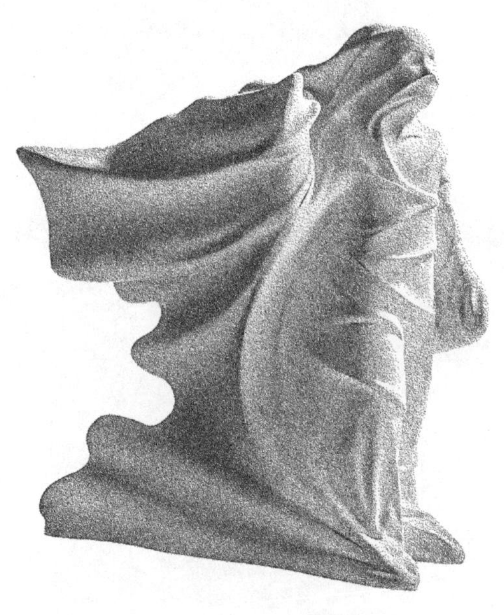

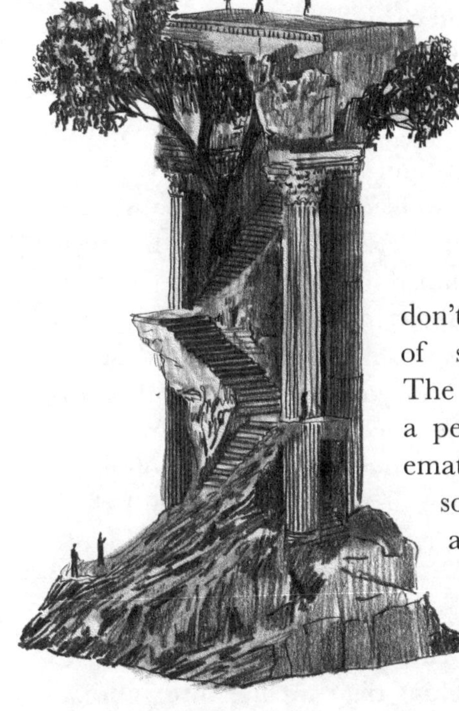

don't believe in the myth of sudden inspiration. The lightning strike of a perfect idea, the cinematic moment where something just clicks and an artist is forever changed. That's not how it works. At least that's not how it worked for me, and it's not how it works for any of the artists I know, whatever their medium. Inspiration isn't magic. It's discipline. It's repetition. It's paying attention to the things that most people don't see. It's spending thousands of hours working and thinking and dreaming. As I once heard another artist say, "Inspiration is for amateurs. I'm a professional artist. I wake up every day and I go to work."

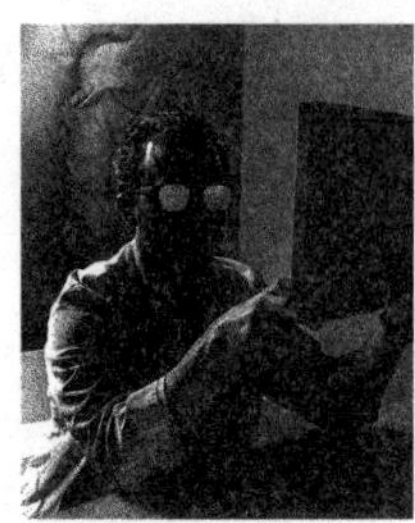

Self-portrait in the studio.

People love the mythology of the genius artist. The tortured soul channeling some divine brilliance, creating masterpieces from thin air. It's a great story, but it's bullshit. Real creativity isn't a gift handed to a lucky few. It's a practice. A daily practice. And every day for an artist is similar to what it is for an athlete or a musician: You work on your craft every day, you make progress, you put in the hours. And the more you work and develop ideas and create and put in thought and practice, the more inspiration you'll have. The ability to see something new in the world is trained, refined, and earned. You have to cultivate it like a craft. If you want inspiration, you have to go looking for it. You have to teach yourself how to see.

When I was younger, inspiration was proximity. It was about what was right in front of me: my neighborhood, the streets I walked, the sneakers I obsessed over, the BMX bikes my friends and I rode, the movies and music that shaped my world. When you're a young artist, your subject matter is inherently limited, because your experience is limited. And that's okay. But I think a lot of young artists struggle with that. They feel like their work has to be big from the start, that it has to be about something profound, something greater than themselves. They think that if their work doesn't carry an immediate sense of importance, it doesn't matter. That's a trap.

I fell into that trap for a while too. There was a moment early on when I felt pressure to make work that was about something big—architecture, history, time, decay, all the grand themes. But that wasn't where my inspiration was coming from. My inspiration was coming from the everyday. The doors photo series I made when I was a kid with my first camera wasn't *about* the doors. It was about pattern and repetition and uniqueness within something that felt homogenous. It was about making art from what I saw every day. It was about taking something mundane and elevating it, turning it into art. At the time, I wasn't thinking about any of that in an intellectual way. I was just drawn to something I saw every day.

In hindsight, that work was foundational. The way I saw form, structure, and hidden meaning in everyday objects started there. I wasn't trying to make a statement; I was just making something I liked. If you keep doing that, over time the meaning will emerge. And that is ultimately what I have done for my entire life and career as an artist. I make art with cars because I love cars. I make art with symbols and icons of popular culture because they are things I love. I make the uniforms for the Cavs because I'm from Cleveland, I love basketball, and they're my favorite team.

And that's the real trick, the real secret, the real practice. That's real inspiration: making art out of what fascinates you, even if you don't know why. If you keep doing that, over time the meaning will emerge. For me, twenty-five years into my career, inspiration is wider, deeper, and more layered. What started with simple explorations of form and decay has evolved into major sculptural investigations of time, material, and historical memory. My work has changed, but the process of finding inspiration hasn't. I still look for the unnoticed details, the hidden patterns, the beauty in imperfection.

"DON'T TRY TO MAKE SOMETHING INCREDIBLE OR POWERFUL. JUST MAKE. TO CREATE SOMETHING TIMELESS AND ALLURING COMES MOST OFTEN THROUGH ACCIDENT AND PRACTICE."

MENTOR NOTE

My Fictional Archaeology series, for example, started as a simple idea: What if contemporary objects eroded like ancient artifacts? That seed of an idea has now developed into an entire universe of work. Similarly, my Architectural Anomalies series began with simple disruptions—breaking the clean lines of architecture by inserting seemingly organic forms into them. But now that idea has expanded into a broader investigation of how space and structure define human experience. And then there are the

Bonsai Speakers and Ancient Speaker sculptures—recent explorations in my work that tie into themes of imperfection and natural decay, combined with hi-fi audio equipment. The outcome is a combination of past and present but not like anything I've ever made before.

"THE QUICKEST WAY TO BECOME DISILLUSIONED WITH YOUR WORK IS TO COMPARE IT TO SOMETHING ELSE. DON'T."

MENTOR NOTE

There's a phenomenon I've come to believe in, something I've experienced firsthand, something any artist can experience with enough persistence, which is that the production of work creates its own gravity. At first, when you're just starting, making work feels like pushing a boulder uphill. Every idea, every piece, every attempt requires huge effort, huge internal force; each piece of work you make leaves you exhausted. You struggle to get noticed, to gain momentum. You fight self-doubt. You question whether your work is good enough, whether anyone will care. The resistance is immense, and you have to push through it every day. But as you keep at it, as you keep producing, keep showing up, something shifts. The weight that was in front of you, that took such an immense effort to keep pushing up that hill, starts to be behind you. You don't need to push the work anymore. It builds and cascades around you. It starts to become easier and faster. And most importantly, it always becomes better. You will have a multitude of opportunities, and your ideas will begin to outpace the number of days available to make them all.

This is why volume matters. This is why persistence matters. The more you create, the harder it will be to ignore you. The work starts pulling people in, attracting attention not because of a single great piece but because of the undeniable presence of accumulated effort.

This isn't just true for artists. It's true for anyone trying to build something: writers, musicians, filmmakers, designers, and entrepreneurs. The people who succeed aren't necessarily the ones with the best ideas. They're the ones who keep going long enough for their work to take on a life of its own.

Resistance is always present in the creative process. That's actually where the idea usually lies. Behind a wall of time. The difference between professionals and amateurs is that professionals show up regardless. They work through the doubt, through the lack of motivation, through the failures. And that consistency, that discipline, creates a momentum on its own.

The work begins to take on a presence of its own. It builds like a snowball rolling downhill in one of those old cartoons, gathering mass and momentum. The sheer weight of what you've created starts to exert a force in the world. And at a certain point, whether the world likes it or not, it's there. It exists. It can't be ignored.

This is what I wish young artists understood: You don't need a perfect idea to start. You don't need a grand vision. You just need to make something. And then make something else. And keep going. Every successful artist, every successful creative, has at some point realized that the work itself is what creates inspiration, not the other way around. You don't wait for ideas. You work and the ideas come.

I still live by this principle. Even now, with years of experience behind me, I don't sit around waiting for inspiration. I show up in the studio. I pick up materials. I start working. And as I do, something always reveals itself. The work leads me forward. Inspiration is a discipline. It's a practice. If you commit to it, it will show up for you. And eventually, if you work long enough, hard enough, with enough conviction, the gravity of your work will pull the world toward you. Art careers aren't built on single moments. They're built on consistent, obsessive creation. The only way to become an artist is to make art—over and over, until the value of the work itself becomes undeniable.

CHAPTER XIV

WHY MY FIRST SHOW COST $1,000 AND NOW THEY COST $1,000,000

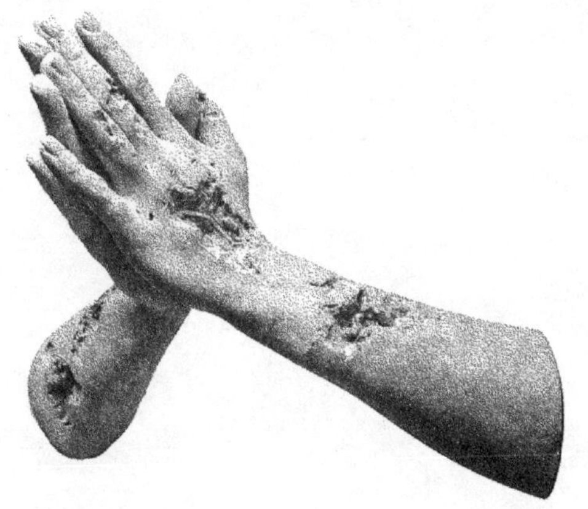

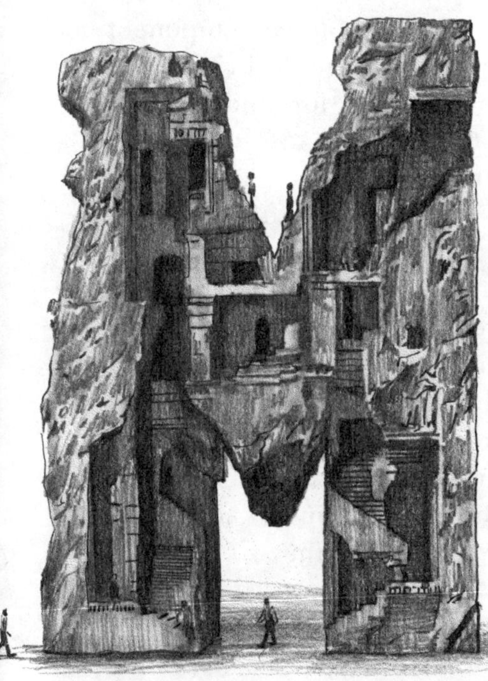

y first exhibition cost me less than $1,000 to create. My most recent exhibition cost more than a million. This journey reflects not only the evolution of my creative process but also the expansion of the scale and ambition of my work.

Back at Cooper, whenever I complained about the cost of materials, my professor Doug Ashford would laugh at me and respond to my concerns with a simple statement: "Eat more ramen." He was unwavering in his belief that an artist's money, above all else, should be invested in their work. Art, after all, can be made from anything. A five-cent pencil and a sheet of paper are enough to create an idea or create a valuable and sellable piece of art. But as your work develops, you realize that materials carry meaning, and the material itself often becomes part of the magic of art. Those materials can be expensive.

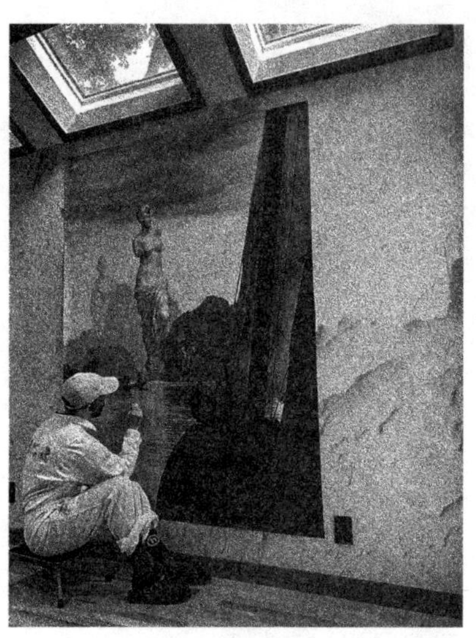

Back to working in two dimensions during the pandemic.

When I was younger, I worked primarily with inexpensive materials: pencil, paper, and cardboard. My paintings were done in acrylic, where the most expensive component was the paint itself. I could create anything for under $100. But when I got to Cooper, that started to change.

Since the pandemic, I've gotten back to the roots of my art making: painting. I used to stretch the canvas first and then paint on it. Now I prefer painting flat against a hard wall. I staple the canvas directly to the surface, paint to the very edge, and then stretch it, wrapping the canvas around the stretcher bar to create an infinity edge. This process removes about four inches from each edge of the painting, so I have to be mindful of where I place important elements. But I love how it makes the painting feel like it extends beyond the confines of the frame—it conveys the idea of endlessness, which resonates deeply with me.

Doug was always pushing me to invest in my ideas, challenging me, asking questions like "Do you want me to call your parents and ask them for money so you can make this the way it needs to be made?" I remember one project in school where I used a hundred sheets of plexiglass, each with a two-dimensional line drawn on it representing my movements throughout the city that day. As the sheets stacked up, they formed a layered, three-dimensional map of my experiences. But plexiglass was expensive. The stack alone cost me around $500—a fortune to me at the time. I had to create prototypes on a smaller scale and sacrifice daily expenses just to afford the materials. More ramen, more plexiglass.

An artist can create with anything, but understanding the significance of materials is a major milestone in an artistic career. The choice to use crystal, marble, or patinated bronze isn't just about aesthetics—it carries historical, cultural, and emotional weight. I once saw an exhibition by an artist who made sculptures from crushed bones, embedding teeth into the pieces. The visceral reactions of discomfort and repulsion became an integral part of the work. Similarly, Paul Thek, an artist from the Warhol era, created pieces that encased rotting meat in resin, introducing decay and time as active elements in his sculptures. Damien Hirst undoubtedly drew inspiration from Thek's approach in his works that use flies or cut-up animals. Every artist looks to the past, learning from what has been done and pushing it further. This extends to materials as well. The first artist to work in bronze must have been astonished by its transformative properties—its permanence, its malleability, its ability to take on different patinas. The medium itself carries meaning.

My first major exhibition in Paris consisted mainly of paintings on Mylar, using gouache—an incredibly inexpensive material. Each piece probably cost me around $80 in total. The sculptures in that show were made from plaster and drywall compound, a material I've used extensively that's found in virtually every building in America. That ubiquity gives it meaning. At the time, I created sculptures of columns that extended from the ceiling and the

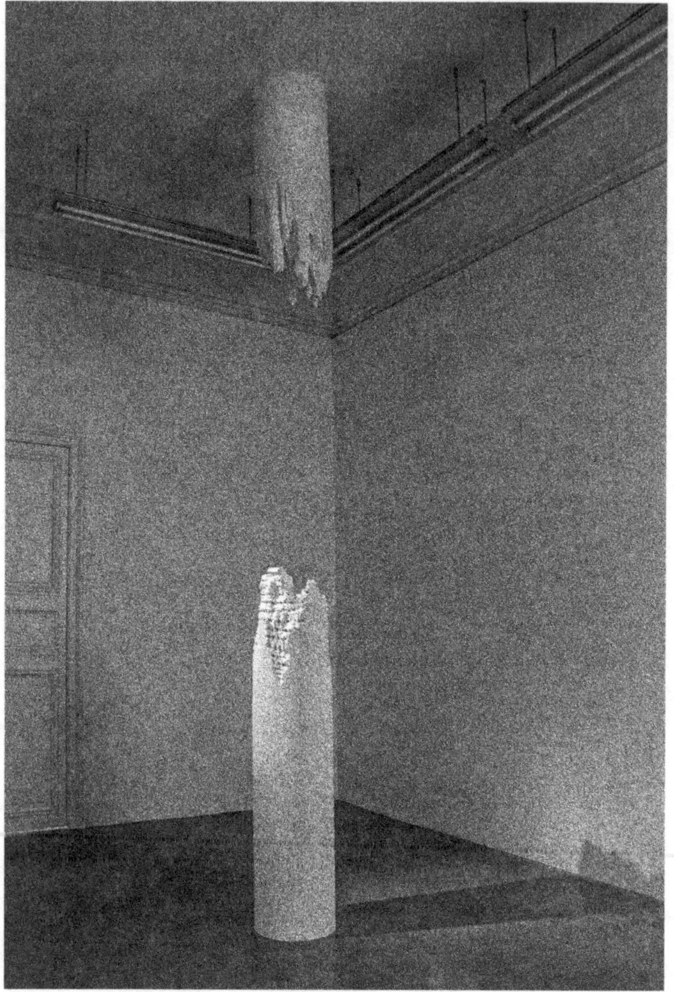

First show, in Paris.

floor but never connected in the middle, creating a visual tension—an architectural impossibility that suggested imminent collapse. The material choice reinforced that message.

These days my materials are instantly recognizable. A viewer doesn't need a label to understand the significance of bronze or crystal. When I create a sculpture from shattered glass, its connotations of fragility, violence, and transformation are immediately evident. My recent exhibitions have reached a scale where production costs can be staggering. For instance, casting all the pieces for the Yorkshire Sculpture Park exhibition cost around $900,000, factoring in fabrication, transportation, and logistical support. At this scale, I rely on teams—engineers, master mold makers, bronze casters. When the molten bronze is poured, I'm observing from a safe distance while professionals in flame-retardant suits handle the process.

Many artists remain consistent in their materials, especially painters. John Currin has been using the same paints and canvases since the mid-nineties. When I was in school, the prevailing belief was that mastering a single medium was crucial to success. Artists defined themselves by their materials—Warhol with screen printing, Basquiat with his expressive, sculptural canvases. But over the past twenty years, that has shifted. Artists today work across multiple media—Koons, Hirst, Murakami. The medium is no longer the defining element; it's simply a vehicle for the idea.

Working at a larger scale, I increasingly find myself drawn to bronze. It's the most expensive material I use, and its production involves a complex network of artisans. Other works, like some of my car sculptures, incorporate expert mechanics, car painters, and German leather specialists. These are functional vehicles, requiring specialized craftsmanship.

From a business standpoint, I've always maintained a rule: If fabrication costs exceed 15 percent of a work's total value, the financial viability becomes complicated—especially when galleries take a 50 percent commission and collectors expect discounts. If production costs consume too much of the budget, there's little left for the artist. Some argue that cost should never dictate creative decisions, but if you want longevity in your career, economic considerations are inevitable. A gallery won't invest in selling a piece with razor-thin margins.

I'm currently working on Speaker Sculptures—classical sculptures of figures who look straight out of ancient Rome, combined with a hi-fi audio system, as if two thousand years had been collapsed—and I'm experimenting with high-resolution 3D printing to create my molds. Previously, I would have sculpted by hand, made molds, and cast in a final material. Now the technology allows for direct fabrication of the molds, streamlining the process and reducing costs. I used to create massive silicone box molds, wasting expensive material. Then I transitioned to paint on silicone and mother molds—a lightweight epoxy shell that minimizes silicone use. These innovations matter; they enable more ambitious projects without unnecessary waste.

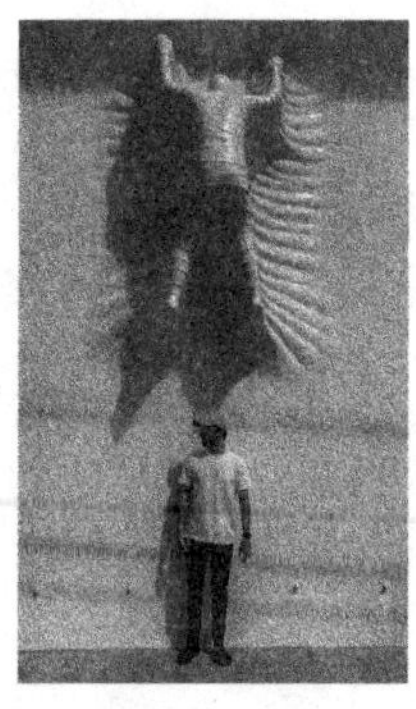

An installation in Dallas.

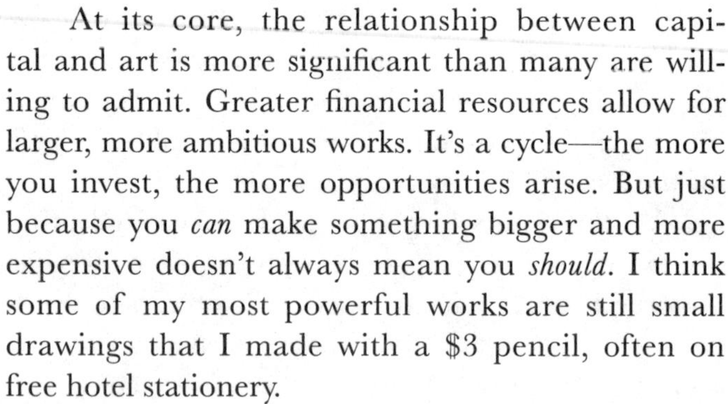

At its core, the relationship between capital and art is more significant than many are willing to admit. Greater financial resources allow for larger, more ambitious works. It's a cycle—the more you invest, the more opportunities arise. But just because you *can* make something bigger and more expensive doesn't always mean you *should*. I think some of my most powerful works are still small drawings that I made with a $3 pencil, often on free hotel stationery.

I often think about my materials in the context of art history—bronze and marble have been used for thousands of years. Some contemporary artists avoid these materials, to distance themselves from tradition. My approach is the opposite. I embrace that lineage. Jeff Koons, for example, largely uses industrial materials, mirroring modern manufacturing processes. My work, while contemporary, draws from the past.

Collaborating with Tiffany & Co. introduced me to new materials and techniques. It was the first time I had worked in jewelry. I made a series of bracelets and necklaces with Tiffany. I produced the cases from bronze with a patina in the famous Tiffany Blue color. It was incredible to work with such a historical American company. After that experience, I designed some of my own jewelry featuring microscopic drawings—an idea sparked by childhood memories of trying to write my name as small as possible. These drawings became pendants, suspended inside of glass casings, almost like wearable paintings. I am now working with some of the best jewelry craftsmen in the world. The techniques involved are remarkable, blending fine art with high-end jewelry design.

Ultimately, size, scale, and materials matter. The ability to command higher prices for artwork grants the freedom to explore new creative territories. Prioritize making the best work possible, but never ignore the economics. You're trying to make a living. Sometimes that means eating ramen, sometimes it means celebrating when you can afford more.

CHAPTER XV

WHY I WAITED UNTIL THIRTY-FIVE TO HAVE

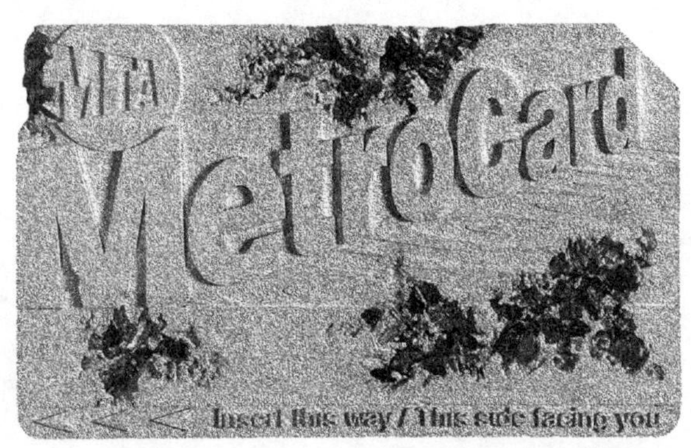

MY FIRST SOLO SHOW IN NEW YORK

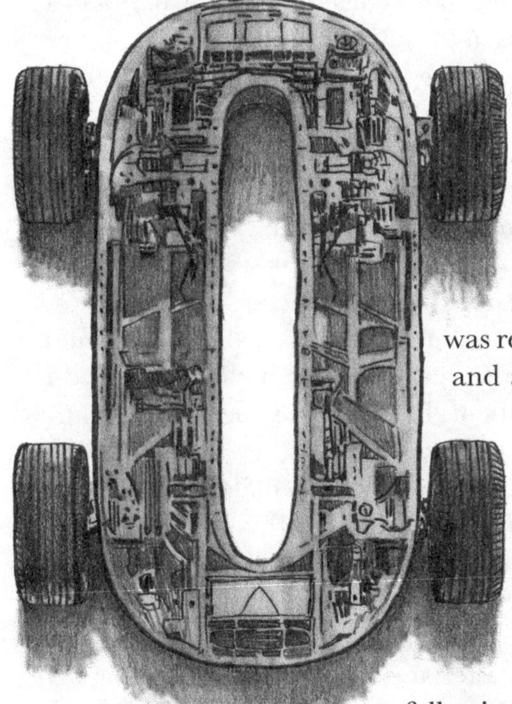

nce Emmanuel was representing me, and after I'd shown in Paris, in Miami, and in a group show at MoMA PS1 in New York, I was starting to attract a following in the art world. But my biggest goal was a solo show in New York. One day, Emmanuel sat me down with news. There was a famous art dealer based in New York who'd bought one of my works a few years earlier, and now that dealer's gallery was offering me a solo exhibition in New York City. I was floored. Somehow it felt kind of like when I was seventeen and Richard called to tell me that I'd been admitted to Cooper Union. All of that emotion rushed back. I couldn't believe it. I was only twenty-six, and I had been invited to show in one of the biggest art galleries in the world, in the capital of art. New York fucking City. It was finally happening.

As soon as I got back to my studio, I started planning the exhibition. Following the approach I'd used when building out a model of Emmanuel's gallery space in Paris, I made a small-scale model of the gallery and began to imagine what kinds of works would be in it. My work had evolved over that period—I was now making a lot of sculptural work in plaster and foam and working with architectural forms that blended natural erosion and structural forms. For the piece I had shown at MoMA PS1, I'd made it look as though a corner of the gallery had been eroded by water. It was similar in shape to an iceberg or a piece of eroded rock. I started to think about the grand gestures I could make in that gallery.

I asked Emmanuel when the exhibition would be, and he told me that they were in discussion and I needed to be patient. I spoke to my mentor a lot during this period. I could see him there in my studio, smoking cigarettes and drinking coffee, leaning back in a chair, talking about my work and helping me think through the process. He always wore monotone clothing during that time. I remember he'd be in this all-white outfit with white slippers, and he'd almost blend into the plaster and foam that was covering my entire studio. I think he was going through a difficult time himself, and he'd often send me texts that were inspirational. It felt like he was talking to himself and trying to encourage himself along the way. He was an artist too, and as with every artist, there are changes in your work and doubts and impostor syndrome and

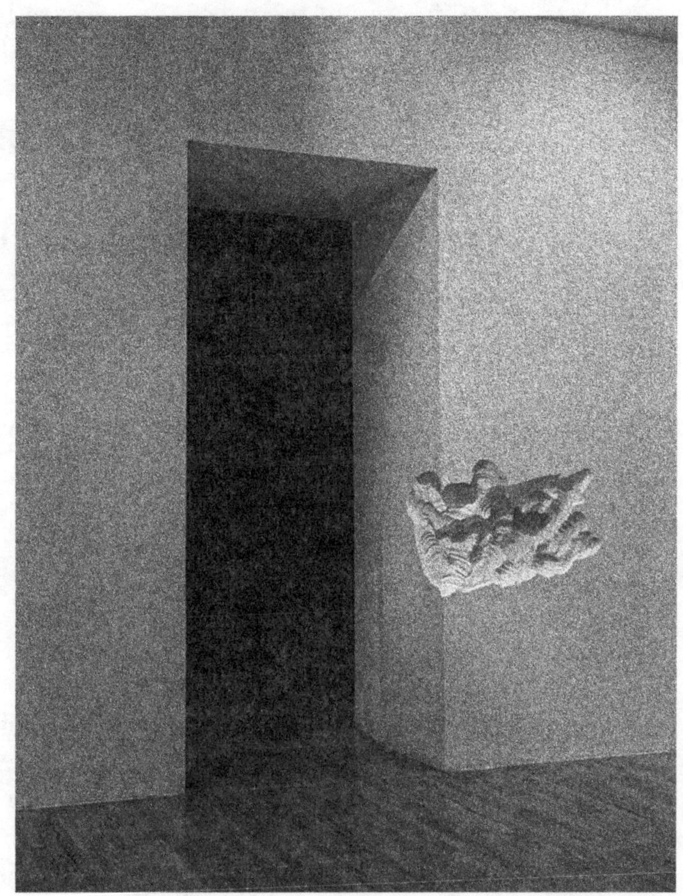

The architectural erosion I installed at MoMA PS1.

all of those creeping anxieties that blend into our world as creators. We talked a lot, but it was those texts I got from him that were so important to me at that moment. As much as I projected confidence outwardly, I still felt like that shy, introverted kid trying to figure out the world. As I stressed out, my mentor sent this:

"DO NOT TRY TO MAKE SOMETHING INCREDIBLE, INSPIRING, OR BEAUTIFUL. JUST MAKE. CREATING AND CRITIQUING ARE DIFFERENT ACTIONS THAT MUST BE DONE SEPARATELY."

The model was built, and most of the show was mapped out. I felt ready.

Then I got a call from Emmanuel: The negotiation had not gone well, and the show was not going to happen. I was crestfallen. *What happened?*

Galleries are in the business of making money. As much as they might genuinely love art and working with artists, ultimately, as in every business, it's about the bottom line. One of the most efficient and common ways to make money is with a quick-strike strategy: Find a hot young artist with a good story, hype the shit out of them, and sell as much of their work as possible as quickly as possible at the highest prices possible. While this often works out for the gallery, it doesn't usually work out for the artist. After the high of the opening and the sales, the market is flooded, and the prices are too high. It becomes difficult to keep selling, and if the artist loses any steam, which all artists do at certain points, the collectors sell, the prices fall, and what was a high becomes a very deep hole. Emmanuel believed that was going to happen with me and this gallery, and he was adamant that not doing the show was the right thing for me.

Emmanuel told me I had two options. One was to go against his advice and do it anyway. He would not stop me, but it could jeopardize our future plans. The other was to trust him and trust that he knew what was best for me. It hurt, and I wanted to do the show, but he had never steered me wrong, so I trusted him. We agreed on his strategy, the opposite of the quick strike. I would keep making as much great work as I could, keep showing it (just not in New York), and keep selling it. We would continue to expand my reputation, both in the US and abroad, and when we reached a point where I had regular and reliable collectors and my work could command a stable price, we would do a show in New York.

It was a slow build. From 2005 until 2015, I was doing two exhibitions a year—in Los Angeles, Amsterdam, Miami, and a bunch of other cities—and showing in art fairs and group shows. It was all simmering and bubbling in the background—no huge crescendo moment. We'd revisit the New York topic regularly, and Emmanuel would say, "Not the right gallery. Not the right timing."

While I trusted him, I didn't fucking like it. It was frustrating. It sometimes kept me up at night. I had friends from school who'd had their first solos in New York and were lighting up the art world. I was happy for them, but I was ready for my turn. I was toiling away in my studio, living in a space with no shower and barely any heat, and I wanted to break out. That was Emmanuel's whole thing. *Be in the studio. Make work. You don't need to worry about anything else.* I wasn't starving, but I was tired as shit of eating ramen. I had just enough to scrape by and make rent. I had enough to get the materials I needed, and

I put everything else back into the studio. By 2013 I had been working as an artist in New York for eight years. Although I had been patient, I *needed* to show in New York at some point.

Emmanuel and I are pretty close. He's a dozen years older than me, but he understands my generation, and we're friends outside of our working relationship. While I waited for my show, his galleries dramatically expanded, and I exhibited in his spaces in Paris, Hong Kong, and Miami. My affiliation with him was allowing me to develop a strong foundation for my profile beyond New York and the US. And the rise of social media and particularly Instagram for art helped create awareness everywhere. There was an "I've seen his work but never in person" buzz and mystery about me. But New York still felt like the pinnacle. I would often walk around the big New York City galleries—Gagosian, Hauser & Wirth, Zwirner—and imagine showing there. The dream never went away.

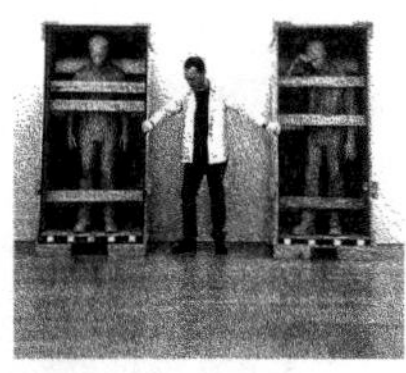

Installing my first show in Hong Kong.

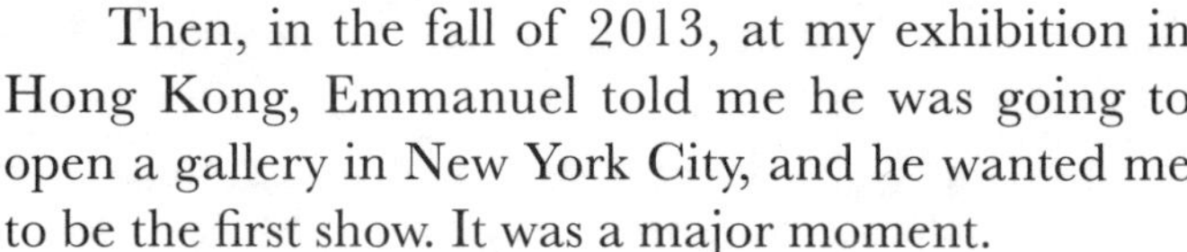

Then, in the fall of 2013, at my exhibition in Hong Kong, Emmanuel told me he was going to open a gallery in New York City, and he wanted me to be the first show. It was a major moment.

I had two years to put it together. Every solo exhibition feels like the biggest, most important show of my life. Deciding what's in it is a way to encapsulate that moment in time. I'm always working in the studio, but when I'm preparing for a show, I'm much more structured. I plan out all the paintings. I plan out all the sculptures. I have drawings or renderings of every single thing that's going to be made. I'm creating with a clear plan of action. I show Emmanuel everything ahead of time, and he might weigh in on which works to include. Most artists don't work this way, but a year and a half before the exhibition, I know every single thing that's going to be in it. For my solo debut in New York, I had a plan on lockdown. I wasn't messing around. I wanted to absolutely crush it.

Emmanuel and I both knew what comes with a show in New York. Your work is going to be looked at and scrutinized and critiqued in a way it hasn't been. Are you ready for that? Are you ready for the interviews? Are you ready for the pressure? I actually didn't know. I didn't know if I was ready for it.

Back when I was offered that first New York solo, I was twenty-six. Even though I'd desperately wanted it, I don't know if my work was mature enough then to carry a space like that, nor was I confident enough in the way that I presented the work—you need a type of energy in talking about your work and a comfort level in having your work talked about. But by thirty-five, when my first solo exhibition actually happened, I had another decade of experience. By 2015 I had matured, my work had weight, and I carried myself in a different way. I was ready. By 2015 I was definitely fucking ready. I had a level of confidence in the work, and in myself, that was completely different.

I decided to go all in with sculptures from my Fictional Archaeology series. The pieces were cast from contemporary objects and re-formed in geological materials, as if they'd been discovered on some future archaeological site or in a future museum. I had first used that method a few years before, when Louis Vuitton invited me to create a book of drawings or paintings describing a place, part of their series of travel books. They told me I could pick any place in the world and they would send me there. Literally anywhere. How fucking cool is that? Around this time, I was walking down Manhattan Avenue in Greenpoint and saw a globe outside a thrift shop. I bought it for $10 and took it back to the studio. Spinning it around, I found this tiny little island in the middle of the Pacific Ocean

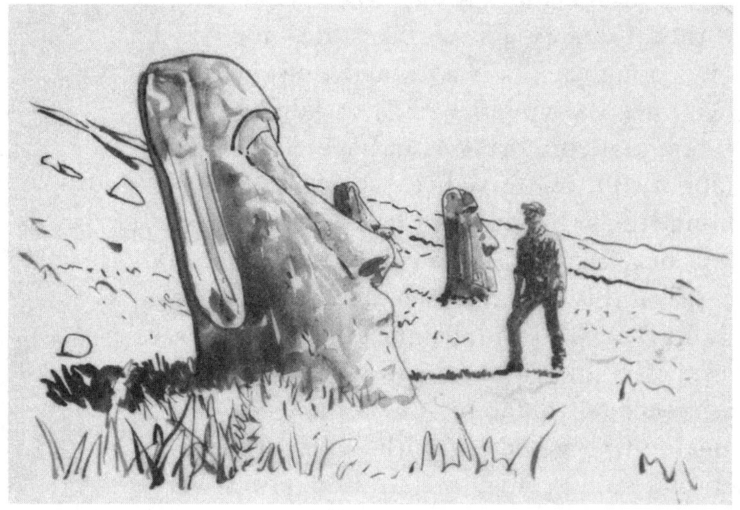

Easter Island.

that might be one of the most isolated places on earth. I looked it up online and then remembered it being famous for these huge statues emerging from the ground.

Easter Island. Most people only go for two or three days, because it's really small. It's super isolated, and there's nothing on it besides one small village and the hundreds of moai statues. I stayed for two months. It's a weird place to be for that long—the type of place that makes you believe in aliens, because it feels supernatural. It's this tiny rock but has an airport big enough to land a 747. The runway stretches from one coast to another. NASA extended the runway in the 1980s as an emergency landing site for the space shuttle because it lies along the launch path for any shuttles that would take off from the West Coast of the United States.

I spent a lot of time going around the island on a quad with a guide and then sometimes by myself. One day I stumbled on this weird NASA installation with a broken-down fence and an old NASA logo. It was abandoned; there were multiple huge satellite dishes and large metal tubes coming out of the ground. If it weren't so remote, it'd be the perfect location for a spooky science fiction film.

When Europeans arrived on the island in the eighteenth century, the Indigenous Rapa Nui people were emaciated, near starving, and there were no trees. No one knows for sure, but one theory is that the trees were cut down to make the statues. Removing the trees radically altered the ecosystem, because the trees created fog and density and held water. They had destroyed the ecosystem. And with no trees, they couldn't make boats to escape the island.

Today, very few boats come and go from the island. Everything that's brought in, from cars and computers to food and TVs, eventually winds up in a landfill on the island. I went to the landfill while I was there, and they were burning trash. There was a pile of old Macintosh computers and a 1990 Honda Civic. Seeing that trash and the other flotsam around the island really got my mind turning. I started to think about the passage of time and how certain eras of the past and present are closer than we're accustomed to thinking. A thousand years from now, when someone goes to Easter Island, those computers will be there alongside the statues. And that's what first gave me the idea for this reverse archaeology exhibition.

When I got back to New York I started thinking about how I could take contemporary objects like computers and cameras and make them into archaeological objects. How could I reverse engineer the idea of archaeology? The idea of materiality in an artwork has always been important to me. We think about traditional art and the traditional materials that are used to create it—paint, marble, metal. Those materials have a history and weight to them. When you make something in marble or bronze, it's impossible to escape the connotations that those materials have in relation to art history. The materials become part of the meaning of the work itself.

But I wanted to ask a new question and push the boundaries with materials, so I asked myself, What if I used other weird stuff that isn't associated with art? Bones or crystals or shredded plastic would have a totally different meaning. My concept was to make objects from contemporary life like computers and cameras but to make them out of materials like volcanic ash and crystal, things that we associate with a geological time frame. In that way the material itself tells the story. It's part of the meaning of the artwork. What I use in each piece is going to tell you something about it that the visual quality doesn't do by itself. I wasn't interested in taking a camera and painting it to look old. I wanted it to have a truth quality to it where you could look at it and actually believe that it might be from a different era. I achieved that through the use of unique materials, specifically geological materials.

When I got back from Easter Island, I started making tests in the studio. Could I cast volcanic ash? Could I cast crystal? What would work and what wouldn't? This was one of the more frustrating times I've had in the studio. I had learned about casting plaster and resin and other materials at Cooper. I actually loved the idea of mold making, how you would break up an object into parts and create a replica of it in another material. Any artist who's worked with mold making knows that it's a magical but highly frustrating experience.

"CREATE TIME AND SPACE IN YOUR WORK FOR FAILURE AND DISAPPOINTMENT. A FAILURE TEACHES MORE ANYWAY."

MENTOR NOTE

The first piece I decided to make was a cast of that original Pentax K1000 camera that my grandfather had given me. I didn't want to ruin the original camera, so I bought a nonfunctioning one on eBay. I first created a silicone mold by slowly painting the silicone onto half of the camera, while the other half was buried in clay. I added layers and layers of plaster gauze to create the mother mold and then flipped it over to the other side to repeat the process. I pulled the plaster apart and took the camera out, and I was left with a highly detailed negative mold. I also found volcanic ash on eBay. I crushed it up further to make an even finer powder and mixed that with a small amount of plaster of paris. I poured the mixture into the bottom of the mold and sealed up the sides with wax so it wouldn't leak out. I could already see this concept fully formed in my mind. I could see the camera made of this textured and flaky volcanic ash. I could see that it looked like a relic. I could see the whole idea in the object. The idea worked.

I left the mold overnight to dry and opened it up when I came back in the morning. As I pulled half of the mold apart, I could see all of the incredible detail, down to the texture in the lens and even the engraved numbers on the shutter speed dial. As I went to pull the second half of the mold, I could feel that the surface was quite soft. I slowly began to peel the silicone off the second half, but that side wasn't as simple. It started to pull parts of the camera with it, and the entire thing crumbled in my hands. One moment of tremendous triumph, and a second later it all literally fell apart. Those are the heartbreaking failures you face when creating art.

I was still working on other types of painting and sculpture during this exploratory period, so it took me almost a full year to figure out how to cast volcanic ash. I experimented with many different casting techniques and materials to bind the ash. Most of the attempts would just crumble in my hands, until one particular cast I made peeled out of the mold perfectly. I was skeptical after so much failure, but this one felt solid. And it was. I had found the right formula. It was proof that the grind had been worth it, that my belief in putting in the effort was going to pay off. Now I could move on to all kinds of other objects: computers, sneakers, basketballs, pay phones. There was such a large variety of things that mark our current era that it became a selection challenge. I wanted the works to look eroded and in a state of decay, but obviously I didn't want them to actually continue to fall apart. It took about two years from the time I had the initial idea to when I had produced a small group of works based on that idea that held together.

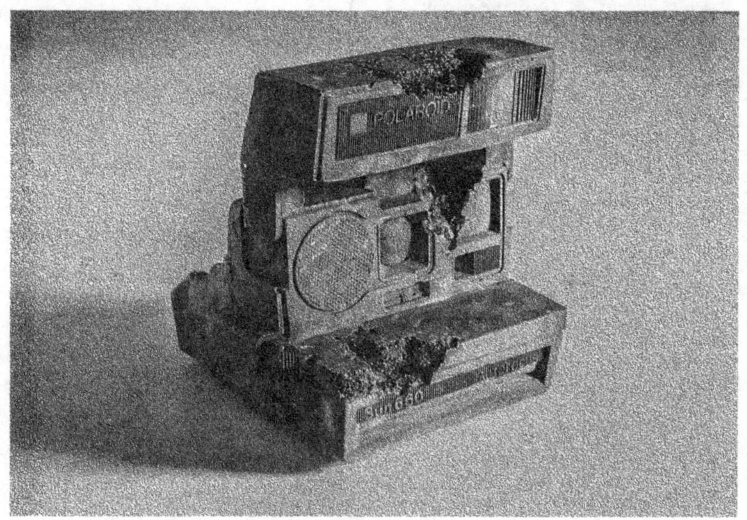

First successful cast in ash.

It's a great example of the volume of work that's invisible to people outside of the process. I spent two years just figuring out the materials. If I hadn't figured that part out, my exhibition would have been dead before it got off the ground. Being an artist or any type of creator really requires unbridled faith. You must constantly keep trying and pushing and failing and trying again and failing again. In reality, the failures never stop. As I sit and write this, I'm still failing and getting projects rejected all the time and trying out new work that doesn't come out the way I intended. Like my mentor says, that is my superpower. Maybe it's stubbornness, but I just don't fucking give up.

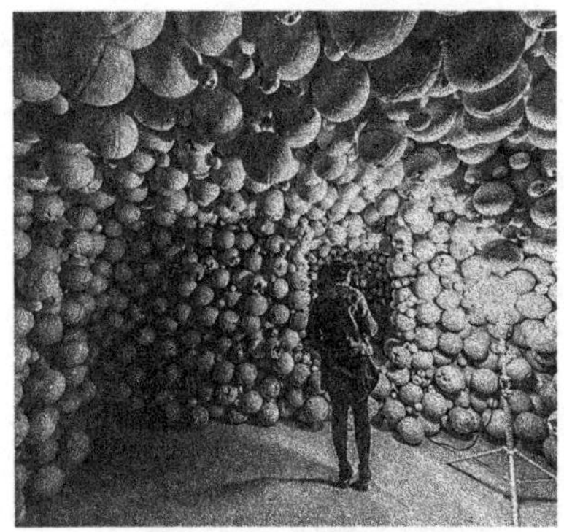

In the cavern built for my first show in New York.

I came to realize later, by accident, that as much as the works look like they're falling apart, they are also coming together, a kind of reverse entropy. I began to use natural crystals in addition to the volcanic ash, and that added a whole other layer of material and meaning. We associate crystals with growth. They form over time—thousands or millions of years—and there's this kind of potential in the works where they're either falling apart or actually growing together.

When the time came to plan the show, I had been working on the Fictional Archaeology pieces for a year or two, and I decided I wanted the show to be about them. I created a focused exhibition that revolved around contemporary sports iconography and objects. There were cast basketballs, cast footballs, a pyramid of cast baseballs, a sculpture of a boxer that was just the shoes and the gloves and the shorts but with no figure inside, though it appeared like one was standing there. All of the objects were cast in geological materials like volcanic ash and crystal.

The exhibition was on two levels, and on the lower level I decided to create an experiential installation, which was a cavern made out of thousands of cast sports balls in amethyst crystal. They had this really intense, deep purple color that came from the amethyst. I always loved the idea of caverns. It goes all the way back to Plato, the idea that the cave is the origin of storytelling. And the cave paintings of Lascaux—people painting pictures on the walls or creating imprints of their hands. There's something magical and historical about it. It was also like going into Superman's crystal Fortress of Solitude. Purple amethyst geode basketballs and baseballs and soccer balls. In the back of my mind, sometimes I try to imagine what scenario would create these works, and this felt like a warehouse of sports balls that had somehow been buried in the ground for thousands of years and had crystallized. To make the balls, I would crush up the crystal and mix it with resin. It was almost like synthetic marble. The casts were 95 percent crystal. The resin is just the binder that holds all those particles together. I experimented with how much I could crush the material into a fine powder to capture the detail and texture of the balls better than a coarser one would. On the basketballs you could read all of the pebbled texture of the leather and even the NBA logo and the Spalding graphic formed in this crystal dust.

I perfected this technique as I was developing the exhibition, and I came to realize that I could actually shape those erosions and have crystals sticking out of them like the inside of a geode. The work felt real. And when I say *real*, I mean it looked like it had been formed over thousands of years, not created in the very recent past. That accident had allowed me to develop this entirely new technique. I'd been able to fully realize the idea I had on Easter Island. *Fictional Archaeology.* The door was opened and a whole universe was inside it.

By the time the show arrived, I had the confidence and experience to execute at the level I wanted. Typically, I'll start installation for a show a week before, with my team. After the previous show gets taken down, the gallery paints the walls white, and all the works get shipped in. One of my favorite times is when the pieces are in the exhibition space but still crated. The crates are open on one side, and you have this moment when you can start to see the potential. It's often the first time that I'm seeing a work in a clean environment. My studio isn't filthy like some studios, but it's definitely dirty. I'm not whitewashing the walls every week and broom-cleaning the floor every day. There's shit everywhere: completed works, half-finished works, work tools, all kinds of stuff. Seeing the art unwrapped and together in that clean environment, even before it's hung or installed, is one of my favorite moments.

It takes about a week to put everything together. And it's an absolute grind getting all set up in the gallery for what amounts to a huge party. When the setup is all done, there's relief, along with some anxiety, because now everything is out of your hands. How the art is received is out of your control. Pulling up to the show, it helped to have a decade of work and critical reviews under my belt. I'd taken in the hate and the critics who blasted my work. I was established in my belief that there will be people who like my work, and if people don't, it's just not made for them. The criticism I frequently get is about my work with brands, and it always hits the same notes: "His work is too commercial" or "He's not an artist; he's more of a designer." At one point this might

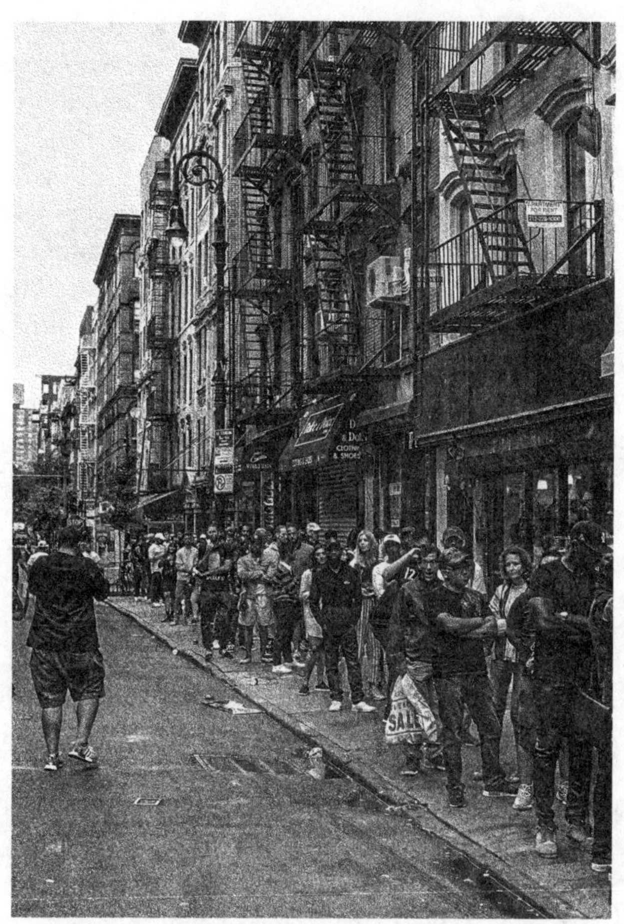

Line to enter my New York solo show.

have really bothered me, but I've trained myself to not give a shit. If you critique how I run my life and my business, you're not saying anything about the content of my work. So it boils down to *Fuck off*. That was the attitude I carried into that solo debut. I knew that the people I cared about would love what I created. That the people who mattered to me would embrace my vision. The rest, I didn't even give them the time.

By this time I had a large following on social media, and the international reach from my past shows also helped turn this into a big show. Massive. The art world, the fashion world, the music people—they all turned out. I showed up to the opening about thirty minutes early, and there were more than a thousand people there. They had formed a line that went south on Madison from Seventy-Third Street down to Seventy-Second, across to Park Avenue, and then turned the corner and snaked back up to Seventy-Third. The police were outside trying to control things. It was awesome. And even better, it was all my type of people. Not the traditional art crowd. This was everyone. What a rush. The feeling of that moment—I can still go back to that night in my mind and get emotional. Emmanuel had never had a crowd that large come to an opening. He smiled and said, "What the actual fuck is happening?" I smiled and said, "You were right. Your plan worked. This is the result of it."

"HERE IS A SECRET. THEY WILL NOT REMEMBER YOUR FAILURES. TAKE THIS AS A LESSON. THIS CAN BE YOUR SUPERPOWER. BE AN EXPERT AT FAILING. THE MORE YOU FAIL, THE MORE YOU WILL SUCCEED."

MENTOR NOTE

The doors opened. It was a blur, as it always is. There are so many people, you get pulled in so many directions. There are collectors congratulating me and asking about the work. There are other artists coming by and talking and showing respect for how much goes into a show like that, the same way I do for them. There are fans who want me to sign books and pose for photos. There's press bombarding me with questions. This was the first time I felt like a celebrity, which is not something I ever aspired to be. There was an after-party. My friends were all there, as were a ton of new friends. It was one of the biggest nights of my life.

I had such a big audience because they had never seen my work in person—proof again that Emmanuel was 100 percent right. The wait had created anticipation of that show, a building desire. I'd announced it almost a year ahead of time, so it had built up this whole countdown. *The show is in four weeks*, then three weeks, until finally it crested the day of the opening. Emmanuel can be obsessed with numbers. He has counters installed in the doorways leading into his galleries, and the show broke his attendance record for any of his galleries. I still hold the attendance record for both his Paris and New York galleries. Every show that I've done has broken the record. I'll have more than fifty thousand people who will come to a show over six weeks. More than a thousand people per day going through your show is pretty crazy. I don't think that type of engagement would have existed without the internet and Instagram.

I waited my whole life for that New York solo. Emmanuel had held it out as a carrot, just out of reach, allowing me the time to develop into the artist I had the potential to become. It killed.

CHAPTER XVI

DIOR AND KIM JONES

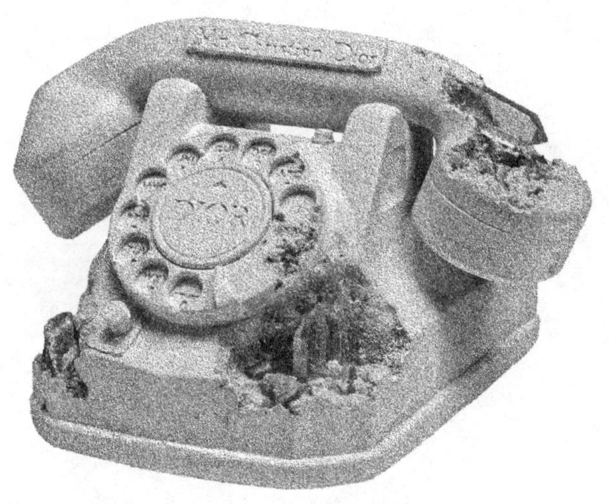

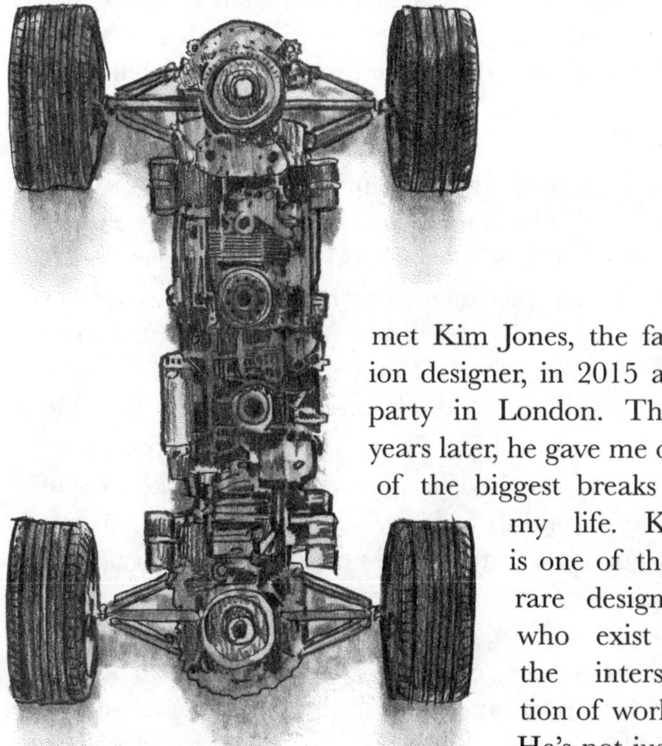

met Kim Jones, the fashion designer, in 2015 at a party in London. Three years later, he gave me one of the biggest breaks of my life. Kim is one of those rare designers who exist at the intersection of worlds. He's not just a fashion designer. He's a cultural curator, a historian of fashion, a collector of art and artifacts, a person who sees the full spectrum of creative disciplines and understands how they can speak to one another. Though there have been others like him, Virgil and

Pharrell being easy examples, Kim was among the first, if not the first, to recognize the convergence of the cultures of art and fashion and music and streetwear.

Born in London, raised in Africa and the Caribbean, and educated at Central Saint Martins art school, Kim has always pulled inspiration from a global vision. Before Dior, he transformed Louis Vuitton's menswear into a bridge between high fashion and street culture, pioneering collaborations that redefined what luxury could look like. When he arrived at Dior, it was clear he was bringing that same instinct for reinvention.

So when Kim reached out to me in 2018 with an invitation to work together, it wasn't just about fashion. It was about creating something that lived between disciplines, something that blurred the lines between sculpture and clothing, between history and the present, between my world and his. And that was exactly the kind of project I wanted to be part of.

But I'd be lying if I said I wasn't nervous.

Fashion was not my world. At least not in the way it was Kim's. By the time I met him, I had worked in sculpture, architecture, set design, and installation but never in a discipline where the work was as fleeting as a fashion show. At some point, everyone in a creative field feels some degree of impostor syndrome, afraid they don't belong and aren't actually any good. It's natural and normal, but it isn't helpful or productive, and I have always struggled with it. After I got Kim's call, I had to keep telling myself, *Don't listen to the voice in your head, don't negotiate with it.*

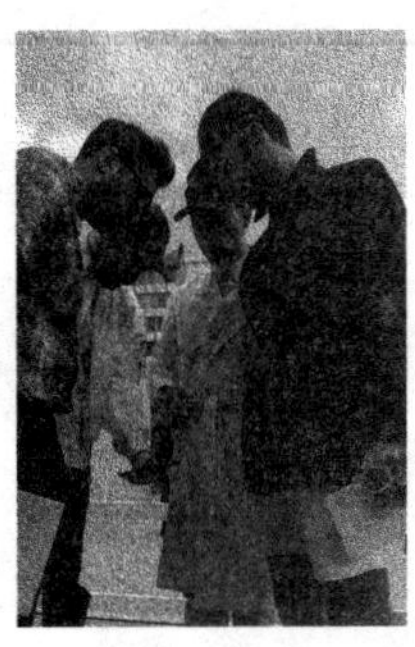

With Chris Stamp, Ronnie Fieg, and Teddy Santis at the show.

In a normal art exhibition, the work lives for months, even years. People can return to it, view it from different angles, let it settle in their minds. But this? This was different. The fashion show was going to be five minutes long, maybe seven. It would only be seen by the people who were in the room, a very limited number. It was also live, so if something went

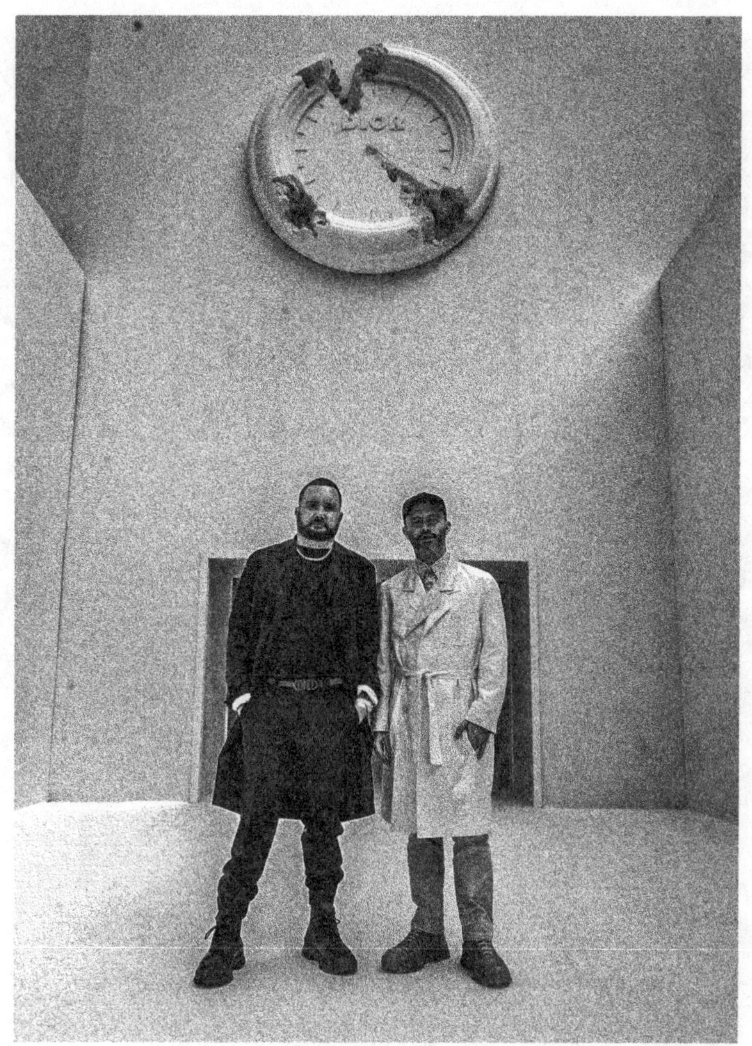

With Kim Jones at the entrance to the Dior show.

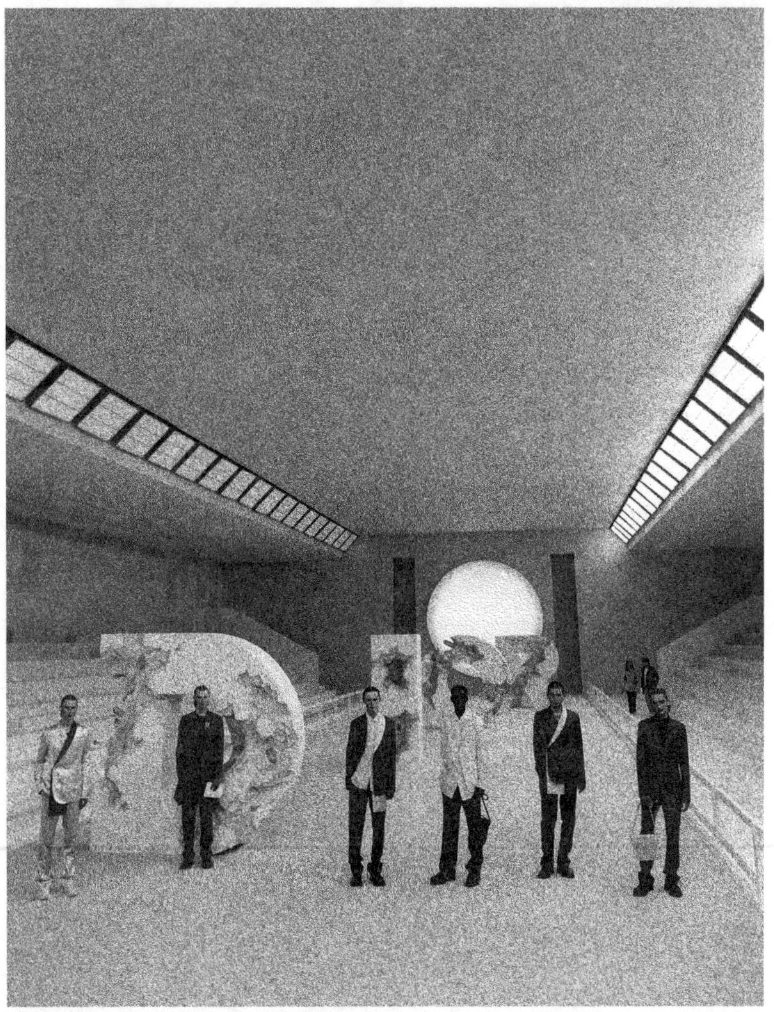

Stage set.

wrong, there would be no way to change it or fix it. A year of work would boil down to a few brief, fleeting moments. A year of work for five minutes.

On the other side, the positive, exciting side—which I always try to embody—was that there would be five minutes to get it right. Five minutes to impress some of the most critical, influential eyes in the world, eyes that have seen it all, eyes that expect surprise, eyes that decide, in an instant, whether something is genius or forgettable. And it wasn't just about me. This was Christian Dior. This was Kim Jones. This was his legacy and the legacy of the most prestigious fashion house in the world. I wasn't just stepping into an unfamiliar discipline; I was stepping into one of the most historic names in fashion. The stakes couldn't have been higher for me.

I knew that people would judge me. Even after more than a decade of working professionally, even with my name established in the art world, this was a new playing field. In the fashion world, I was an outsider. And in a space that moves as fast as fashion, an outsider has to prove themselves quickly or they're instantly dismissed. I felt the weight—and the fear—of that every single day.

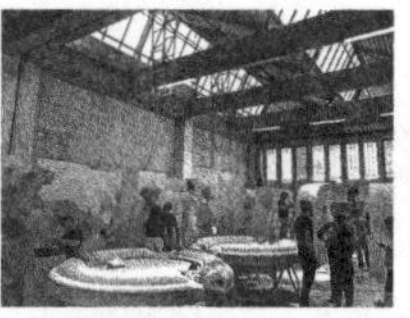

Working on the Dior stage set.

Kim and I knew from the start that this collection had to do something completely new. It couldn't just be clothing inspired by my sculptures; it had to *become* sculpture. My work has always played with the passage of time, with the way objects erode and transform. We had to find a way to capture that texture, decay, and crystallization in fabric, leather, and metal.

The suits in the collection weren't just tailored garments. They had sculptural weight, with structured silhouettes that felt like they were formed from stone rather than woven fabric. Some pieces were printed with eroded textures that made them look as if they'd been dug up from an archaeological

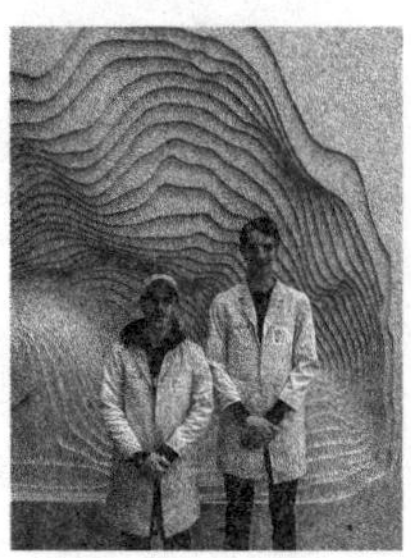

With Alexandre Arnault.

site—an extension of the work I'd been doing. Others incorporated metallic embroidery that mimicked the way minerals crystallize over time. It was unlike anything that had been done in fashion or art. The work was a huge challenge for me, a huge risk. And with great risk comes great reward. If it works. Five minutes. It had to work.

One of the things I love and admire about Kim and have in common with him is his ambition. We were not going to play it safe. The first thing we decided to make was a pair of crystal boots, an idea that felt completely insane. Kim and I were both obsessed with pulling it off. Together with Dior's footwear designer Thibo Denis, we designed boots that appeared to be made out of crystal, from the sole to the upper; they were completely clear. Cinderella's slipper, but a heavy, chunky boot. It took six months to figure out, but once we did, the effect was stunning. Luxury and a Future Relic at the same time.

We carried the concept forward into sneakers with sculptural, encrusted textures. Dress shoes with rough, almost geological surfaces. And then jewelry. Bold, ambitious, beautiful. The rings, pendants, and brooches weren't just accessories; they were wearable artifacts, each piece looking like it had been buried and rediscovered, marked by the passing of time. We used the finest materials: pure metals and the best available gemstones. Every piece in the collection was touched by this idea of erosion, of time leaving its mark, of beauty found in imperfection.

As we made progress, Kim and I started thinking about how the spectacle of the show could match the spectacle of the items we were making. Christian Dior's office was legendary. It was the space where he worked, designed, sketched, where he built the foundation of one of the most iconic fashion houses, where he forever changed fashion and changed the world. After he passed, no one else was ever allowed

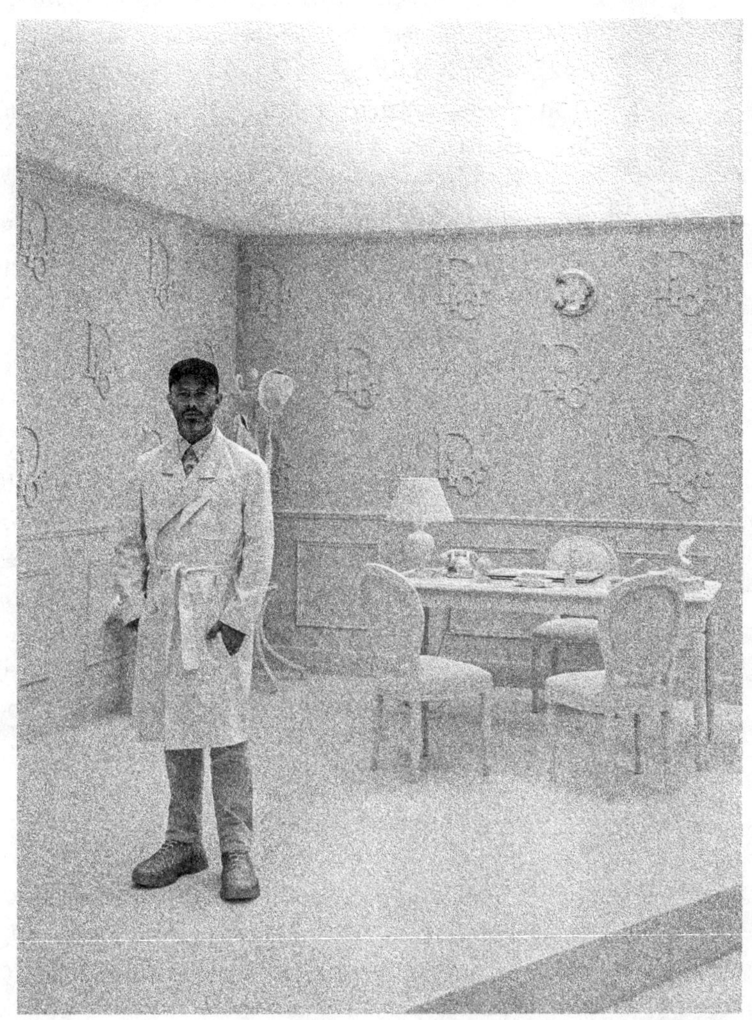

Christian Dior's office, reconstructed.

to work in it, and it was sealed off from the general public. I decided to bring it back, but in a way that fit within my own world.

I reconstructed his office as an all-white, calcified room, a ghostly, eroded version of the original, as though it had been suspended in time, turned to stone over centuries from lack of use and isolation. History, frozen. A memory made physical. Not just a stage design but a statement about legacy, about how time affects everything, about how art and fashion are always in conversation with the past. It became part of the runway set, a space the audience walked through to get to their seats, providing an experience before they even saw the collection itself.

By the time the show started, there was nothing left to do that I could control. The work was done. The clothes were made. The set was built. The models were lined up, ready to walk. I took my seat next to my friend Virgil Abloh, watching as the lights dimmed, as the first note of the soundtrack played, as the first model stepped forward onto the runway.

And for a moment there was nothing but silence.

The flashes started. The cameras. The murmurs. The movement.

Five minutes.

Just five minutes.

Sink or fucking swim.

The models moved through the calcified Dior office, past the textures and surfaces we had spent months perfecting. Just as we envisioned, the collection was sculptural, the pieces moving with weight and structure, as if they had been carved from stone yet somehow still breathed and were somehow still wearable. I saw heads nodding. I saw people leaning forward. I saw cameras capturing every detail.

But I still didn't know. Was it working? Was it enough?

And then it was over.

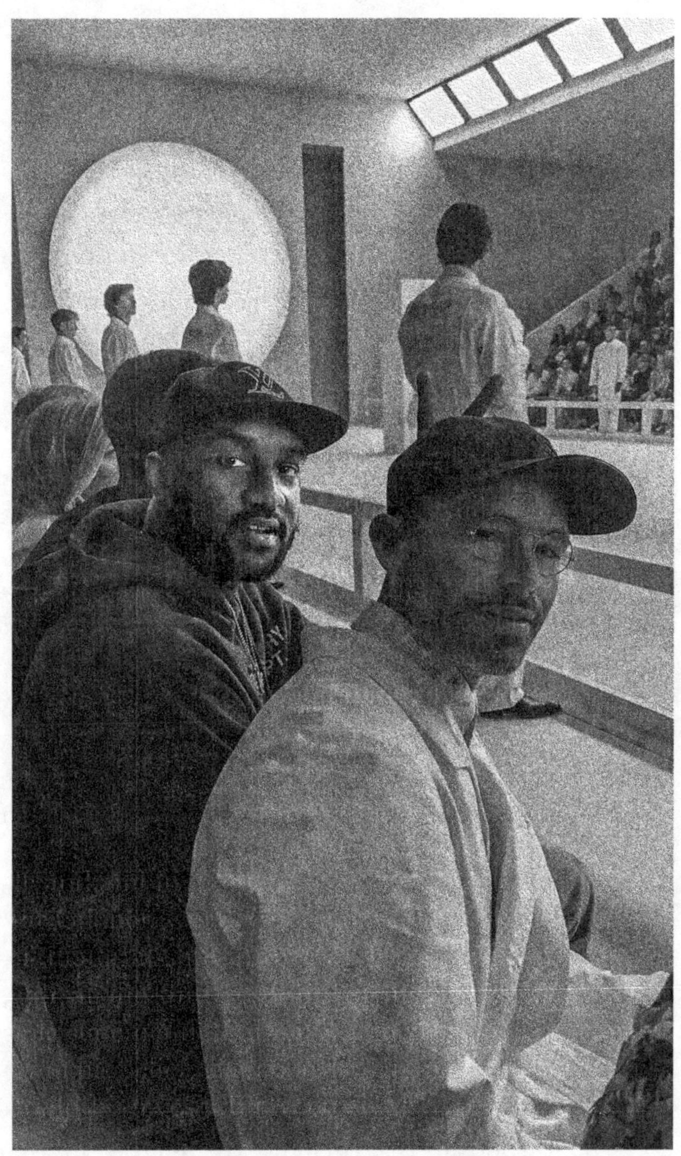

Sitting with Virgil Abloh in the front row at my Dior show.

Five minutes had passed. The final model walked. The music faded. And for a moment—one endless, terrifying moment—there was nothing.

Just a pause.

Silence.

And then, thankfully, the applause started.

And it didn't stop.

It wasn't just polite applause. It was real. It was loud. It was sustained. With profound relief and joy, I exhaled for the first time in what felt like hours. Kim walked out to take his bow. He nodded at me. I nodded at him. We both knew. It had worked.

The response in the following days and weeks was overwhelming. The reviews were all raves. Critics called it one of the most inspired collaborations in recent fashion history, praising the way we had fused disciplines, the way the collection felt like something entirely new yet deeply connected to Dior's history. The commercial success was immediate: Pieces from the collection became some of the most sought-after items that season, selling out almost instantly. As we stood up after the show, I remember Virgil turning to me and saying, "You know you just changed the game, right?"

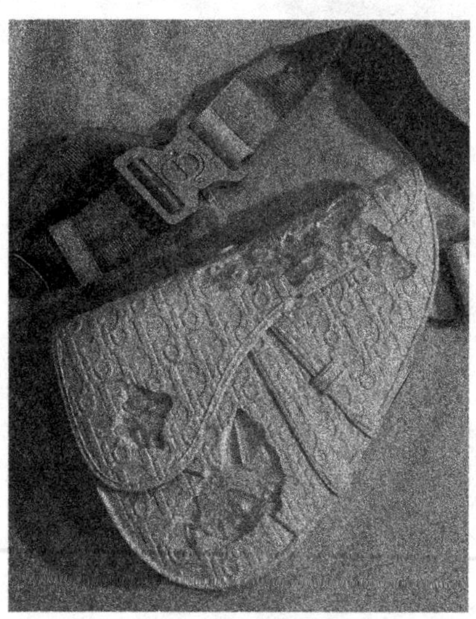

One of the very limited Saddle bags that I produced with Dior.

That stuck with me. I remember it as clear as day, like a photo, or more like an Instagram reel. Because as much as this had been a milestone in fashion, it was also a milestone in my career, a confirmation that the barriers between art, fashion, and design don't have to exist.

That was the last time I saw Virgil in person. The following March we all went into lockdown for the pandemic, and we never crossed paths in real life again. He died from cancer about a year later, leaving an indelible mark on so many of the creators of our generation. I miss him greatly.

Looking back, I see this project as proof that art doesn't have to stay in one place. It can move, evolve, take new forms. It can find new life through collaboration. Because at the end of the day, that's what this is all about: pushing the work forward, expanding the possibilities, creating things that didn't exist before and which will outlive you.

CHAPTER XVII

HOW DO YOU RUN A BUSINESS WITH THIRTY EMPLOYEES

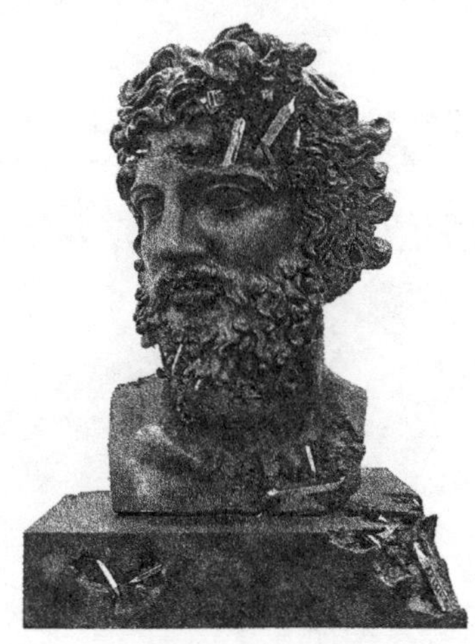

WHEN YOU WENT TO ART SCHOOL?

"I'M NOT A BUSINESSMAN.
I'M A BUSINESS, MAN."

—JAY-Z

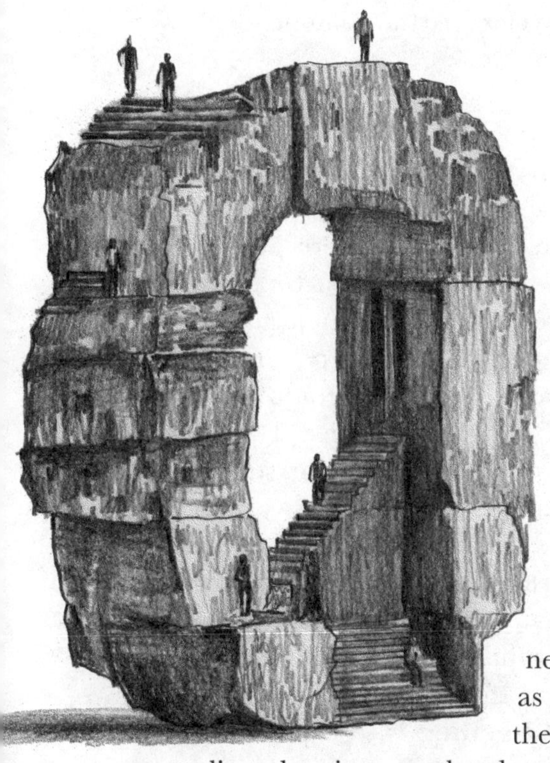

ne of the main motivations for writing this book is this chapter. To be a successful artist, you must also be a successful businessperson. In fact, as an artist, *you* are the business. From my earliest drawings to the doors series, I knew I wanted to be an artist. What I didn't know was that I'd need to understand taxes, hiring, firing, marketing, networking, and the countless other tasks that come with running a business. Cooper and my mentors gave me a foundation in creating my art, but figuring out how to be an entrepreneur? That was all on me. There were many moments, and sometimes there still are, when I had no clue what to do. I just had to figure it out.

Warhol nailed it: "Being good in business is the most fascinating kind of art. Making money is art and working is art and good business is the best art." He understood that the business itself *is* the art. His genius was using the mechanisms of capitalism—buying, marketing, and selling—to bring art into the world. If you're reading this and thinking, *No, art and capital should never touch*, then I suggest you take an art history class. Art and money have been married since antiquity.

In 2007, when I got my studio in Brooklyn, I had been working with Emmanuel for two years. He had galleries in Miami and Paris, and my work was gaining interest in New York. I was twenty-seven, had a Brooklyn studio where people could visit, and had shown at MoMA PS1's *Greater New York* exhibition. I was getting noticed. But just a few years earlier, I'd had no connections, no money—just $700 in my bank account when I graduated. I went to the studio every day, nine to five. Days, weeks, months, and years of grinding. Ramen, studio, sleep. Over and over again.

I had no safety net. My parents weren't wealthy. I didn't have a trust fund. I had nothing to rely on but my dedication and drive. Some nights I would lie awake thinking about whether I could even afford my rent that month. There were times when I considered getting a side job, but I was too stubborn. I knew that if I divided my energy, my art would suffer. So I just kept at it. I failed repeatedly. I created work that didn't sell. I put in effort that led nowhere. But I kept showing up at the studio. I knew that, one day, something would give.

I realize now that I was making sacrifices I wasn't even aware of at the time. I rarely socialized, I didn't take vacations, and every dollar I made went straight back into my work. Some people look back at their twenties as the best years of their life—full of exploration, travel, or relationships. I look back at mine as a blur of barely sleeping, barely surviving, scarring my hands and twisting them with carpal tunnel, pouring everything into my work. It wasn't easy, but I wouldn't change a thing. That level of focus was what made the difference.

My world opened up when Emmanuel got my work into art fairs. A show in Amsterdam in 2008 with Ron Mandos was my first experience outside of Emmanuel's galleries. It was a pivotal moment: Not only was my work being seen but I was finally making enough money to support myself. Paying rent without stress was transformative. I wasn't a starving artist anymore. But there were constant doubts—about my direction, my career. Looking back, I made barely anything, yet it felt like a fortune to me, just to be able to cover basic expenses.

Until 2009 I worked entirely alone, which meant that everything from concept to execution fell on me. But then I hired Tim Stanley, and this was a turning point. For the first time, there was an extra set of hands to help me lift and move things, cut things, and execute artworks. This was critical in allowing me to think bigger. It also forced me to consider what kind of leader I wanted to be. I had never been anyone's boss before, and suddenly I had to figure out things like delegation, communication, and making sure he was paid on time.

As my studio grew, I had to learn not just how to hire but how to lead. Managing a creative business is different from managing a corporate team. Artists need space to explore ideas. They need to feel supported. But at the same time, there has to be structure. I had to learn how to balance those things, and it wasn't easy. I made mistakes. Figuring out hiring, payroll, HR—it was trial by fire. But even though managing people was a whole new challenge, I always viewed my studio as a family. I hosted dinners, held summer retreats in upstate New York, brought in former Merce Cunningham dancers and other artists.

When I first moved to New York, I was struck by the fact that galleries were free. Wealthy collectors funded them, but anyone could walk in and experience the art. That idea of accessibility stuck with me. Art should be available to all, even if owning it isn't. Social media has taken this principle even further, allowing artists to instantly showcase their work to a global audience.

In 2012 my studio had eight full-time employees, and I launched Arsham Editions with the goal of making my work more accessible by using less expensive materials. I started with a Future Relic cast of an old cell phone. The original work was made out of crystal and volcanic ash—materials that are hard to source and expensive to work with. The Editions version was made out of plaster and broken glass, which were significantly less expensive, and I could make ten of them in a day. I premiered the original run of five hundred at Art Basel in 2012. They sold out in a day, for $500 each—obviously still expensive, but attainable for many more people. I was stunned. Clearly there was an audience of people who wanted to own my work but at a lower price point. Even after the gallery took its percentage, it was by far the most successful day of my career up to that point. The model was proven.

The Editions became a vehicle for cash that I could pour back into the studio, helping me fund my other, critical ventures and creative opportunities that were not themselves generating money. The Editions

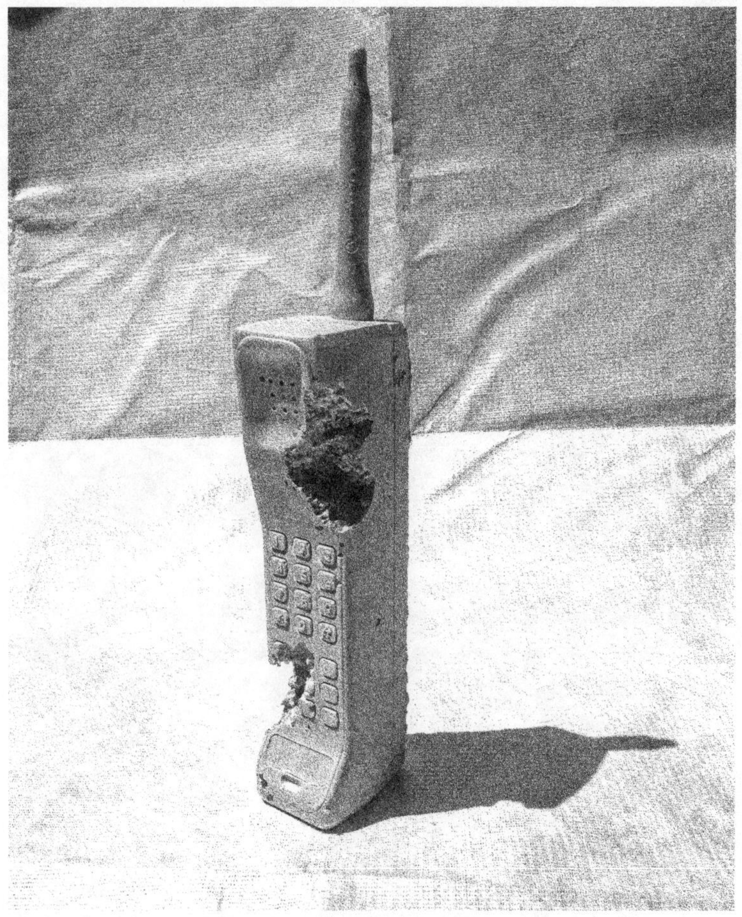

First Future Relic Edition.

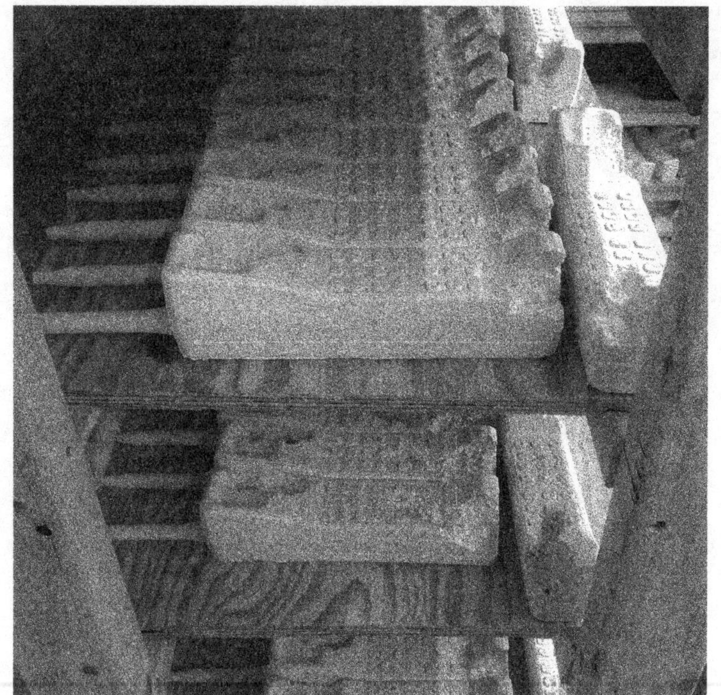

Editions.

opened my work and my ideas up to a much bigger audience while providing increased capital resources that allowed me to expand my creative capabilities. How people live with this work is pretty fucking cool. "I gave your work as a gift to my son, and he still has it . . ." The stories always make me smile.

I'm not the first artist to use this approach. Nineteenth-century artists were doing this with lithography, and then Picasso took it even further. Then Warhol saw what Picasso had done from a business perspective and turbocharged it, making thousands and thousands of editions. I saw what they both did and believed it would also work for me. As much as I stress taking risks as an artist, I also believe in taking them as a businessman. This one worked, and it still does.

To successfully scale a business from a one-person operation to one that fluctuates up to thirty employees has stretched me as much as developing my art has. Here's what I've learned:

MANAGING PEOPLE

HIRE FOR STRENGTHS YOU DON'T HAVE. I needed people who were better than me at fabrication, business management, and logistics.

FIND PEOPLE WHO UNDERSTAND YOUR VISION. A strong studio assistant isn't just skilled; they understand the creative goals behind the work.

BE CLEAR ABOUT ROLES. In the early days, roles were fluid, but as the business grew, it became essential to define responsibilities.

LET GO OF MICROMANAGING. I had to trust my team and focus on my own strengths.

PAY PEOPLE WELL. Early on, I didn't have much, but as soon as I could, I made sure my team was fairly compensated. Today my staff have very competitive salaries, and they all receive full health benefits, a year-end bonus, and a 100 percent matched 401(k) plan. I take care of my people.

KNOWING THE BUSINESS SIDE

UNDERSTAND CASH FLOW. Revenue fluctuates, and managing finances properly was critical to sustaining growth.

BUILD LASTING PARTNERSHIPS. Creating long-term relationships with galleries and collectors helped build stability.

INVEST IN THE RIGHT TECHNOLOGY AND INFRASTRUCTURE. Whether it was hiring specialized mold makers or setting up production for larger-scale works, I often had to invest long before I would see the results, but it was necessary.

BALANCE CREATIVE PROJECTS WITH COMMERCIAL WORK. Finding the equilibrium between personal projects and brand collaborations was crucial.

PROTECTING YOURSELF FINANCIALLY

I never thought I'd need to understand taxes, payroll, or financial forecasting, but as my career grew, those skills became essential. Some of the financial lessons I've learned include:

GET AN ACCOUNTANT EARLY. This has saved me from countless financial mistakes.

PLAN FOR SLOW PERIODS. Art sales can be unpredictable; financial planning helps you weather the lean months. I save a lot and live well below my means. In the beginning I tried to save 10 percent of my income every year. Now I try to save 50 percent.

UNDERSTAND LICENSING AND IP. Owning your intellectual property is key to long-term success.

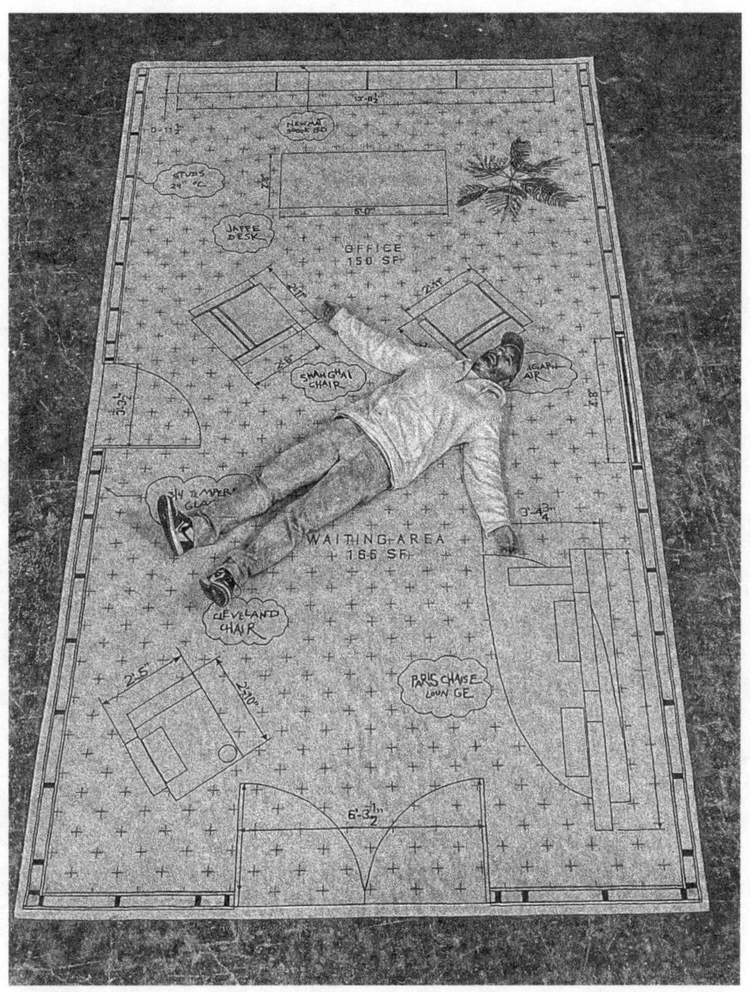

Lying on top of the rug that I produced for my first furniture collection.

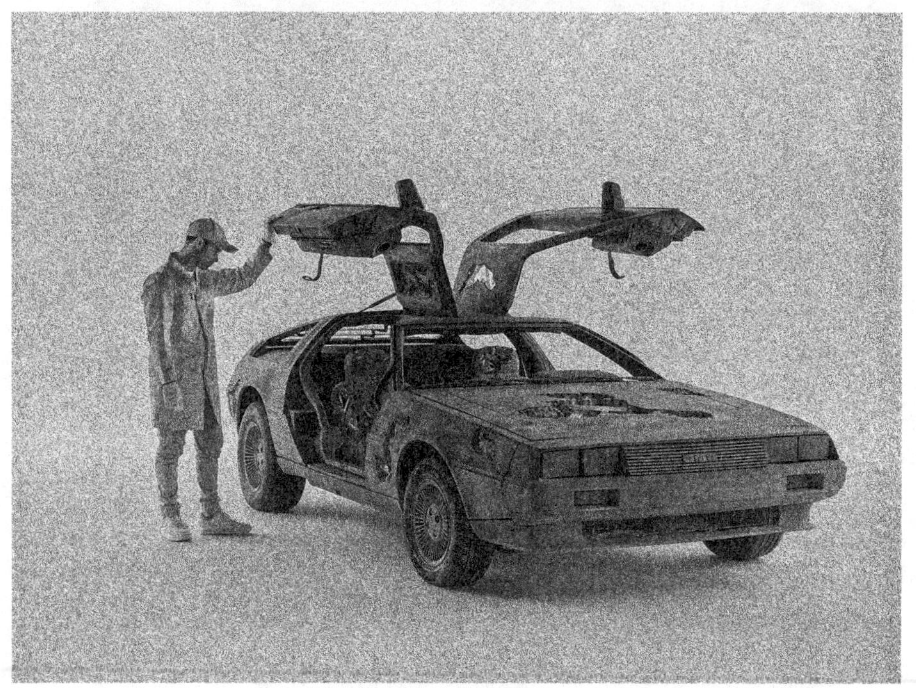

With the first major car artwork I made, a DeLorean.

DIVERSIFY INCOME STREAMS. From selling original work to prints, collaborations, and even furniture design, diversifying income has been crucial to my ability to continue making art.

Today my businesses include Arsham Studio, Arsham Editions, my design studio Snarkitecture, a furniture line, and a car division that creates one-of-one vehicles. Collectively, the businesses generate millions of dollars a year. My staff includes mold makers, designers, archivists, business managers. Despite all this, I only spend about 50 percent of my time making art. The rest is running the businesses, traveling for exhibitions, and visiting the bronze foundry. I've accepted that, as a boss, I need to be both creative and strategic. If something goes wrong, my team looks to me. I've learned to be tough but fair with my people. I'm obsessive about details, but I've also learned to delegate.

Running a business wasn't part of my art school education, but I've embraced it. A lot of artists resist being "business people." I see it differently. Business is an extension of my art. It allows my work to reach more people, to be sustainable, and to grow beyond me. That's the real challenge: building something that lasts, something bigger than yourself.

As I look back, I realize that running a business as an artist is a unique challenge. It requires both creativity and discipline. The balance between creation and management is delicate, but ultimately, the ability to scale, to reach more people, and to create new opportunities for my art has been worth the journey. And that? That's also art.

4

CHAPTER XVIII

FAITH AND WHY IT MATTERS

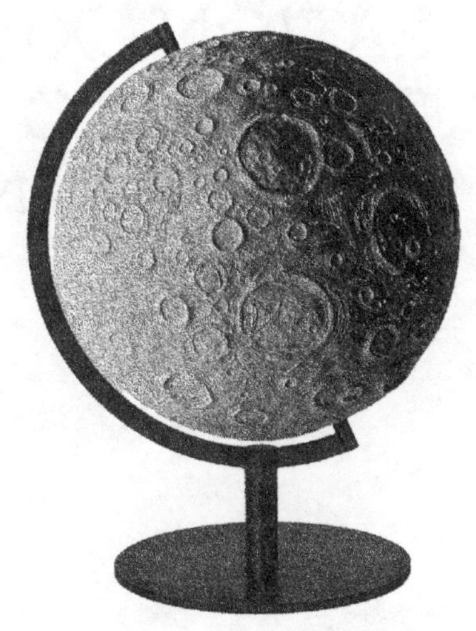

"INSPIRATION EXISTS,
BUT IT HAS TO
FIND YOU WORKING."

—PABLO PICASSO

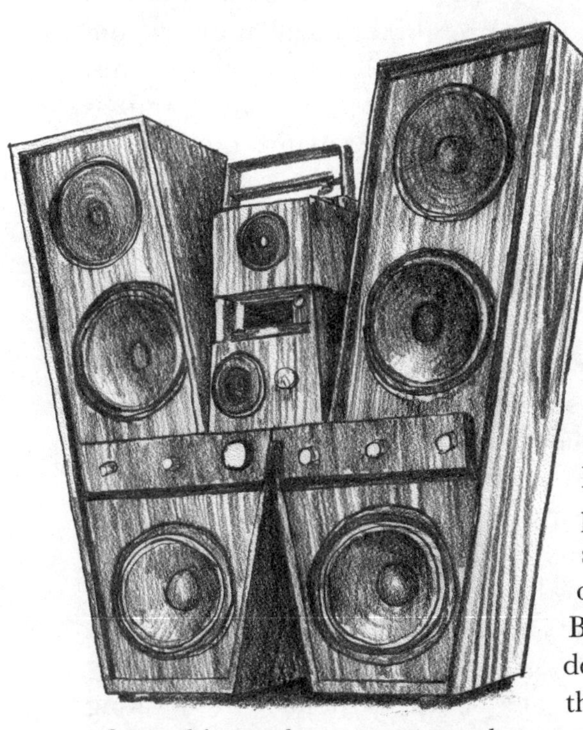

hen I was in high school, my girlfriend Ren's family practiced a specific form of Japanese Buddhism derived from the teachings of a thirteenth-century monk named Nichiren Daishonin, who had a unique interpretation of the Lotus Sutra. The practice involves daily chanting of *Nam myōhō renge kyō*, a phrase that expresses their devotion and is a core aspect of their faith. After chanting it, they would recite a selected section of the Lotus Sutra a set number of times. The religion emphasizes meditation, and since Ren and I were together at a time when I was trying to figure out my future, it had a profound impact on me. Their home had a massive shrine with an enormous scroll, a bell, and incense, all integral to the practice. Sometimes we would chant for hours as a group, with the rhythmic repetition creating a melodic, meditative experience. The idea was to clear your mind, but in reality, the process allowed for intensive focus.

"LIVING TRUE TO YOUR AUTHENTIC SELF WILL OFTEN CAUSE PROBLEMS WITH PEOPLE WHO LIVE BEHIND A MASK TO CLOAK THEIR INSECURITIES."

MENTOR NOTE

Like most high school romances, the relationship didn't last, but her family's influence on me did. I have meditated for decades, with a focal point for my practice that has shifted over time. When I was considering Cooper Union, I focused my attention on being admitted there. It became a process of almost manifesting the goal, actively working toward it while aligning my thoughts with that reality.

For years, I didn't consciously connect my projected intentions with that outcome, but over time I've become more deliberate about manifesting outcomes. Looking back, there are countless examples—securing gallery representation, creating a specific body of work, or even buying and restoring a historic Norman Jaffe house. I envisioned renovating a mid-century home on the water long before it became a reality.

A major challenge for young artists is understanding that success isn't guaranteed, even after decades of work. Many people give up because the uncertainty is crushing. Visualizing my success and meditating on it helped guide me. It's not like it's magic and happened overnight—it took ten years before I could even move out of my tiny studio. In a way, I had just enough success to survive. But while I was just barely surviving in that small Greenpoint space, I believed in the possibility of something greater, and meditation, mentorship, and a kind of blind faith helped me make it real. As an artist, sometimes that's all you have—faith. Waiting for success to fall into your lap without you driving it? That's never going to happen.

During my years in Greenpoint, faith, intention, and meditation weren't just abstract ideas; they were daily practices that kept me moving toward my vision. Even when it felt absurd—even when people around me doubted me—I stayed the course. I was often told, "Bro, this isn't going to work. You're living in a shitty studio. You're not represented by a major gallery. You've had one show, and it wasn't even in New York." But I recognized small hints of progress: *Greater New York* in 2005, followed by my first exhibition with Emmanuel in Paris. Those moments reassured me that momentum was building.

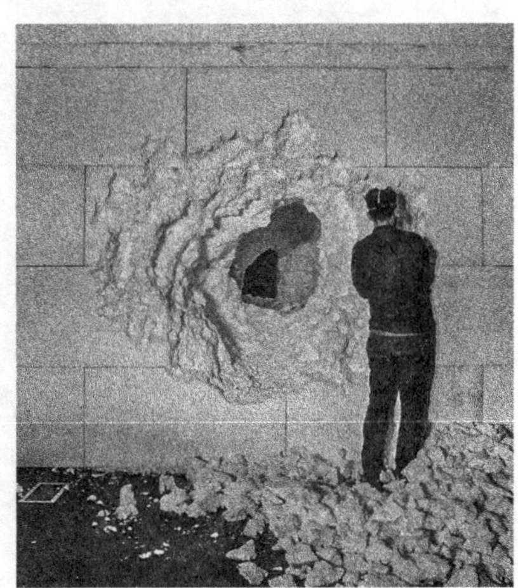

Exhibit at Storefront for Art and Architecture, 2011.

Beyond that, I had an almost ridiculous, stubborn faith in my potential. I firmly believed that if I worked long enough, something would happen. There was no timeline—I had accepted that it might take forever. It's not easy to keep going for ten years without any certainty—it takes a lot. Some might call it foolish, but I see it as strength, willpower, and faith.

Having a direction, an imagined future, makes the path easier. You will face doubt from yourself and

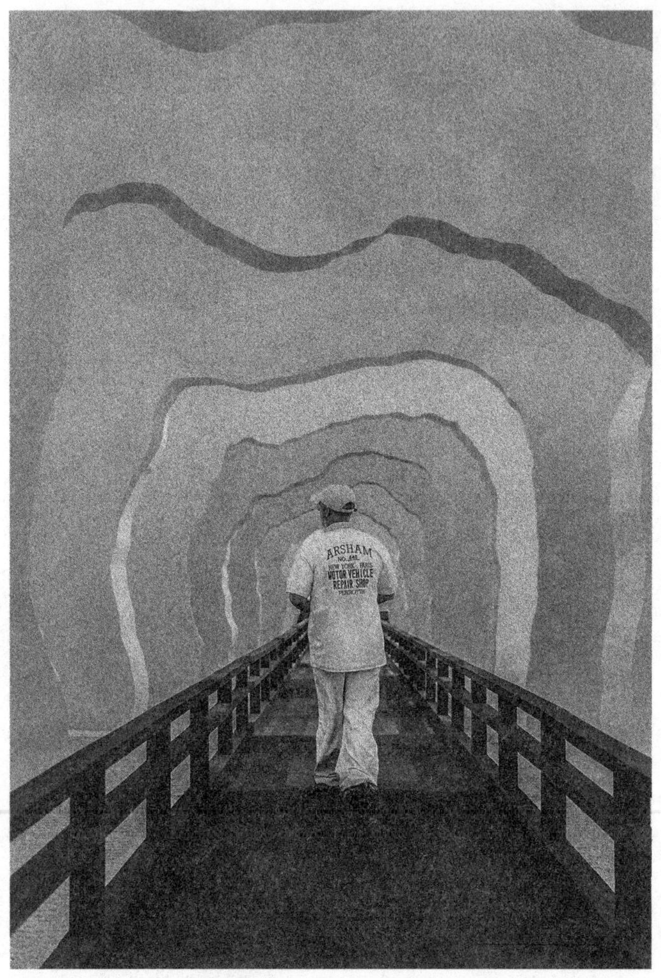

Eroded walls installation in Bangkok, 2024.

others. One of the biggest obstacles is the internal voice whispering, *You've worked hard enough today. Take a break tomorrow.* That's bullshit. You know what needs to be done. Stop negotiating with yourself. Get the work done. No alternatives.

I have a daily sauna-and-cold-plunge routine. Every single time I step into that thirty-eight-degree water for three minutes, it sucks just as much as the first time. Every time, before leaving the sauna, a voice in my head says, *Maybe I don't need to do this today.* That's the negotiation trap. The easiest life hack? Don't negotiate with that voice. Hold yourself accountable. Apply that same principle to your work. Faith means not only pushing through doubt but refusing to entertain the idea of quitting. When I'm in the water, I often imagine scenarios that I would like to see happen. I try to envision them. This is a mental trick, training your mind to prepare for a certain outcome. Do this consistently and you will notice yourself unconsciously doing things that will move you toward those goals. The inverse is also true: If you dwell on negative possibilities and things you don't want to happen, then you are training your mind to accept and prepare for those possibilities.

Two key elements matter. First, that voice of self-doubt, like an enemy—don't engage. Second, establish a routine. It doesn't matter what it is, but be consistent. I treat my art like a job. I go to my studio every weekday, from 9 a.m. to 5 p.m. If you treat art like a hobby, it will remain one. But if you commit to it like a profession, it becomes a necessity, like breathing. This takes years of practice. Every successful creative I know—filmmakers, musicians, painters, writers—shares one trait: they put in the work every day, believing that eventually someone will recognize it. Faith means showing up, even on the days when you're terrified, doubtful, or convinced your work is garbage.

"HAVE YOU EVER WOKEN UP OUT OF A BEAUTIFUL DREAM THIRTY MINUTES BEFORE YOUR ALARM, AND YOU REALLY JUST WANT TO GET BACK INTO THE DREAM?

MAKE YOUR LIFE FEEL LIKE THAT."

MENTOR NOTE

You might think self-doubt disappears with success, but it doesn't. Younger artists sometimes assume I wake up every morning thinking, *This is amazing. I made it.* The reality? Every day is a challenge. I'm running a business, managing exhibitions, balancing family life—all while fearing that it could all disappear and I could revert to that shy seventeen-year-old. The fear of losing everything never fully goes away. My wife, Jacqueline, teaches yoga and has a profound connection with the idea of manifestation. She is a powerful force in my life and is constantly pushing me to stay focused on my goals, to keep that faith.

Faith in your craft is essential. If you don't believe in yourself, you have no chance. Convincing yourself is the first step to convincing others. People ask if I worry about younger artists surpassing me or about losing relevance as I age, but instead of worrying about that, I invest my energy in mentoring others. I want to do for them what my mentors have done for me. If we invest in one another, not only does the art get better, but our lives get better.

My confidence in my process has allowed me to work in spaces well beyond the usual boundaries of the art world. While others focus solely on gallery representation to get their work out into the world, I collaborate with global brands, I work on album covers for musicians, I work with athletes. I operate on a whole different and ever-expanding playing field, because I trust in my ability to create valuable work in unexpected areas.

David Kohler approached me about a collaboration. We produced a ceramic sink, using 3D printing in a way it never had been. I told Kohler's team, "We'll release it on my website, and it'll sell out within an hour." They were skeptical. But it sold out in thirty minutes. That faith in my work opened doors—eventually leading to the idea of a golf course sculpture park. That opportunity wouldn't have existed without a fundamental belief that I could create value in places others never imagined.

Without faith, you have no chance. It's not blind faith; it's intentional. As my mentor says, "Envision the goal and move toward it." The goal may evolve, but you're always progressing toward your best possible future. Some days, progress is slow—just inches down the field. Other days, it's a thirty-yard gain. But as long as you keep moving forward, eventually you'll reach the end zone. Have faith—you'll get there.

CHAPTER XIX

DREAMS DO COME TRUE

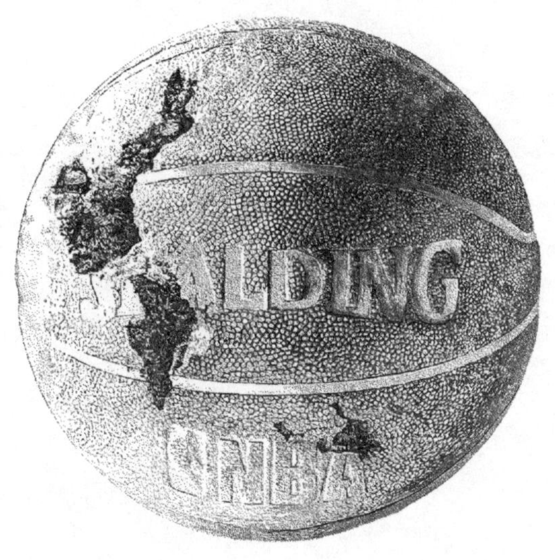

1

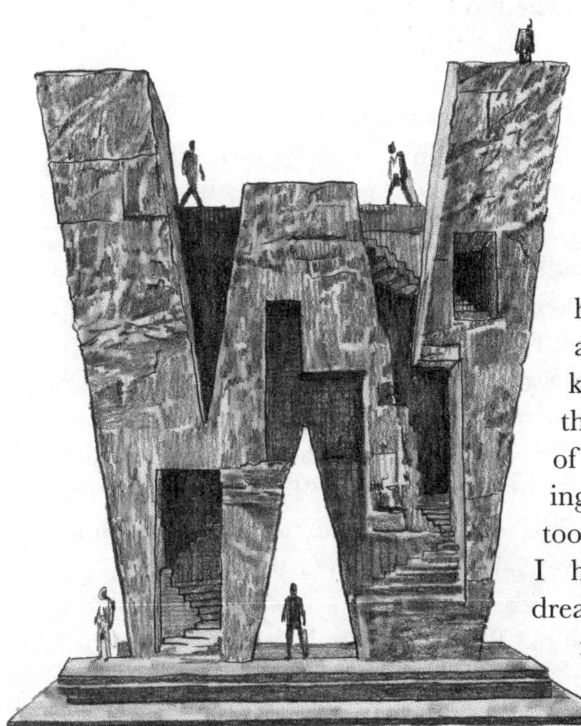

hen I was a little kid, before the dream of becoming an artist took hold, I had other dreams, often revolving around sports. Although we moved away from Cleveland when I was still young, I was there long enough that it's my hometown, and I remain a die-hard Cleveland sports fan. Like my interests in popular culture, music, and fashion, my interest in sports has had a foundational influence on my art.

My own time as a Cleveland sports fan started in the 1990s, following the Cavaliers teams built around Mark Price and Larry Nance and Brad Daugherty and later Shawn Kemp. After my family moved to Miami, it was tough not to root for the Heat, since all of my friends were big into the Heat. When LeBron James left Cleveland the first time and went to Miami, I wasn't sure what to do. I love LeBron. He's an Ohio kid, we're roughly the same age, and now he was suddenly playing for the Heat. Should I root for him, for them? I decided not to bandwagon the Heat and kept rooting for the Cavs. When LeBron returned to Cleveland and led the Cavaliers to the 2016 NBA title, that was the highlight of my sports fandom.

Dan Gilbert had bought the Cavs in 2005, and after the championship win in 2016, he decided to renovate and expand the arena. Dan had the idea of installing a portion of his family's art collection inside the building, and it turned out that the Gilberts owned some of my work. I had shown some pieces at Library Street gallery, in Detroit, and it so happened that Dan was from Detroit and that's where he started his business. I received a call from the gallery saying that the Gilbert family wanted to commission a piece to go inside the arena. The piece would sit right at the VIP entrance to the luxury suites. I don't think I've ever said yes to a job faster.

As the arena was being renovated, I created a piece that looks like a basketball thrown against the wall. Its energy is grabbing the wall, moving so fast that it's pushing the wall and creating this folding and rippling motion in the surface. It's a larger piece, around twenty feet across. The ripples keep unfolding, and you can see it when you're walking through the concourse. The majority of fans see it as they walk to their seats. Thankfully, the piece has become a fan favorite. People are always posting pictures of it on social media. They take photos with their kids or stream themselves as they stand near it. I couldn't have dreamt of a better outcome, but it turned out that creating that sculpture was only the beginning.

I had been talking to a number of people in the Cavs organization directly about what I thought of the Cavs' jerseys and their logos: "You just won the NBA championship. You can't have this ugly mustard yellow on everything and all over your social media." In passing, or maybe even as a joke, one of them said, "Why don't you come and do some design work for us?" It soon became more of a real conversation about how a creative director could be a real benefit to the team and the franchise. At the time, *creative* work in the NBA consisted of sports marketing people hiring a bunch of graphic designers. The whole design language in the NBA was a take on Marvel movie posters. They'd take a superstar like LeBron and use a range of Photoshop filters over him, typically in a gritty, dark black-and-white photo of the player drenched in sweat, with loads of grain added. It was a formula, and, to be frank, it was shit. This was at a moment when there was real crossover happening with the NBA and culture, a moment for collaboration in those areas. Sneaker fashion and art were coalescing when we started talking about this arrangement in 2018. This was an opportunity: The Cavs could be the first team to hire a creative director to create a consistent, dynamic, relevant, high-quality franchise-wide look to manage everything visual for the team.

As much as we believed this was a no-brainer, it took a long time to get the commissioner's office on board. I quickly found out that trying to get anything done with the league is super complicated. Everything we work on, whether big or small, has to go through multiple levels of approval. It happens that way because, while the owners own the team, they don't own the IP to their logos. To protect the value of the franchises, it's actually a good system. It allows for visual consistency and keeps the look and feel the same across the league. The league owns everything and then licenses it back to the teams. But it's a pain in the ass to work with. After all my care to make sure I never gave up my own creative IP rights, here I was, working for the Cavs and finding out that these ultrawealthy owners didn't even have control over their teams' designs.

We finally got approval to make the relationship real. The idea was that anything visual—social media, photography, all of the graphics, the uniforms, the merch—would be under my purview. There was a lot to do, and I was excited to get to work. I went to Cleveland and redid everything. I kept the original "C" logo, but I redesigned the Cavs logo. It was completely new, though I made it look as if it had been there forever. It contains references to past Cavs logos and has a refined vintage feel. The 2016 colors were wine and mustard, a horrendous shade of yellow. I hated it. The fans hated it. It was a big, big thing to move to the gold we settled on. We announced it in a full-page ad on the back page of the sports section in the Cleveland *Plain Dealer*.

As part of my deal, I also own a percentage of the team. I'm not going to say it's a big percentage, but it's still skin in the game. Having an ownership stake was really important to me when I joined up—not just because I was a lifelong fan but because I wanted to help transform what this team could mean, both to the city and at a national level. Before 2016 and before LeBron, the Cavs were considered a mid-tier NBA franchise. They're now in the top tier with the Knicks, Lakers, Bulls, Celtics, and Warriors. Below that top tier, selling merchandise outside of your home market is an uphill battle.

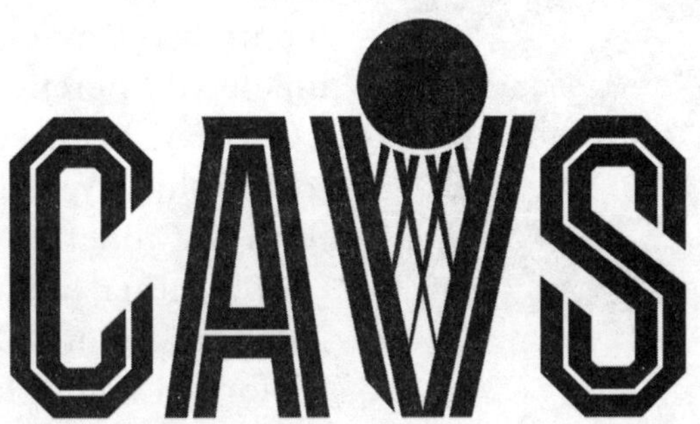

The new Cavaliers logo that I designed.

Part of my rebranding efforts and what I wanted to bring to the team was the creative vision to change that. Unlike the control factors that exist between the league and the individual teams, the NBA is incredibly permissive with its merchandise licensees. Teams don't have control of anything in a printing—not what gets printed or how many or the color quality. I was adamant that we work to simplify and better control what was getting printed. When I started, there were forty-one different versions of the logo and nineteen different color schemes. They had been layering shit on top of shit. We still had graphics from the nineties. Graphics that people either didn't use or didn't know how to use. Different graphics for television, for T-shirts, for the court. It was a hot fucking mess. I insisted on going with three logos, two colors, and a streamlined design language. I believed that if we made these changes, our brand recognition would go up. *We're going to have the C, we're going to have the Cavs logo, and we're going to have one that pays tribute to the city and the state: "The Land."*

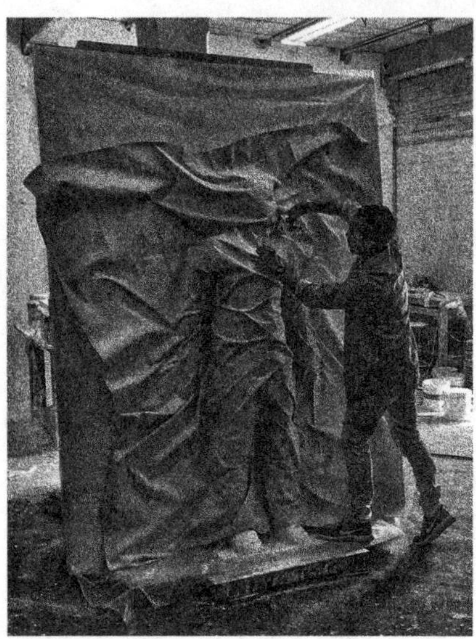

At work.

The stripping away and cleaning up was the first move. The new gold was step two. Step three was completely altering our photography. You want the fans to see the players as the amazing athletes they are. We have everything close up. You see players' faces, you see sweat. We tell more stories about who the players are, what they're doing off the court. Obviously, fashion has become a big part of the NBA. When it was done, we took out the full-page ad in the *Plain Dealer* to announce the changes, with a letter from me to Cleveland. I still have the original framed on the wall of my living room.

Most of my work for the Cavs is done in the offseason, with two years' lead time for approvals and production. Once the season begins, I focus on promotion and signings when I'm in Cleveland. During the offseason, I might look at something related to the Cavs four or five times a week. Once the season starts, design is locked in, so for me it's all about the games and networking for the franchise. I've hosted groups of people at the Barclays Center, in Brooklyn, when the Cavs play the Nets: fashion and music people like Nigel Sylvester, Alton Mason, Bloody Osiris, and others. We give out custom Cavs jackets to help create a new, influential Cavs fan base in New York.

Since I started, our merch sales have increased 450 percent, with a large portion of those sales coming from outside of Cleveland. We attracted more fans to the gear with merch drops using the City Edition jersey. Each season, I linked the jersey to something dope in the city. The first year we did the Rock & Roll Hall of Fame. Another year we did the Metroparks, with a vintage striated graphic on a white jersey. The year after that we created a jersey called "The Land," a reference to the unique history, resources, and culture of the city and the state. It was the bestselling City Edition jersey in the league. Darius Garland, one of the star players, told me he and the team loved wearing "The Land" jersey and that they hadn't lost wearing it the entire season. Even if we had never sold a single one of them, that feedback from Darius would have made it worthwhile.

As a Cavs fan growing up, I never would've believed that years down the road, I'd be designing the team jerseys. If you'd told me I'd have an ownership stake, I would've laughed at you. Who would think that a career in art would lead to a

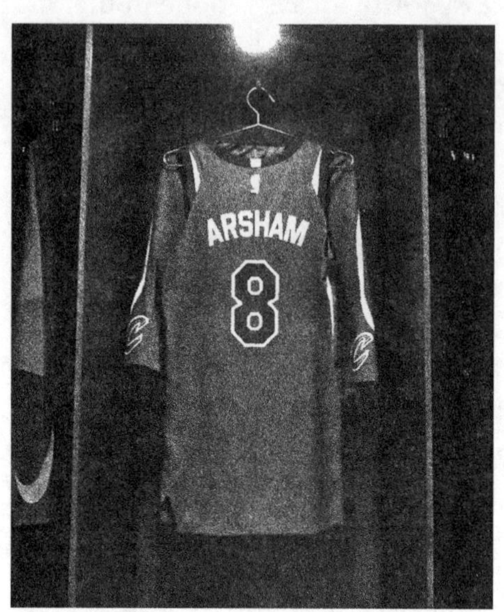

Dear Cleveland,

I am honored and thrilled to be joining the Cleveland Cavaliers as Creative Director.

I was born in Cleveland. I am a 3rd generation Clevelander and my family traces its roots back to 1908 when my great grandfather first arrived as an immigrant to build his life here. He came to this country with nothing and like many hard working Clevelanders, he built his business from the ground up. My Grandfather and father both graduated from Cleveland Heights High school. It's a place that has heavily influenced me, from the rushing waters of Chagrin Falls, to the Pizza at Geraci's, to the autumn in the Metro Parks. My father lives part of the year in Chagrin Falls, my cousin is Executive Chef at Toast CLE, and my Uncle is a Surgeon who has been affiliated with the Cleveland Clinic for many years. The Land is in me.

I will be bringing my two decades of experience as an Artist to tell the story of our Team, our community, and our City. I am a visual Artist and I have shown my work from Paris to Tokyo, from Rio to Shanghai. Now, I'm bringing my work home. Basketball, as a global phenomenon, is a reoccurring theme in my work and I am a longtime Cavs fan. However, most people don't know about these strong personal ties I have to Cleveland.

Cleveland is an iconic American city, and the people of Cleveland have immense pride in their hometown. To join the Cavaliers as Creative Director, and to have the opportunity to help shape and lead the team's visual identity as we look ahead to the future, is honestly a dream. It's a life moment for me.

If you see me around town or at a game next season please say hello. I'm here to tell your story, too.

- Daniel Arsham

ARSHAM STUDIO

The full-page ad on the back of the newspaper to announce my appointment as creative director.

career in the NBA as well? Looking back at the criticism I've faced for not focusing solely on art in the capital-*A* Art World makes me laugh. I'd have missed out on living a dream I never even had the audacity to dream. If I can do it, so can you. Dream fucking big. Go for it. You never know: Those dreams might actually come true.

CHAPTER XX
THE MENTOR

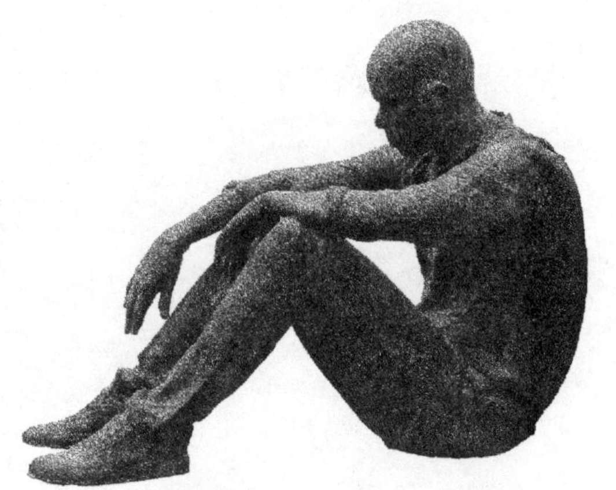

7

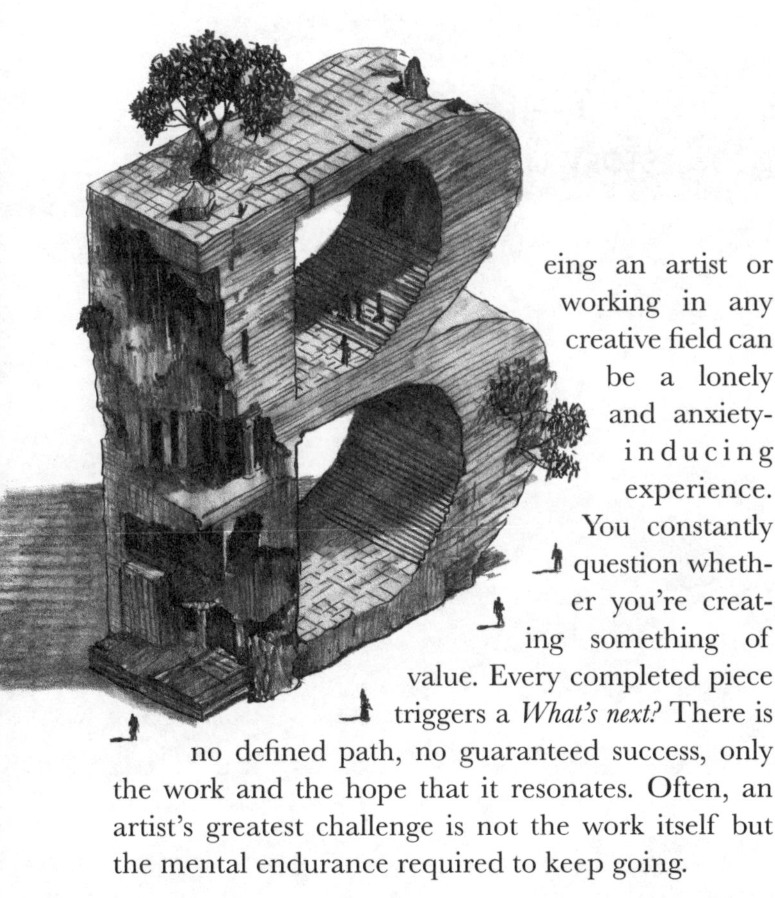

Being an artist or working in any creative field can be a lonely and anxiety-inducing experience. You constantly question whether you're creating something of value. Every completed piece triggers a *What's next?* There is no defined path, no guaranteed success, only the work and the hope that it resonates. Often, an artist's greatest challenge is not the work itself but the mental endurance required to keep going.

> Embrace difficulty and disappointment—they will make for a great story one day.

MENTOR NOTE

For as long as I can remember, I've wanted a mentor—someone to guide me both personally and professionally. I've had plenty of close relationships throughout my life and career, and there were key figures who played a significant role in shaping my artistic development. The first was Mary Johnson, my high school teacher. Though I loathed her architectural drafting class and performed terribly in it, she later taught my portfolio class, which was a much better fit for me. Mary was more than a teacher; she was a working artist, someone who had firsthand knowledge of the creative world outside of school. She challenged me to find my artistic direction, knew how to push me without breaking me, and encouraged me in ways I didn't fully appreciate at the time.

Mary had a deep curiosity about the world. She lived in Paris for a time and wrote a book about a famous house there, Maison de Verre. She had unique perspectives on architecture, shaped by her experiences growing up in Africa. She noticed details in buildings that others overlooked. Her ability to see things differently made her a valuable guide in my early years, teaching me that curiosity and perspective are essential traits for any artist. Her guidance wasn't always direct—she didn't sit me down and say, "Here's how to be an artist." Instead she opened doors of thought, asked the right questions, and created an environment where exploration was encouraged. That is often the best kind of mentorship—not spoon-feeding answers but inspiring self-discovery.

When I arrived at Cooper Union, another mentor emerged: Doug Ashford. Doug wasn't just a professor—he was an artist, someone who had walked the path I was on and understood the struggles I would face. Midway through my first year, I considered dropping out. My friends in Miami were already making art, getting attention, and I felt like I was wasting time in school. Doug gave me the tough love I needed. He told me he'd kick my ass if I left Cooper, reminding me of the effort it took to get in and the value of staying the course. I stayed.

Doug also taught me about sacrifice. When I complained about spending money on materials for a project, he reminded me that I had a job at the library and told me to get more hours if I needed to. He made it clear that, as an artist, my work had to come first, and sacrifices were necessary. Those lessons stayed with me long after I left school.

But after college, something changed. The structure was gone. There was no professor guiding me, no class deadlines pushing me forward. I found myself searching for someone to help me navigate the real-world challenges of building a career, handling press interviews, and managing the business side of art. I never found that person. Instead, I became my own mentor. The mentor texts? I sent them to myself.

It started small—writing down thoughts, lessons I had learned, things I wanted to remember. I would keep notes about things Mary, Doug, Hans, Emmanuel, or Merce had said, as well as advice I'd read from artists like Warhol, Duchamp, James Turrell, Dalí, and Manet, who've spoken to me through their methods and philosophies, pieces of advice that struck me as important. Over time I realized that I could take this further. I started texting myself messages, affirmations, reminders, insights.

I imagined stepping outside of myself and seeing my situation from another perspective. *What does Daniel need at this moment?* That question became the foundation of my self-mentoring practice. I began sending myself messages as if they were coming from someone else. Sometimes they were words of encouragement. Other times they were hard truths I needed to hear. The voice that answered that question soon became embodied too, the guy smoking and drinking coffee in my studio, as 3D and real to me as I am.

The first message I sent myself was simple: *Keep going.* I was at a low point, doubting my path, feeling overwhelmed. Seeing those words on my phone, as if they'd come from an outside source, gave me the push I needed.

From there it became a habit. Every time I faced a challenge, I would imagine what a mentor would say to me. The messages evolved, becoming more specific, more personal. I didn't realize it at the time, but I was training myself to be my own guiding force.

As I moved further into my career, I realized that mentorship isn't always about having a single figure guiding you. It can take many forms. Some mentors are direct teachers, but others are people we observe from a distance, individuals whose work and approach to life inspire us to be better.

I started looking at mentorship as an ongoing process rather than a fixed relationship. This shift in thinking allowed me to find guidance in unexpected places. Conversations with fellow artists, books by creative minds, interviews with industry leaders—all of these became sources. I would take notes from speeches, study the careers of artists I admired, incorporate lessons from people I had never met.

"IF YOU CAN GET PEOPLE THAT MAD ABOUT YOUR ART, YOU'RE DEFINITELY DOING SOMETHING RIGHT."

MENTOR NOTE

There's a misconception that mentorship has to be a structured relationship, where someone formally agrees to take you under their wing. The truth is, mentorship can be fluid. And it can be brief: A single piece of advice from the right person at the right time can be as valuable as years of guidance.

Eventually, as I gained experience, I found myself in the position of a mentor to others. It happened naturally—young artists would reach out for advice, ask about my process, or seek guidance on how to navigate the industry.

At first I felt unqualified. I was still figuring things out myself. But then I realized it isn't about having all the answers—mentorship is about sharing what you've learned. It's about being honest about the struggles and the triumphs, about helping others avoid the mistakes you've made while encouraging them to take their own risks.

One of the most rewarding aspects of mentorship is seeing someone else succeed because of the guidance you've provided. It reinforces the idea that knowledge and experience are meant to be shared. If someone had taken the time to mentor me when I was younger, I know it would have made certain aspects of my journey easier. By mentoring others, I can be the person I once searched for.

Mentorship doesn't exist in a vacuum. It thrives in a community. Artists, designers, musicians—anyone in a creative field—benefit from surrounding themselves with a network of people who challenge, inspire, and support them.

Being part of a creative community means having access to a wealth of shared knowledge. It means being able to call on others for advice, to collaborate, to push each other forward. Some of the most influential mentors in my life were peers, people who were on the same journey as me but had different perspectives and experiences to offer.

When I started sharing some of my self-mentor messages on social media, I was overwhelmed by the response. People would message me asking, "Who is your mentor? Can they be mine too?" They didn't realize that the messages were me speaking to myself.

Mentorship, in any form, is about pushing yourself forward. Whether it comes from a teacher, a friend, or your own voice, it's one of the greatest tools an artist can have.

Use it. Nurture it. Pass it on.

"DO NOT ACCEPT MEDIOCRITY FROM YOURSELF."

"GOOD ENOUGH IS NOT GOOD ENOUGH."

"THERE ARE NO REFUNDS ON TIME SPENT UNWISELY."

"KEEP GOING."

MENTOR NOTE

CHAPTER XXI

MY LIFE TODAY

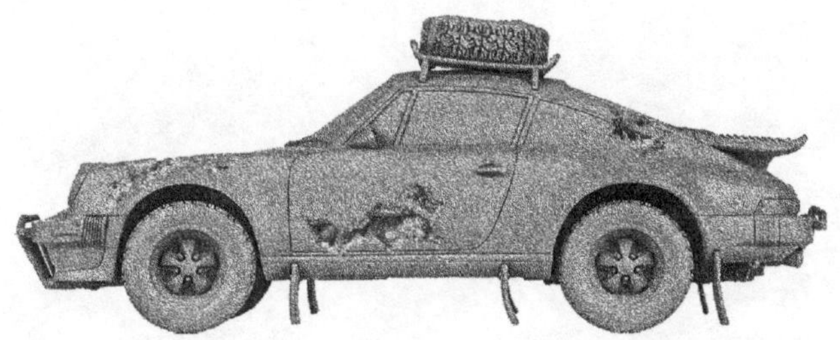

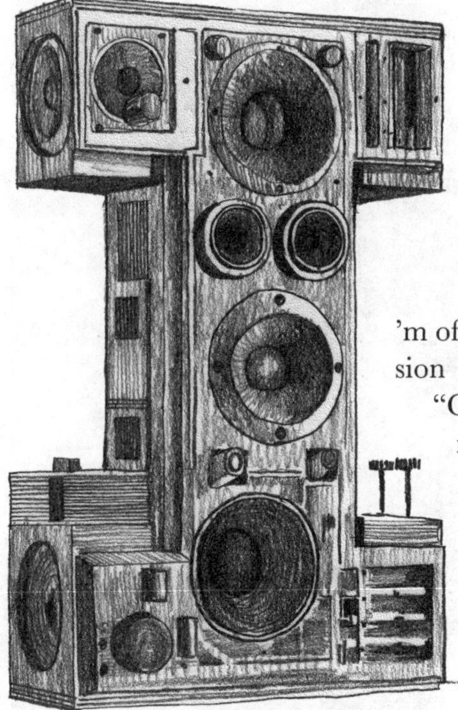

'm often asked some version of this question: "Given your commercial and financial success, why keep going? Why keep pushing?"

I feel incredibly fortunate for the success I've had in my life and career. I dedicated myself to it completely, and while I've had some good luck, I've also worked relentlessly for everything I've achieved. But the grind I chose isn't like other grinds—I love what I do. Being an artist isn't just a job; it's something I can't imagine ever giving up. It's a fundamental part of who I am.

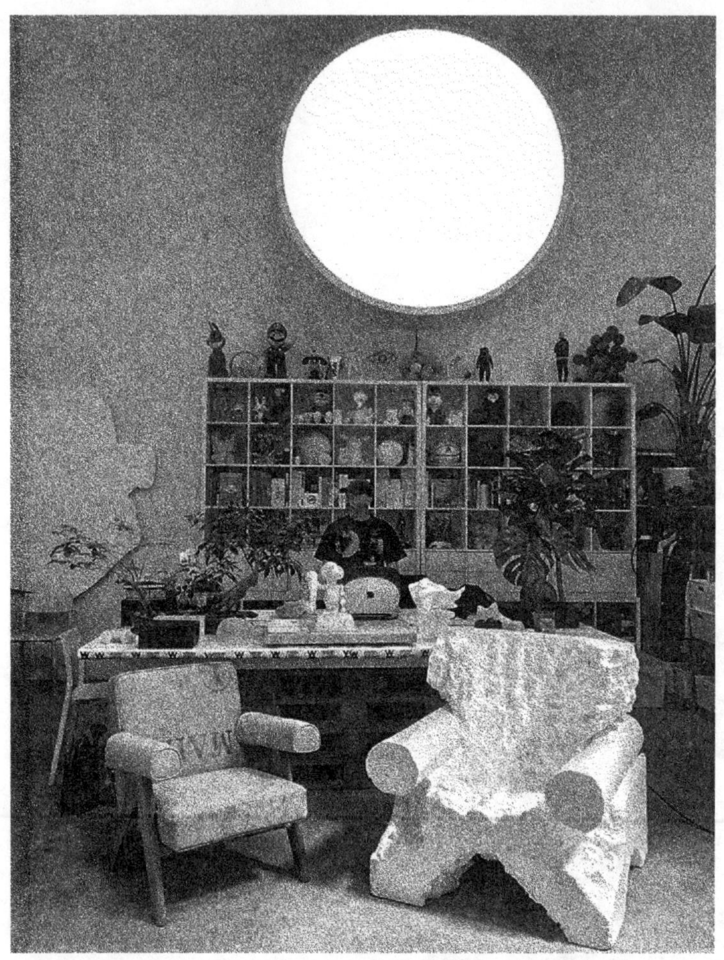

In the studio.

The creative process fuels me. The idea of stopping, of "retirement," doesn't make sense to me in the way it might to others. The need to create is constant—it doesn't turn off, it doesn't pause. It's always there, lingering in my thoughts, pushing me forward.

When I was younger and struggling, I'd sometimes wonder why I didn't just go into finance, wear nice clothes, sit in an office, and not have to worry about my next paycheck. But even though the thought crossed my mind, I knew I couldn't do it. That life would have suffocated me. Most of my days would have been spent in a dull, cubicle-filled hell. Art gives me freedom—freedom of thought, expression, and schedule but, most importantly, freedom from a boss. If you're successful, you can shape your life however you want. But on the flip side, art never ends. There's no retirement from it. I've fantasized about saying, *I've done enough. I've shown everything I have to offer.* But I know that's just a fantasy. I'll always be chasing the next project, the next goal—maybe one more museum show, maybe a major retrospective. Maybe something I can't even imagine yet.

Art has become as natural to me as breathing. If I go a few days without drawing, I feel off, like I'm not fully alive. Gregory Crewdson once described this compulsion during a lecture I attended years ago. He referenced the movie *Close Encounters of the Third Kind*, where Richard Dreyfuss's character becomes obsessed with sculpting Devils Tower, a rock formation in Wyoming. He shapes it out of mashed potatoes at dinner, out of shaving cream in the bathroom—he *has* to create it. That's how I feel about making art. I don't believe this compulsion is something you're born with; I believe your body learns it through repetition. Over time, it becomes a necessity. There's a rush in completing a work—a massive dopamine hit. But creativity isn't just about inspiration and dopamine; it's about discipline. Some days, nothing comes out right. The sketches feel forced; the colors don't blend. But I've learned that those days are just as important as the ones where everything flows effortlessly. You can't reach the breakthroughs without pushing through the resistance.

Since I still crave that feeling—need that feeling—I know I'll always keep going. But beyond my art, there are so many things in my life that bring me joy: my children; my wife, Jacqueline; sitting by the ocean on a warm afternoon; and a new obsession—golf. I've spent much of my career fully immersed in the studio, obsessively focused on my work, missing out on relationships or losing them to the grind, but over the past few years, especially since the pandemic, I've put a lot of energy into finding balance. Before the pandemic, I traveled 60 percent of the year—for exhibitions, research, and meetings for art, design, fashion, and automotive projects. Any given week, I could be anywhere in the world. I loved that period. Travel has always fueled my creativity, exposing me to new ideas, materials, and people. But the pandemic forced a reset. For eighteen months I didn't travel at all. I fell into a different rhythm, one that prioritized my health.

During that time, I also started seriously painting again. My early exhibitions, from 2005 to 2012, were mostly paintings. Then, for almost a decade, I didn't exhibit a single one. Part of that was because I was always on the move. I don't like to get started on a painting, leave it unfinished, and come back to it. It never feels cohesive. During the pandemic, I finally had the space to paint uninterrupted. No travel, no meetings, no distractions. It gave me clarity about where I wanted to focus my energy. Since then I've committed to fewer projects but larger ones. My work now is much more hands-on—I'm drawing nearly every day, spending focused time in my studio. Since I shifted my focus to a more balanced life, my daily routine has become much more structured. When I'm in the city, my schedule is highly regimented. I get to the studio at nine in the morning and stay until five. Those are my firm studio hours now. During that time, I try to eliminate distractions—I don't check social media, I don't take unnecessary meetings. My time in the studio is sacred.

Mornings usually start with a quiet period in which I review work from the previous day. I'll walk around the studio, look at what's in progress, and mentally map out the plan for the day. Drawing and painting are the core of my practice, so those take up the bulk of my time. I've structured my schedule so that I can spend at least four to five uninterrupted hours creating. During this time, I wear noise-canceling headphones—sometimes even with earplugs underneath—to block out all external noise. It's the only way to fully immerse myself in the work. There's a level of meditation in this process, a rhythm that you fall into where everything is flowing.

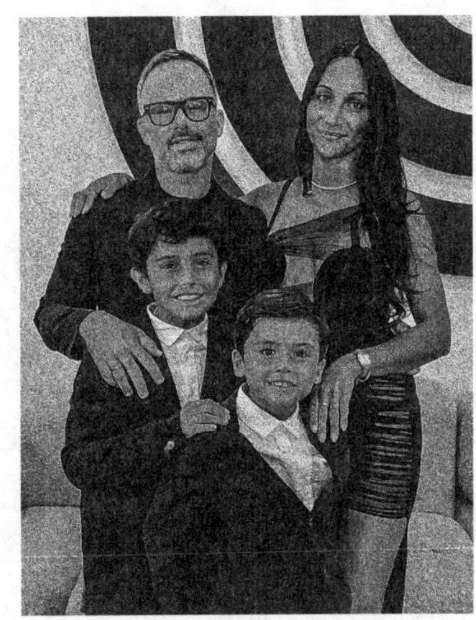

With my family.

Afternoons are typically reserved for administrative tasks—checking in on projects, reviewing exhibition designs, and meeting with my team. My studio operates like a well-oiled machine, largely thanks to the people I work with. The business side of things interests me less these days, and I've begun to pass most of that off to the team so I can focus on passion projects and major exhibitions. One of those is a mid-career survey exhibition that started in California and went to Korea. It includes a thousand objects—everything from my Cavaliers jersey designs to my car projects, sculptures, and paintings. We even re-created my studio in the exhibition, with my desk, my shelves, the helmet I designed for Lewis Hamilton, my Dior collaborations, and my Adidas sneaker designs.

Beyond exhibitions, I'm also exploring new creative territories. I've always been interested in architecture—not just from a collector's perspective but as a creator. I've restored homes designed by famous architects, making careful additions that respect the original vision. Now I want to take that a step further and build something from scratch. I want to create a space where every detail—from the light switches to the landscaping—feels intentional, an extension of my artistic identity. I've been sketching designs, studying historical architecture, and thinking about how a home could be both a personal sanctuary and a living piece of art.

"WHATEVER YOU MAKE, IN WHATEVER INDUSTRY, THERE WILL BE PEOPLE WHO FIND A WAY TO KNOCK WHAT YOU DO. REMEMBER ONE THING: NOBODY WHO IS DOING MORE THAN YOU WILL EVER HATE ON YOU."

MENTOR NOTE

There are so many areas I want to explore: industrial design, experimental sculpture, jewelry, film (which I would like to return to), and even music. Each project presents a new challenge, a way to stretch my creative abilities and test the limits of what I can do. I want to create art that isn't confined to traditional spaces, that exists in ways people don't expect, whether that's a sculptural installation in a remote desert, a film that challenges visual storytelling, or an immersive space that blends architecture, light, and sound into something completely new. Looking forward, I see endless possibilities. I want to create immersive spaces that redefine the way people experience art. I want to collaborate with more visionaries, pushing boundaries in ways that haven't been done before.

For me, the work is never finished, and that's what makes it all so exciting. There is no end to the ways I want to challenge myself. Whether it's working with new materials, redefining how art interacts with the public, or simply pushing my own creative limits, the future excites me. I don't want to slow down—I want to keep moving, keep evolving, keep making. That's what keeps me alive. And that's why, no matter what I accomplish, no matter how many milestones I reach, I know I'll always be looking toward the next challenge, the next inspiration, the next piece of work that will consume me completely. Because that's the reality of this life—art isn't just something I do. It's who I am.

I've come to understand that success—real, lasting success—isn't built on inspiration alone. It's built on showing up. On doing the work when no one's watching. Coming to terms with failing, and failing again, and still choosing to keep going. If there's any truth I can offer, it's this: You don't have to wait for the right moment. There's no right moment. There's only the decision to begin. And to begin again. The dream doesn't show up fully formed. You build it. One sketch, one idea, one risk at a time.

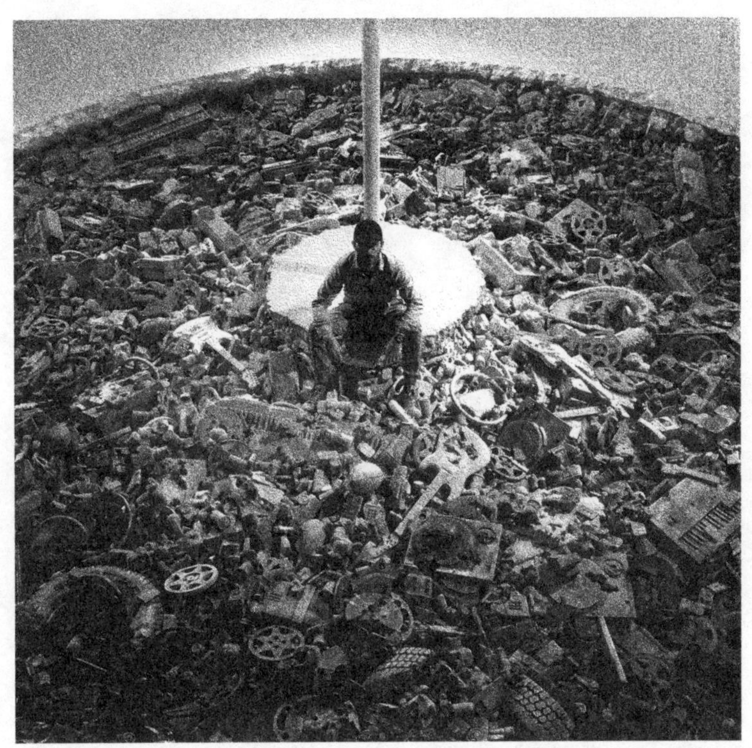

Surrounded by Future Relics.

ACKNOWLEDGMENTS

This book could not exist without the many people who have shaped my path. To those whose stories appear in the book, and to the countless others who offered guidance, support, and belief in moments when I needed it most, I am deeply grateful. Your presence has left an imprint on my work and my life. Every page carries traces of the friendships, collaborations, and lessons that have sustained me. My story would not be the same without you.

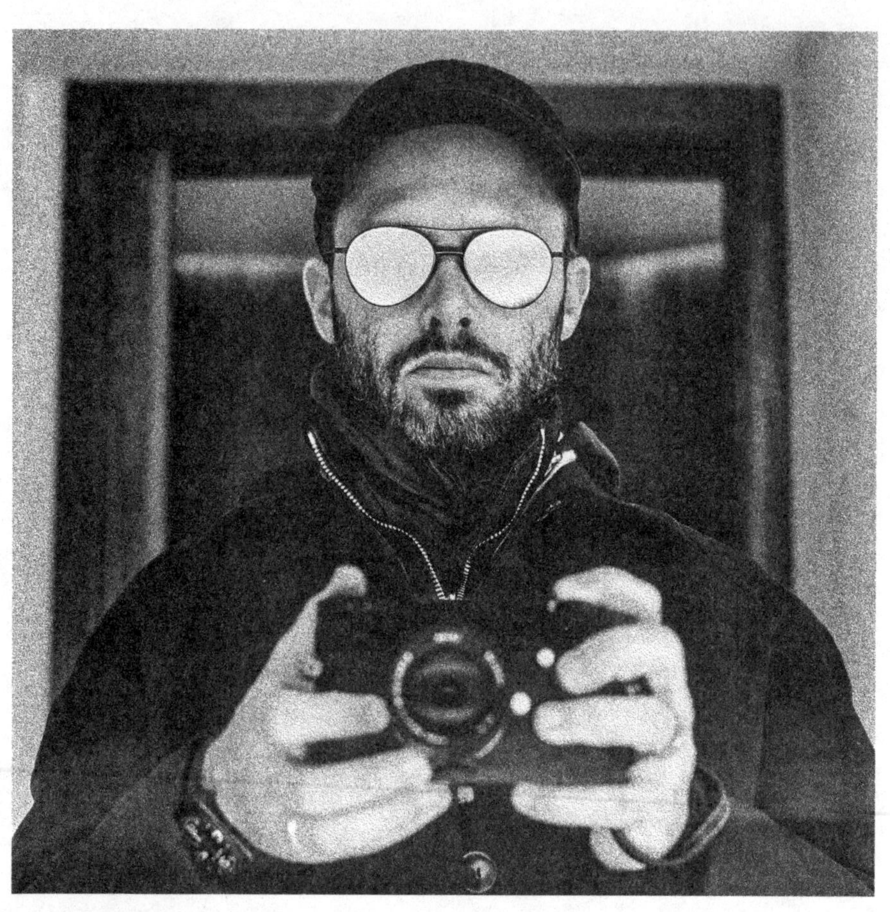

ABOUT THE AUTHOR

Daniel Arsham is an artist whose work blends sculpture, architecture, performance, and design into a singular vision shaped by time, memory, and material experimentation. His now iconic "eroded" aesthetic—artifacts rendered as if excavated from the future—has become a signature visual language that speaks to impermanence, nostalgia, and transformation. Born in Cleveland and raised in Miami, Arsham's work is in the collections of the world's most acclaimed museums, and he has collaborated with major brands from Dior to Adidas.

PERMISSIONS

CELL PHONE IMAGES ON PAGES 6, 65, AND 170 COURTESY OF SHUTTERSTOCK.
INFRARED IMAGE ON PAGE 173 COURTESY OF NOAA.
DISPLAY TYPE SET IN TRILLIUM COURTESY OF HOUSE INDUSTRIES.